Enlightened Authentic Self

Complete Guide of Awakening to Your Natural Full Consciousness

Sat Mindo Dev

New Humanity *Divine Marga*

Enlightened Authentic Self

Complete Guide of Awakening to Your Natural Full Consciousness

Sat Mindo Dev

Copyright © 2023 by Sat Mindo Dev
Published by Sat Mindo Dev
Cover Design: Sat Mindo Dev, Lyonne Premananda
Email: satmindo@yahoo.com
www.SatMindo.org

Meditation practices in this book are those made public by Sat Mindo Dev and New Humanity Divine Marga in publications, and Satsang talks. It does not include the more specialized meditations given by Sat Mindo in his discourses to members of the New Humanity Divine Marga.

The author of this book does not dispense medical advice or prescribe the use of any technique as a form of treatment for physical, emotional, psychological or medical problems without the advice of a physician, either directly or indirectly. The intent of the author is only to offer information to help you in your quest for emotional, physical, and spiritual well-being. In the event you use any of the information in this book for yourself, the author and the publisher assume no responsibility for your actions.

"All know that the drop merges into the ocean, but few know that the ocean merges into the drop." (Kabir)

"Here is a man of truth, great compassion, and honor. The sparkle in his eyes reminds me of the infinite. Nothing can contain him. The heaven and stars sing to him. This man walks on earth so that others can return home." (Lyonne Premananda)

Sat Mindo Dev is a spiritual teacher, author and founder of Divine Marga and New Humanity Foundation. For over a decade, Sat Mindo has been assisting spiritual seekers worldwide in opening to Non-Duality, Enlightenment, Divine and Natural Full Consciousness.

Sat Mindo offers crystal-clear insights on the steps of Enlightenment, supporting and guiding you through every aspect of awakening to your Natural Self (Sahaja Consciousness).

Sat Mindo holds weekly online Live Meditation Meetings, Satsang, Meditation Teacher Training Courses, and International Retreats.

This book is dedicated to all Beings in the Universe who wish to return to the Freedom, Joy, and Peace of their Natural Full Consciousness.

Acknowledgements

I am grateful to so many people, too many to mention all by name. So, I just want to say "Thank you" to all those who have been my helpers and my guides, to all our community.

I would like to express my special gratitude to my beloved Lyonne Premananda, for her love and support in so many ways beyond compare.

To my parents, Milda Damalienė and Bronius Damalis, for their love and support throughout my life.

To our close team members, Manvir Dhinse, Mechele Tison, Anneke Arweiler, Helena Johansson, Temida Magrin and Nicole De Leonardo, without whom this book and many beautiful projects would not have been possible.

To Anders Mannseth and Ronald Guzik for their contribution to this book.

To Moira Cross, Rasa Sagė, and Andreas Ullrich, for their suggestions, ideas, and proofreading.

To all Beings who have been connected with me to create this beautiful manifestation.

To the Self, without whom nothing ever exists or happens.

With Gratitude
Sat Mindo Dev

TABLE OF CONTENTS

CHAPTER FOUR

Levels of Consciousness 143

CHAPTER FIVE

Spiritual Myths & Clarity 238

CHAPTER SIX

Consciousness Integration 271

CHAPTER ONE

Enlightened Authentic Self

Full Consciousness is the Natural State - called Sahaja. It is the end of the search as natural openness is awakened – restful, aware, and alive. It is closer than the blink of an eye. It is our Awakened Authentic Self.

Clarity of What is and What is Not Enlightenment

What is authentic enlightenment really about?

Authentic Enlightenment means awakening to your true Self, realizing your own essence right here. It is not about becoming somebody else, but it has all to do with you and opening to the Self that you are. It has all to do with overcoming and transcending inner limitations, suppressions, and conditionings that limit your consciousness.

What is left, once these belief systems and identifications are cleared, is your Natural Essence, your own pure and boundless Consciousness.

There is no longer the need to identify that you are this particular idea, or this particular feeling inside, or that you are only the boundaries of your skin, or that you are only what you know or feel as yourself that is subject to change.

Once you are able to see beyond conditioning and false identifications, what remains is your natural, very familiar sense that you are, that you exist, that you have always existed.

Essentially, you are your pure Consciousness, untouched by limitations and by thoughts or emotions. Thoughts and emotions happen in your awareness, but they do not limit you.

In your deepest essence, it is that pure Consciousness, which is liberation and freedom from all that is unwanted. It is freedom from deepest feelings since you are the context in which everything happens.

It is important to understand that Enlightenment is not about thoughts and ideas, feelings, or energies. It is rather all about your Essence Self and stabilizing as That.

It has nothing to do with any idealizations, but all to do with you, simply you, and finding yourself most deeply. All the saints and teachers are here to help you find your essence. They are your guides to your true Self, the way showers to your own pure Consciousness.

Enlightenment is available to everyone. Wherever you go, it is all about you. You always ARE wherever you go.

In a practical way, what does it mean to be Enlightened or Self-Realized?

Being Self-Realized means being your unconditioned Self and knowing absolutely your true Self and living your life too. If you are chasing another life, you are limiting the potential of your own life.

However, if you think that all your problems will be resolved, you will suddenly have no issues, you will have perfect health, that money will pour upon you, that all relationship problems will be solved, and your kids will become angels – that is merely an illusion.

Becoming Self-Realized has nothing to do with what is outside of you. Since you have seen through those illusions and transcended those limitations, you can live your life fully and naturally, unobscured by what is happening outside of you.

You can live your life deeply. You can indeed live your life totally as you are now, without inner suppressions or separations, without contradicting or opposing yourself.

You should not have any limitations or even judge yourself; that is even worse. You can live fully and truthfully now, you can live honestly and nakedly now, and you can live Absolutely as you really are. That is your Enlightened Authentic Self.

Is it realistic that Enlightenment can happen to anyone?

Enlightenment is becoming more available due to the accessibility of Enlightenment teachings and many more available Self-Realized teachers. Many enlightened teachers these days offer Satsang and initiations into higher Consciousness.

Although exploring different teachings, teachers, and possible paths is good, you should always examine what is best working for you right now.

3

You should also be dedicated and sincere, and see what helps you most to move forward, to come increasingly closer to your Natural Sahaja Self.

It is becoming more realistic than ever to become Self-Realized because many enlightened teachers are becoming more effective in helping others in more direct ways.

There is also no longer the need for any particular ceremonies, rituals, or buildings, such as churches, ashrams, temples, or monasteries. There is no need to travel anywhere.

When you see different kinds of teachers, you will understand that they are all unique in their own way. Therefore, you should find someone who resonates with you and explains things most simply, in the most understandable way, and in the most relatable way.

Is there a highway to Enlightenment?

There is no longer the need to meditate for 40 years, engage in various rituals, etc. It is good to realize that every meditation technique has a specific purpose.

One of humanity's greatest gifts has been the Levels of Consciousness[1], revealing the exact steps towards Enlightenment, where each stage has a different process and effective practices.

The highway effect of Enlightenment is through Full Consciousness Transmissions[2]. It clears your energy field and your mind and easily assists in deconditioning. As a result, the conditions, identity, and various corners of the

---

[1] See Chapter 4 'What are the Levels of Consciousness?'

[2] See end of book 'About Full Consciousness Transmissions'

ego-knot are very quickly cleared, amplifying the Natural True Self that you are.

Consciousness transmissions have been known to be offered by some enlightened teachers, but these were very exclusive due to previous limitations, such as transportation, technology, and so forth. However, consciousness transmissions can now be done online, and thus, you may receive them at home.

What is the difference between now and 100 years ago?

Around 100 years ago, the only way you could meet an enlightened teacher was by taking a boat to cross the ocean or hopping on a horse for a long ride. It could be that you may have heard stories about them and then decided to go on a journey for a few months to meet a guru in a remote area, such as the Himalayas, Tibet, or some other place. Travel was a considerable limitation in the past, and then, things became more accessible with transportation, especially with technology.

Becoming Self-Realized has never been easier in the whole history of humanity due to the ease of travel and technologies, such as the internet. Another important aspect is Planetary and Galactic energetics, a new cosmic cycle in which we are now.

With the upcoming Golden Age, all the energies in the whole solar system are lifting. They are very supportive in so many unseen ways for your well-being and awakening, as well as for raising your consciousness.

These energies have intensified mainly in the last 30 years and are currently intensifying every single year. The planetary energies of the earth's energy grid are being restored and are becoming purer and on a higher vibration. The surface environment is resonating at a higher frequency as a whole. Therefore, human beings living on Earth as part of it are receiving these higher vibrational energies as well. This is indeed the main reason why more people are suddenly interested in awakening, meditation, and enlightenment.

What are the criteria for Self-Realization?

Willingness, dedication and honesty, not giving up when the first challenge manifests itself, or even the second challenge, the third, and so on – commitment and determination, but very simply put, willingness.

The saying 'if there is a will, there is a way' is quite apt here. I have met many people who were willing and opened up to high levels of consciousness. I have further met many intelligent and high achievers in the material world who lacked willingness, and they did not go far as they fell back to their minds.

Intellectual, intelligent, and rich people who have many activities in their lives often fall back because they lack one simple thing, willingness. They further lack dedication, persistence, and determination. Willingness is, however, the main quality required.

Can I be enlightened and still live a normal life? If I become enlightened, can I still have family, friends, and work? Because I've seen many teachers simply sitting on a mountain, doing nothing, or seated on a chair and just talking.

As you may have already recognized, yes, you can still do what you do. You can have your relationships, family, and work. You do not have to change your life to start realizing who you really are. In essence, you do not need to change anything in your life.

If you naturally feel that there is the need for a specific change that you want, maybe to move to a better, quieter area, or to find work that is slightly less demanding, or perhaps your relationship has always been problematic, suppressive, and/or abusive, so you decide to make a change – these are natural changes towards a more harmonious and better life, and you now have the strength and inner support to do that.

You would naturally want to improve your life as you go along, but I never tell anyone to change this or that. Many of my fellow spiritual explorers have not changed their outer lives at high levels of realization. I usually say, it is all good where you are, as you are, and let us meet and work on your Self-Realization. That's it. It's very simple.

There is a Zen saying: 'Before enlightenment, I was chopping wood and carrying buckets of water, and after enlightenment, I was chopping wood and carrying buckets of water.'

You can still have relationships, and your relationships improve because you no longer subscribe to abusive behaviors. You would have more understanding, love, compassion for your partner, and a deeper connection with your partner.

Your relationships and family life would improve, and you would have a much better connection with and understanding of your family. You would understand your parents, your partner, how they are, who they are, their life or challenges,

7

their good and bad sides, and accept them fully as they are.

You can still have friends, and those who never had a good interest in you would fall to the side, and the real friends who genuinely love you would stay. You would find new friendships that would be more enriching, supportive, closely connected, and deeper. Regarding your work, you have to be practical and realistic as you need an income, you need to pay your bills, you still need to sustain yourself with food and have a roof over your head.

The only natural thing that would need to change is that a highly stressful, mentally straining environment might not be suitable in the long run. However, I never say that you have to quit your job. Simply find a middle way to make it all work.

Perhaps, instead of being very stressed at work, you might prefer to have more free time for yourself and your family to find the right work-life balance. Everything comes into a more natural balance; thus, highly stressful situations are no longer preferred, with fewer ego needs, like gratifications and desires.

A more balanced way of life, in the long run, is usually preferred, and you can still absolutely live your life as it is now, and make gradual improvements over time, if you wish. It is absolutely okay as it is.

Why do enlightened teachers say different things?

If you follow Buddhist traditions, they have their language, terminology, rituals and traditions, and you need to decipher them.

I remember long ago that Buddhism was a big interest of

mine, but then, I would question, why this ritual? What is it for? I do not understand it. I was hence not interested in what I did not understand. I never followed blindly.

That was my approach to inquiry. Come to India, to Indian spirituality, with an abundance of Sanskrit language and yogic language. In the Hindu tradition, there are many rituals and ceremonies as well. Again, you have to decipher them, understand them, and figure out what you are truly looking for and what is working for you now.

Are you looking for a cultural experience, or are you looking for Self-Realization?

Different teachers have different backgrounds, whether religious or cultural, or simply put, different ways.

Each being has its preferences. Some are more heart-centered, and thus, they are focused more on devotional aspects, while others are more inquiry-focused, and hence, they can explain everything clearly and easily.

What are the main ways of Self-Realization?

From the highest perspective, there is a direct path of Self-Enquiry and the path of Devotion.

The direct inquiry path looks directly at who I am and how I can realize my true essence, while determining the quickest and most efficient way.

In the devotional path, the aim is to surrender to the Divine thereby becoming One with God, Self, Consciousness.

There is also an Ascension path which is about raising energetics to a higher domain of existence. It is about energetic cleansing, raising vibration, and transcendence. It involves connecting with higher planes of existence and with related beings on those higher planes. The goal of ascension is essentially to ascend to the higher planes of existence. It is a total transformation.

Therefore, we have so many healers, light workers, and channelers, as well as many teachings about higher dimensions that are so exciting, albeit confusing.

Ascension involves the whole universe, the universal structure. It is a vast subject, and it takes all life to learn. It is thus good to be clear about what you really want.

If you are interested in Enlightenment and Self-Realization, there is a direct path of Self-Enquiry and devotion. However, many spiritual teachers who have attained Self-Realization continue integrating deeper into consciousness by working on their energetics, thus we could say that they are continuing their work on Ascension Path.

Why aren't there many enlightened people?

There are more enlightened teachers these days than ever in human history. It is becoming increasingly supportive to awaken to Full Consciousness[3] due to all the conditions and circumstances we have already spoken about. This phenomenon is becoming much more common than at any previous time in our history.

What happens to the physical body after Enlightenment? Can it improve your health?

In essence, your physical body and the nervous system relax

---

[3] See Chapter 4

more. This happens because the body is no longer being suppressed. It does not have to keep any heavier emotions and no longer feels stressed since the mind is constantly distracted and keeping all attention only in the head thereby enabling your physical body to relax more.

It may depend on how you have lived your life, your genetics, and if you are taking care of your physical body throughout your spiritual journey. For example, becoming vegetarian to be lighter makes it easier for digestion, while you do not ingest antibiotics via meat, chemicals, and so on, thereby improving your health.

Your health improves when you change your diet, eat more healthily, and spend more time with your body, in your body, and support your body.

If you become self-realized, your body is still the same, but it would adjust and become more relaxed. Emotional extremes, highs and lows decrease as your traumatic responses to life heal. The body does not release as much adrenaline and other hormones when this happens. Your body does not need the energy to obtain balance after emotional episodes, and thus, more power is available for healing.

When there is no more mental, psychological, and emotional heaviness, the body feels much lighter and much more enjoyable.

Do you become immortal after Enlightenment?

Once you see that you are the eternal, pure, and boundless Consciousness, you will know that you can never die, that you were never born, and that you have always existed.

Your physical body has its own way. It would live its own way and pass on its own accord. The question here is, who are You?

There is no more fear about bodily existence or physical garment. There is indeed no more fear that, for these 80 years, you wear this particular bodysuit, and then it will be dropped. You are boundless Consciousness as you have always been present here.

Your focal point would perhaps shift into another bodily form in another place or dimension in the next lifetime. However, as the true essence and identity, you are this pure Consciousness, shining through everything, through all forms and spaces.

Only in this instant, in this life, you are more focused on this particular body and locale, and it's okay. This lifetime is a beautiful and unique experience. It is challenging in its own ways, but equally beautiful in its own ways.

As soon as this garment wears out, you receive another one. We can see so many life forms around us. There are so many plants, animals that have consciousness, so many human beings, so many cosmic beings and other non-human beings, and the whole universe is full of life.

Therefore, you can rest assured that there would be the next body to inhabit if you want to because they are so plentiful. That is the nature of consciousness – being able to experience multiplicity while being ONE.

The whole universe would still be here, and you would experience it differently. It would be further highly likely that, since you have come to your Self-Realization, according to the natural laws, the next lifetime would be more conscious.

Most likely, you would not fall back into being an animal or human again; more likely, you would become someone or something else supportive of even higher consciousness and higher vibration, or you might choose to return fully to the Source and stay as Source itself. That is indeed the most likely thing to happen according to the natural laws of the universe and your will.

There is nothing really to worry about in the larger sense. Enlightenment is the most beautiful, special and most important thing that can happen to you in this lifetime, even in many lifetimes. You truly start living fully and absolutely.

You spoke about the path of Ascension and Self-Realization. I feel they are very connected. I think they are both happening to me. My question is whether they can both happen at the same time.

Yes, for some people, both can happen. My advice is to recognize what you are doing. If you are drawn into, let's say, channeling things, lightwork, etc., you need to understand that it has to do with global ascension, with your ascension, and this is usually not so much about Self-Realization and Enlightenment.

Many aspects of ascension work can focus on universal maintenance and matters, like helping other sentient beings and raising global consciousness, which is very important.

For most people, Self-Realization involves some energy work. Meanwhile, for all people, some energy work is involved because some healing and deconditioning needs to be done.

Some energies need to be healed and taken care of, as well as some techniques and meditations to learn for a myriad of purposes – to live a more harmonious life.

Some ascension techniques are supportive. In terms of Self-Realization, certain energy work is supportive and is taught by us towards achieving Self-Realization.

The direct path of Self-Realization is not a mental one either. It does not entail sitting down and questioning yourself, "Who am I?" until you get the answer.

According to Ramana Maharshi, the inquiry 'Who am I?' is for those who have already done some yoga, meditation, and preparational work, and for those who can go deep within and meditate and contemplate meditatively upon it. This inquiry is for mature souls. The same applies to devotional practices. They are most effective when one is at a certain level of spiritual maturity.

I know that many people treat Advaita (Sanskrit: without duality) and Non-Duality[4] as a philosophy, but these are not for intellectual understanding. You would not go far with your mind adopting this approach. You cannot transcend the mind with the mind.

A direct path is a path of meditation and a deep inquiry or devotion. Some energy work is involved in it too. Teachers' grace and consciousness transmission are vital for openings to the highest levels of consciousness.

---

[4] See Chapter 4 on Level of Consciousness Non-Duality (Pre-Enlightenment)

Are there any sacred texts that can assist?

One of the Kung Fu movies featured a most sacred temple that housed the most sacred artifact with the most sacred wisdom. The most advanced Kung Fu grandmaster was guarding this artifact, protecting it with the deepest Kung Fu wisdom, and defending it for the student who was genuinely ready for it.

The dark opponent challenged the most eager student, and a huge fight ensued between the two to determine who would have access to this most guarded, most valuable wisdom of Kung Fu mastery.

In the final battle, the good guy defeated the bad guy. Having proved his worth to the master, he entered the temple. The master greeted him and gave him the sacred artifact.

Upon opening the artifact, all he saw inside was…a Mirror! That was the most guarded, sacred, and highest wisdom of the Kung Fu martial art. When you are truly ready, you see your authentic self.

Therefore, you similarly become very interested in sacred texts and books of deepest wisdom. The most sacred wisdom is your present pure Consciousness. The mind cannot hold onto it. Consciousness is open.

Your present pure Consciousness is the most sacred thing! Knowing this and that would save you a big journey, many troubles, and fights. What you truly seek, the ultimate thing, is your own present pure Consciousness, but you must prove it to yourself.

Many beings in the past spoke about Enlightenment. It seems that people hold particular ideas about it and how it is supposed to be. It can seem beyond one's reach.

Many ideas can be suppressive. Therefore, if you get rid of those ideas, you would be much closer to yourself. Ideas have a specific meaning in your mind. They have a certain distance, and they have created a certain distance from you.

Maybe one or two ideas have inspired you in the past. Moreover, maybe one or two of these ideas have assisted you in challenging times. They thus served their purpose at that time as inspiration and moral or psychological support.

You have to examine what you think about enlightenment. You have to unlearn many things because you want to be open and free.

However, you do not have to go to any extremes. All you need to do is simplify and examine very closely which idea truly does what for you. Just break it down to absolute simplicity and observe if this is helping you or not.

Because, as I have said, right from the beginning, it is all about you and your awakening to the Natural Sahaja Self.

That is why it is good to closely examine any idea, belief, association, or idealization. Is it helping you or supporting you right now? Maybe it was in the past, but that has now become the past. What about right now, which is fresh and new?

Check your past and what you still carry. If something was helpful yesterday, it does not mean that it is helpful today. Heraclitus once said:

"No man ever steps in the same river twice, for it's not the same river and he's not the same man."

If a particular meditation practice has been beneficial for the last five years, two years, or one month, it might not be helpful now and in the future.

You must constantly examine yourself, double check yourself, put yourself in the clear Mirror of Consciousness of Now.

What I call the Mirror of Now refers to seeing what you see in the mirror of now. See what you know, what you feel, what you think, and what you do. Is it still helping you to become more natural and more of yourself, more of your real Self, natural Self, free Self, spontaneous Self, and effortless?

How do I stay on the most optimal path?

It is essential to be vigilant, to keep your focus on the Self, on God, softly and naturally.

Then, from one moment to the next, you can have this intention to perfect yourself, to continue transcending, healing, opening, and ascending, which is very supportive.

If you have that intention, you would continuously be on your most optimal path. There is nothing wrong with having amazing experiences. Being in Full Consciousness, you can surely enjoy many amazing experiences without side-tracking into any distractions from your ultimate goal.

Regarding perfection, is it possible to transcend human nature?

Firstly, you need to perfect your humanity. That is the first step to help you truly understand that it is okay to be human, to have no judgment about yourself, no resistance to being yourself, no judgment about your body, having the body, and being in the body.

You have to perfect your humaneness and to absolutely acknowledge yourself the way you are first before you can transcend human nature.

Then, out of that absolute acknowledgment of who you are, you eventually begin to transcend the human limitations with compassion and grace.

That is how you may rise and become a divine human being. You are still human, but have become a divine human or perfected human being. Therefore, you have no resistance to being human and no judgment of being the way you are, or the way someone else is. That is real unconditional love and an integration phase of consciousness.

Through that unconditionality, higher qualities emerge, namely, total acceptance, nonjudgement, humility, and compassion.

Seeing Your Natural Self

"I searched for God and found only myself. I searched for myself and found only God." (Rumi)

How does the Natural Self feel like? Is it the same as an opening of the heart and a feeling of love? Is it the quietness of the mind? Or a certain peaceful place inside?

The starting point is that your Natural True Self is always here. Most simply, it is a realization, a recognition that there are distortions that arise and that are here, which hold a distance from being your natural awakened Self.

Any thought, if it is believed in, creates a distance because your attention goes into that bubble of the thought, and your attention is absorbed in that thought pattern or belief.

Identifying with emotions means that your attention goes into emotions, and you reside in feelings, not in your open self. There is a certain sense of discomfort, of your attention living in your thoughts and emotions.

Even residing in energies and spaces still create distances, as it doesn't feel that it's you, that it's natural, so even the light-love energy, no matter how beautiful, cozy, and nurturing it might be; you can't sustain it forever because something else will come up and take you out of it.

When we speak about the Absolute Self, it means being absolutely your Self, without any distance, any sense of separation and not excluding anything from here and now.

We should not idealize the absolute Self either, as if it's the highest God of all or the most divine being of all.

Many seekers are searching for the most divine being but one needs to awaken to the question of what are you looking for? For something "most"? It's still someone else, something else, something higher, someone more grandiose; it's a trap of "more," creating more distance from your True Self here and now.

We must come back again to see that what we want to find is our essence Self. Then you might say: how can I absolutely want myself if I don't like myself? Well, what you don't like are the limitations within. That's what you don't like.

What you don't like are those problematic emotions, confusing thoughts, worrying feelings, those dark corners that you try to avoid. That's what you don't like about yourself because you experience those things, and they are challenging.

Buddha's observation is rather pertinent here, in that these are diseases of the mind. These are the diseases in oneself.

Therefore, as the doctor would say: "let's come back to the natural, healthy state, and you will feel just fine; you will feel well." Generally, everyone feels quite healthy, unless one feels a certain pain. This is a moment of realization that your body is not feeling well, and now, this pain is here, and you have to do something about it.

Otherwise, when you are healthy, you forget the body because you do your own thing. Similarly, the things you do not like inside you (i.e., doubts, worries, confusion, sadness, and so on) are also akin to diseases (i.e., mental, emotional, and psychological distortions); hence, you do not like being sick.

You should not identify with a sickness, although everybody does that, to a certain extent, with such laments as, I have many worries, I am very confused, and I am a very emotionally unstable or angry person.

People have identified with illnesses and diseases and have somehow ignorantly accepted these illnesses and normalized them, which is rather paradoxical.

Finding yourself is finding your healthy self, that is, the way you would feel when the illnesses are healed.

Therefore, you would love living, you would love being yourself, and you would want to be yourself and nobody else.

The essence of a search

The most direct way of finding yourself is that which brings you closer to your true Self, that which brings you closer to your Natural State (Sahaja Consciousness).

A search is embarked upon when something is missing in one way or another. Either one does not see things as perfect, is not as happy as one would like to be, does not feel love as one would like, or does not have peace of mind.

In essence, one feels that something is missing, that something is incomplete and, intrinsically, there is something wrong with one's mental-emotional-psychological-energetic component. In a larger sense, if we take out the religious and spiritual aspects, it is the resolution of these inner distortions that one is looking for.

There is the need to have absolute clarity in one's search. Anything that takes power away from a human being is not healthy, no matter how lovely, promising, or grandiose it sounds. Anything that takes power away and puts it into the hands of an organization or into the hands of a world religion, or even worse, in the hands of the government, is not healthy.

The most direct way of finding yourself is that which brings you closer to yourself, that which brings you closer to your Natural Self, to your Natural State (Sahaja Consciousness).

At some point on the path, we must examine whether we are still worshiping the sages who have been guiding us, like Buddha, Jesus, Shiva, Krishna, or any angelic or cosmic beings. Are we still relinquishing our power to anyone else than our own beloved Self, our pure Consciousness?

In the devotional path, for example, when one is entirely devoted to Lord Krishna, one might lose oneself in that divine aspect, and give all power away to that divine entity, while forgetting oneself.

Devotion is needed at certain times on the Path to Enlightenment, but eventually, it is about returning power to your own Self. The healthiest path is that which helps you to be one with yourself quickest, to abide in your own pure Consciousness.

In Ascension teachings, being in the Light and Love, being with angels, or being in higher dimensions, people can easily get lost in them. It becomes another subject-object relationship.

After examining all the paths humanity has taken throughout thousands of years towards Enlightenment, in essence, it is all about focusing on Self-Realization and what is already here and what has been overlooked all along.

What would feel like the most real you? What is already here and now as the unchanging you?

It is not about losing yourself in some energy field, in some kind of space or another dimension. It is about becoming your Self fully, becoming truly your Self, becoming free from limitations, from mental-emotional-psychological distortions.

We can see that the path presents many pitfalls and traps as one subscribes, knowingly or otherwise. Something is at times helpful at the beginning; for example, devotion to a higher being is helpful initially, but eventually you need to return to your Self fully. There needs to be a balance.

I have witnessed many ways in which people can unknowingly or unconsciously create even more distance from themselves on this journey to the Self.

If one starts to idealize what one ought to be, one creates more distance from oneself, even with good intentions.

On a mass scale, religions became dogmatized, mentalized, and systemized. Consequently, they created more distance from actual liberation, the actual self-love being, and the true oneness with oneself. That which makes more distance is not supporting liberation.

What is my closest Self?

Your closest Self is the present openness, naturalness,

effortlessness, aware and awake emptiness.

Your essence is pure Consciousness. You do not have to focus on it unless you want to verify that you are aware, but you always are.

Natural Consciousness, natural openness, natural boundlessness, natural lovingness, peacefulness, and joyfulness – that is your natural true Self. That is how you feel when these mental, emotional, and psychological illnesses and distortions are healed, resolved, and transcended.

You have many ideas of what you want at the back of your mind. Many ideas arise which can distract you. These are optional.

What is that you need to know clearly at the back of your mind? What are you really looking for? That is the biggest question of all. What are you truly, absolutely looking for?

If you say love, bliss, and happiness, no, that is not the thing. If bliss comes, it comes, and if love comes, then it comes. If it is in the background, it can remain in the background. If it opens your heart, it opens your heart. And if something closes your heart, it is not a problem, it is all fine. It is just what happens.

What you are really looking for is your present, awake, aware Self. That is the real thing. I say it is a real thing because, otherwise, you would be chasing that which is a distraction, which is only temporary. You would spend so much time, money, travel, and so on, and some of those things can create even more distance.

That which is real sometimes sounds too simple. Do not

believe in it, thinking that the picture of the Saint is closer to your heart than yourself in your own heart.

When you examine what is in you, you will find that you are relinquishing your power and keeping that distance willingly in many ways. That which is real in yourself is your own pure Consciousness, not a form or shape of anyone else, unless they help you see your Self more clearly, in which case, it is all good.

Healing those inner distances and distortions is something many people fail to take seriously because they are more excited about something which is hypnotic, sparkling, hallucinating, like altered perceptions and temporary feelings, or some high experiences, which are all temporary, of course. People seem to like temporary, but then, become disappointed when they are gone.

There are so many things, like self-help books, religious and spiritual paths, that can be used 'on the way'. Of course, you need to choose something that is helpful to you.

My biggest message is finding your Natural Self, your absolute Self, and no one else.

Can one get trapped in Spirituality?

Yes, simply put, anything that keeps distance, anything that is an ideology, somebody else's preferences, rather than yours, is essentially keeping a certain distance from yourself.

You want to be yourself in your healthy and natural state, a boundlessly open state, and an absolutely self-aware state in order to heal those distortions that keep distance.

Another excellent teaching by Papaji is to 'stop the search'.

That moment you stop your search, what you find is that which is here, but many people experience certain conditions because they stop the mind so suddenly.

It is like you are driving a car in 5th gear, and somebody shouts to stop your car now! Therefore, you pull the handbrake, the tires begin to screech, the brakes are hot, and you feel your heartbeat pumping in your chest because you have stopped too fast. Since there was momentum, it might feel too sudden.

The healthy side of the teaching of 'stopping the search' is generally for those who are in Presence Consciousness[5] and are more mature beings who can reflect deeper on what they are genuinely looking for.

Any technique, for example, 'stop the search', 'who am I?', or 'surrender to God', may have a limitation because they are suitable at a particular stage in your Self-Realization journey.

No single technique will liberate you. Many try to present the ultimate technique, and although they are wonderful teachings, there is no single technique that will do it. They are merely supportive tools.

A healthy way to go about it is to reflect on all techniques and teachings maturely, see what helps you most now, and evaluate your progress. This way you will gain more clarity about what you are doing.

---

[5] See Chapter 4 on Level of Consciousness Presence (Third Awakening)

Being Your Self - the Deepest Acceptance

Your pure Self is yourself that is not obscured and colored by any experience. Your pure Self is the Self that is not colored by thoughts and emotions, not affected by energies in your experience.

At the deepest level you are always your Self, you cannot not be your Self, no matter what you do. Your Self is always present. Your Self includes everything you experience, including your deeper beingness.

It is the more limited being that can be caught up in mind, emotions, body and sensations. The challenge, of course, is that there are unwanted aspects. Therefore, how do we find okayness with all that is? How do we find acceptance with the present thoughts, feelings, energies, or even pain that we might experience?

To find this okayness with all that is here, step slightly back or above your involvement with thoughts, emotions, and energies.

Even if you are at a higher consciousness trying to find completeness, it is still the same, it is actually here.

Okayness recognizes that there is someone here, and this someone is what you may define as the one who is engaged with thoughts, emotions, and energies, and this someone is experiencing these wanted and unwanted activities.

As you play this someone, you may recognize that what is

being experienced is okay, despite being unwanted.

We may say that it is a larger acceptance of the IS-ness of what is. Even if something is unpleasant, it already is. In a larger context, it is also okay since it is already happening.

You begin to observe that suffering is in the lower personality, in the lower self, which is both experiencing and resisting the experience, while complaining and trying to avoid or escape something unpleasant.

That resistance, avoidance, or denial contributes to suffering. Therefore, no one has managed, in a larger sense, to escape suffering by avoiding it, resisting and denying that which is uncomfortable or challenging.

To go another way about it is to find the bigger okayness with what is. First, you acknowledge that there is avoidance, resistance, and a certain denial of that which is unwanted.

It is okay since it already is. It is good to soften resistance, avoidance, or denial. Intrinsically, suffering, by definition, arises from resistance, avoidance, or denial. There is nothing wrong with having a challenging moment. There is indeed nothing wrong in having some anger, and in experiencing that which is unwanted.

To find okayness is to recognize that nothing is wrong with what you are experiencing. Even if you perceive it as unwanted or wrong, there is nothing wrong in having this experience. This is called 'the human experience' or 'being human'. This is called 'being the way that you are'. There is nothing wrong in having your preferences and your personality. There is nothing wrong with having your unique problems.

There is a societal assumption about societal programming that something is wrong with being yourself. You should be perfect, and you should not have this or that feeling. Societal programming is very judgmental.

A great example has been given by Albert Einstein. One day, he wrote the following on the board:

$9 \times 1 = 9$

$9 \times 2 = 18$

$9 \times 3 = 27$

$9 \times 4 = 36$

$9 \times 5 = 45$

$9 \times 6 = 54$

$9 \times 7 = 63$

$9 \times 8 = 72$

$9 \times 9 = 81$

$9 \times 10 = 91$

Chaos erupted in the hall because Einstein had made a mistake. This was Einstein! How could this genius get such a simple equation wrong?

The correct answer for 9×10 is 90. All his students ridiculed him. Einstein waited for everyone to be silent, and gave a powerful lesson that no one would forget:

"Despite the fact that I analyzed nine problems correctly, no one congratulated me. But when I made one mistake, everyone started laughing. This means that even if a person is successful, society will notice his slightest mistake. And they'll like that.

So don't let criticism destroy your dreams. The only person who never makes a mistake is someone who does nothing."

This clearly illustrates a big social program functioning in Western society that creates an impossible standard and expectation. Mass media is trying to portray that the standard man should be perfect, fit, and rich, and that the standard woman should be beautiful and fit, like an athlete.

There is imprinted suffering associated with these standards. Therefore, to find okayness with whatever is happening to you is to recognize that it is okay to have these emotions. It is even okay to have these thoughts in your mind, and to have physical pains and discomforts.

Have this fundamental remembrance at the back of your mind. Remember that it is okay to have these thoughts and feelings. Yes, it is okay.

It is okay to have these discomforts or even pains. Acknowledge that it is okay to feel what you feel and think and have these thoughts, even negative ones. It is okay to experience what you are experiencing.

That would most likely remove 50% of your psychological suffering. That is indeed the most crucial step – step number one that is called ordinarily being yourself.

Why am I putting so much focus on this? Because if

everybody internalizes this, and emphasizes that it is okay to think, feel, and experience all that we are experiencing, then half of the suffering would be removed. Half of the suffering would no longer be present throughout our lives.

Of course, as you move into spirituality, you uncover challenging emotions and past experiences, and you start trying to deal with them. Again, many people would fall into the same trap of not being okay with what they experience.

On a higher, Non-Dual level[6], there is usually an assumption that there should not be any thoughts. Thoughts might be a simple invitation to slow down and balance yourself, which is why thoughts arise. Your natural system invites you to slow down and balance yourself.

Even the 'I' on a higher level arises only as an invitation to slow down and balance yourself. It is thus okay to experience the 'I' at a Non-Dual level of consciousness.

It is okay to have some thoughts. There is nothing wrong with that. You are no longer identifying with them, so why resist them?

You see, this is where the trap lies. In other words, there is an immediate judgment that you should not have thoughts, and you should not feel your 'I'-ness or yourself. Consequently, this judgment creates an inner conflict, and you suddenly resist that which is naturally occurring. Even if it is your identity, the past identity, if it is arising, it is okay.

Let it arise, come, and go. Without resistance, there is no problem. A problem is only a problem because it is created

---

[6] See Chapter 4 on Level of Consciousness Non-Duality (Pre-Enlightenment)

31

by the ego fixation that is not okay with it.

The actual acceptance, or the absolute Self, allows everything to be here, to come, and to let go. Even if past thought patterns arise, that is fine too. Would the sky resist any clouds?

There is a reason why thoughts may come back. Even if you may have experienced some challenging moments and your past identity seems to contract and catch you in the moment, it is also okay because there is a reason for it.

In the absolute sense, there is no more identity. Even if your body is contracting, your energies are contracting, and you feel this uncomfortable 'I' feeling, but it is also okay.

Allow that for a few moments, and you will see how quickly it passes. However, there could be a judgment of falling back into your identity, or you might start assuming that you should not have these thoughts anymore since you are so enlightened, you should no longer feel these feelings, or you should even erroneously think that you should have no more pain.

They are all spiritual delusions and wrong assumptions. It is resistance to life that is called ignorance and self-created suffering as nobody else causes that.

The real okayness is to first foster a mental attitude that it is fine the way I am, it is fine that anger or sadness is appearing in my Awareness. It is okay.

Let yourself be as you are. Therefore, if you let yourself act out conditionally and you have an Awareness that you are doing so at that very moment, that is also fine. It is okay. There is nothing wrong with being slightly conditional for a moment. However, suppose there is resistance or judgment. In that case, that is a much bigger problem because you would not only be acting on your limitations but also justifying them and sometimes even fighting in the name of that limitation.

One of the biggest causes of suffering is self-judgment. Indeed, self-judgment is a huge obstacle to your Natural Full Consciousness.

Self-judgment arises because of resistance to what is here, and judging what is here, rather than allowing what is here to be with okayness and going beyond it, thus removing the resistance and associated suffering.

I invite you lovingly and compassionately to deeply allow this way of okayness to sink in, and to have unconditional okayness.

A little precaution, of course, is that, if you do something bad or harm others and justify it by claiming that it is okay, that is no excuse to intentionally harm others. I trust that you are a responsible human being.

Unconditional okayness is direct. It is this instant awareness of these thoughts, and it is okay. There are these feelings, even if you act out conditionally; thus, recognize that it is okay that you just acted out, as long as you are aware of it, then it is not acted out unconsciously.

Of course, if there are other people involved, you may need to apologize. It would immediately open all the doors.

This unconditional okayness would remove half of your life's suffering right away. It applies to every higher level of consciousness as well.

One of the last tricks of the mind is to judge that you should not have the 'I' identity. That is indeed the paradox of it all, and the last trick of the mind.

If you sit down and tell yourself that it is okay to have an 'I' identity, it is okay to have this last sense of separation, you will see how quickly things dissolve, with no resistance, no denial, and avoidance. It just dissolves it all.

That is a very big problem for people in non-duality and higher levels of consciousness because they are now 'spiritual', and they think they should not have this or that.

It is neither authentic awakening nor absolute awakening. There is still more work to be done.

Essence of Your Authentic Self

What is the pure essence of Being? Is it absolute unconditional okayness with myself?

The pure essence of yourself is the recognition that you are always your Self. Actually, you are always being your Self. It is rather that, sometimes, you are slightly mixed up with your experiences.

At other times, you are too involved in the experience, or you are somewhat lost in it. Nonetheless, you must remember that you are always yourself. Even in the most extreme cases, if you feel that you are not yourself, how would you know that? You still know deeply that you are yourself simply because you are not feeling like yourself. You are able to see that, even in extreme cases.

If you have paranoia, delusion, or psychological issues, you will still know that you have an issue and that there is something wrong. It only means that, in your experience, there is something wrong or unbalanced, or that there could be a huge challenge at that moment.

Most purely, you would recognize that you are always your Self. This is not merely your experience. This 'I am myself' sensing is always actually pure.

Upon closer inspection, it is always actually pure. It is always actually unconditional and transparent. The purest Self is not mixed with experience, thinking, feeling, sensing, energies, etc.

It is akin to a disturbance in the lake. You cannot see it clearly, maybe half a meter down. The visibility is, however, clear when the waves or ripples in the lake subside and all the mud settles.

Similarly, when it comes to being the essence of your Self, when all the emotional, mental and energetic stuff settles, there is this clarity that you are your Self.

It is not the classical stillness or silence that is rather a half-truth or half-reality. Classically, people think you need to be silent, or there needs to be stillness.

People try to become frozen in silence or in stillness, without moving at all. Some people go into that space of stillness, and they fall into nothingness. A few moments later, they emerge from meditation as if they have just had a nap. They even claim that they had an amazing spiritual experience, where there was no one, and now, they emerge from meditation, and here they are.

You might notice that, oftentimes, I do not use the word stillness or silence because pure consciousness is beyond silence or noise. It just allows the silence, and it enables the noise and silence – it doesn't matter to consciousness itself.

It is always here, open, and present. Similarly, your essence of Self is eternally here, always present and alive.

Your essence Self is very simple. It need not be fireworks and explosions of light, with your Kundalini shaking, or some cosmic experience.

These are energetic experiences. Your natural being is obvious when your experience, whatever form it takes, settles down.

This is the Self that the mystics spoke about. It is rather simple. Everyone feels themselves to a certain degree. Besides, only your involvement in an experience creates a certain covering or veiling of it.

How do our interests affect our Self-Realization?

The simplicity of Self is the biggest value of your Being.

I find that the best question to ask is: 'What are you interested in?' You would immediately notice that people reply with certain subjective or objective experiences. I am interested in spirituality, I am interested in arts and music, in learning about this, or that.

Indeed, nobody would say, I am interested in being myself, I am interested in just being aware, in being present, because it has no objective value to the mind.

At higher levels of consciousness, seekers would say, I am interested in mantras, devotion, and finding God, which is another goal.

Admittedly, we can say that it is a noble goal, but seeking God is still a search because it is a goal. Therefore, the simplicity of being your Self here and now is ignored and overlooked.

You are thus filled with more spiritual desires, all new forms of desires. They are higher level desires. You previously had worldly desires, and now, you have spiritual desires.

Nonetheless, despite upgrading your desires, you are still ignoring the simplicity of your Natural Self.

What if I have self-judgment?

Being okay with yourself is fundamentally essential. Irrespective of the level of consciousness, it is fundamental to be okay with yourself and remove judgment.

You should not give your power away to the inner critic, thus being okay with whatever is arising in you. Of course, it is better to do it with a more meditative approach, rather than just being on your phone checking social media and telling yourself that you should be okay. It is rather a slightly deeper inquiry.

You need some more Presence to do that, to have a deeper, contemplative okayness.

At higher levels of consciousness, there is nothing wrong in having spiritual challenges the way you have them. There is nothing wrong if you feel blockage. There is truly nothing wrong with that.

There is nothing wrong if you have thoughts. Why shouldn't you have thoughts? What is the problem with your thoughts? However, if you are resisting your thoughts, if you are judging your thoughts, then there is a resistance to what already is here.

There is nothing wrong in feeling the way you feel, having thoughts, having energetic blockages and disbalances, and having your past traumas.

There is additionally nothing wrong in having an identity if you are okay with having an identity in this unconditional way. You would see how quickly your identity would fall off.

You would say, 'Oh! My pride came up', and 'Oh! It's okay. My pride came up'. There's no more fuel, it just comes up, and it falls off.

Whatever arises in you, welcome it with okayness. Then, you would see how quickly things unwind, get relief, and fall off, or they would be processed much smoother, effortlessly, and spontaneously.

Effortlessness arises because you are fine with whatever comes up.

There is a certain unconditional, Non-Dual integration if we speak on a higher level. The more time you spend being okay with yourself, the more things arise and fall off the horizon for you, and you eventually polish yourself, albeit with this attitude of okayness.

It is a much more enjoyable journey not to judge yourself. Resisting, judging, avoiding, and denying – it is such an arduous journey, and a very tough road.

Sooner or later, you must stop thinking that it is wrong to have a thought, identity, or blockage.

Coming to the Essence Self is when the water settles. Your body is present, and your essence is very simple.

You sense that you already are, even in the transitory meditation of 'I AM' or being you. When you are in that place of 'I AM' or being you, it is good to know that you are you - simply for the sake of being.

Of course, maturing into your 'I AM' is much needed to cleanse yourself from lower experience interactions. It is a transitory state until you reach the absolute 'I Am That'.

Being your Self, or 'I Am That' is being okay with what is here, since there is no more resistance, no more identity. Even if identity is there, it is okay, but it arises in you for a while and then it falls off.

Most of the time, I accept myself and the unwanted parts. How can I accept myself fully and not be involved with the unwanted parts?

You can always come back to your center and notice that you are now engaged with the wanted or unwanted. You always need to return to the neutral ground, which is your center, but the center is actually centre-less. It is the present space, the present emptiness where you know that you were engaged with the wanted or unwanted.

Therefore, just remind yourself gently to come back, to return to the center, to this neutral ground where things arise and fall back into.

It is okay if you notice that you wander here and there, or that you engage with this or that. Always remind yourself gently to come back to the neutral ground without judgment.

When you learn to return to the neutral ground a thousand times, you will be good at that.

How can I settle into my Beingness?

Recognize the profound simplicity of just being here. Practice slowing down any movements and activities and recognize the simplicity of Being. This is called Beingness.

Simply be here, and value this present Presence of being here. Being neutral helps not to want and not need to resolve something.

Start to practice to Be for the sake of Being, and Being Aware, in time, becomes more natural too.

Full Consciousness is Natural

When the muddy water calms down, your Natural Pure Self shines through.

What does it mean to be the Natural Self? How would I feel in Full Consciousness?

Consciousness has many meanings; many concepts may come up. However, consciousness is about you. It is all about you.

It is about your own Self and what is natural to you, and how to be more open and more Natural Self in your own way.

To know what Full Consciousness is and what is natural to you, first, I will tell you what is Not natural to you. For example, having doubts is not natural; it is a mental problem. Having worries is not natural, nor are anxieties. Acting out on emotions is not natural, although it is natural to feel emotions. For example, it is not natural to act out, speak out of anger, and say things that you would not want to say. That is not natural.

There is indeed nothing wrong if emotions come up as life goes by, but it is not natural to dwell on feelings, to get lost in emotions, to be in them, so much so that they influence your thoughts and take over, leaving you with no control over emotions. That is not natural.

It is natural to be Open, to be Present, to be Here and Now fully, and the proof of that is your own body. It is always present, and it is always trying to cope with everything that is occurring in you right now. It is always trying to be balanced, harmonious, as open as the body can be.

Therefore, we can say that the body has its own consciousness, sometimes referred to as body consciousness. Luckily, it does not follow the mind too much because if the body were to suddenly start following the mind, then there would be chaos, many more disbalances and subsequent diseases in the body.

The body itself is thus a very natural organic energy system. It is okay to feel the body, to be in the body, to experience the body. What is not natural is to be alienated from one's own body. It is not natural to be only in the head, to be lost somewhere in the mind, to be on some kind of cloud, to be lost in emotions, or to be only in energy and ignore the body.

People who are more sensitive to energetics tend to prefer being in a particular space, in a certain energetic experience. They start to ignore the body, and the body always reminds you that it is here, in the present.

It is, of course, not natural to keep the diseases of the mind, such as doubts, worries, confusion, and dwelling on emotions, including sadness, depression, and so on.

Meanwhile, it is not natural to dwell on preferred good feelings, such as, clinging to excitement only, because clinging makes you less present and less aware.

It is entirely natural to be content with anything present here. Even if it is very simple, very natural, it is natural to be satisfied with what is here. Even simple things are okay.

It is natural to fully acknowledge what is present, not to avoid, resist, or deny anything. It is not natural to try to avoid certain emotions, deny certain inner feelings, or escape your present moment. That is what I call 'being alienated from yourself', from the present moment. That is not natural.

Escapism & Separation

On higher levels of consciousness, people tend to want to be only in heaven, and thus, they start to unconsciously alienate themselves from the present moment. Especially in the New Age movement, there is a tendency to not feel at home here, on this earth, wishing to be on another planet or dimension. That is again another form of alienation from the Truth and Reality of the Now, from the Living Presence of God, from the Living Presence of Consciousness itself.

Therefore, one would wish to be somewhere else, rather than in the now, being somewhere in a concept, an idea, a certain feeling, rather than in the Present Moment. Any preference to be somewhere else than in the now is not natural, no matter how beautiful it may be.

One question though, what is that 'somewhere else'? It has a certain feeling. It is rather a clinging to a certain feeling, an attachment to a certain emotion, a certain experience.

Paradoxically, speaking from the highest level, it is a denial of the present moment itself. This denial of the present moment is, in essence, a denial of the existence of the Divine, of the present moment, and the rejection of the existence of God Now, of Consciousness, or the Aliveness of Life itself.

Any preferences for being somewhere else, rather than in the here and now, include a certain avoidance, resistance, and escapism. Similarly, energetically speaking, when people start to get into deeper meditation, as they experience higher dimensions and various experiences, they begin to cling to them and yearn for an escape from the present moment.

At the lowest levels of consciousness, you are present only in the body, and you identify only with the body and do not feel comfortable; thus, you seek something else. People try to escape the body and physicality for a mental reality, which is not natural. Meanwhile, when people gain more control over their emotions, they start escaping into their preferred feelings.

People are constantly creating certain utopias, certain escapisms. As we live in a technological age, people are also escaping into computer games and virtual reality.

Undoubtedly, that would not work out well. First, you cannot fix your actual energy blockages in virtual reality. Second, you cannot become Self-Realized there, and third, your Soul will not be freed in a digital reality either.

These are just mechanisms to further alienate people from the actual universe, from the actual present consciousness. It is another trap of separation, the actual wound that created all these problems in the first place.

Limited consciousness is a wound of separation, trying to avoid present challenges, and compensate for the original problem. If we honestly examine the present moment, Full Consciousness means that you are no longer fragmented, no longer trying to fragment yourself further into something else, no longer trying to abide only in a certain fragmented consciousness, into a partial consciousness, such as mental consciousness, only body consciousness, only emotional consciousness, or only energetic consciousness. Full Consciousness is becoming whole again.

What is the real meaning of ONE?

Full Consciousness means that you are absolutely here, and there is no more fragmentation, no more avoidance, no more denial, no more escapism, and you have learned how to meet everything here, no matter how difficult it is.

Since people do experience challenging emotions, certain past traumas can emerge. It is, we can say, a habitual instinct to try to not experience again that which is unpleasant, but that, paradoxically, does not serve well in the long run.

Therefore, in Full Consciousness, you learn how to meet whatever is here and whatever arises within you. It is a real meeting of 'Everything that is here', the Is-ness of NOW.

Absolute Self is the same as Full Consciousness, where Absolute means ALL, without any exclusion. It is literally, absolutely everything. Absolute self is absolutely all included. Therefore, if there is trash in the street, it is also a part of the Absolute. You are not pretending that it is not there. What is here, is here. That is the deepest acceptance.

Is physicality separate from spirituality?

The idea of separation is also reflected in spirituality due to the common knowledge that the majority of people are living in a materialistic reality, while spiritual people are living in a spiritual reality. However, why would there be two realities? There are no two realities. There is just one reality, physical and spiritual are actually ONE. Absolute includes consciousness and energy too. In Hindu tradition, it is known as the Oneness of Shiva and Shakti.

This world features an abundance of nature, animals, trees, and so forth. Therefore, all that is here is here, and if, through meditation, you start to experience altered states or higher experiences, such as other dimensional experiences, they are also here, including everything in them. That is why there is no separation, you cannot separate anything from the NOW.

All is Absolutely ONE. Not only is everything connected, but it is all Absolutely ONE. Therefore, any separate concepts fragment one's experience. Any separate beliefs and ideas limit one's own full potential and one's complete openness.

So why then does each person have a different Worldview?

If you hold any particular worldview, if you see the world as something negative, well, we need to be honest, that is your own stuff. It is how you see it, how you feel about something, but it is only partial in its wholeness. You are limiting yourself from the wholeness, from the totality of all. Therefore, any particular worldview is a limitation, and any particular perception of the present moment in any way is a limitation in itself. It is a fragmentation into a more limited consciousness.

It is not natural to be limited. It is not natural to see reality as only one slice of cake from the whole cake. It is not natural to look at the globe and only see the South or North of the globe. Since the globe is a sphere, it is a complete 360 degrees object. Any perception of the present moment in any way is thus a limitation in itself. It is a fragmentation of consciousness.

How does Mysticism relate to Absolute Self?

People commonly tend to form certain particularities in spiritual life and spiritual communities. While it is healthy to have an open mind, to assume that all is a mystery,

Mysticism is however also a limitation of one's intelligence and consciousness. If one cannot explain something, one does not need to perceive it as a mystery.

One can simply admit that one cannot explain it, and that is fine. For a person living in the Middle Ages, our lifestyle today would be a miracle. Similarly, our current lifestyle would very likely be perceived as primitive by someone 1,000 years more advanced.

Essentially, there is no mystery in the universe. It is all known. It is all created by the laws of the universe, by how things work in the universe. Consciousness is the creator of all.

Is Allowance a form of Natural Self?

Allowance is natural, but resistance is not because resistance is an immediate limitation. When you resist something, you are not allowing the life force to flow through you in whatever form it takes. You are not allowing life force, even if it emerges as some sadness, you are not allowing it to flow through you to be processed.

It is not natural to keep emotions because that is unhealthy. Emotions accumulate, they get stored in your subconsciousness, and are forced into your unconsciousness. Subsequently, you start dreaming all sorts of things, and you begin experiencing continuously repeated episodes of recurring problems. That is not natural.

Constant repetition of the same problem is not natural. It only means that you have not dealt with it in the first place. It comes up again, and if you are not processing it, it will come back. The universe has a certain balance and harmony. Things come back for you to rebalance, re-harmonize, and process.

What happened in the past, happened. It is gone, and it is futile complaining about it. If you however hold any feelings, you need to process them and heal them. That is what needs to be done.

What is Judgment?

Judgments are limiting negative views, and one of the core issues of humanity's consciousness. Judgment is hence a denial of Now. It is a negative component that immediately denies the existence of something which is judged. Judgment immediately blocks the fullness and wonder of understanding a difference, of the multiplicity of experience.

Judgment is a big blockage of consciousness, and I would encourage everyone to closely observe if anything is judged at any time because that is a huge blockage of your Self, and you would not want to do that.

Do people in higher consciousness have issues? They seem to be quite happy.

It gets somewhat more subtle as you grow in your consciousness because you start to experience more subtle, energetic experiences. Consequently, you begin tapping into higher dimensions, into higher energetics. You may want to be only 'there', and not here, which is Avoidance, let's be honest.

Another issue with spiritual seekers is that they tend to cling, keep, and attach to only positive experiences. They start to avoid everyday life, their families, friends and work. These are avoidances and resistance to the wholeness of NOW.

Spiritual seekers might start to avoid the normality of life, the normalcy of their own ordinary experiences. Isn't that another form of separation? Shouldn't spirituality imply unity and absolute oneness, no matter the level of the soul's development?

Can you say that the cat is not spiritual, the mouse is not spiritual, and troublesome human beings are not spiritual? Isn't everything spiritual? These false ideas and judgmental spiritual concepts are also judgments. Please get rid of them since they are not serving you. Indeed, they are not helping you since they are not natural, and they are avoidances. You do not want to do that.

At any level of consciousness, as one grows increasingly more, one has to constantly check in with basic things, with oneself, to determine whether anything is avoided, whether anything is resisted or denied, because these are some of the biggest separations, whether they are called spiritual or not.

How about people awakened to Non-Duality[7]? They seem to be 'Above' the problems?

On a higher level are 'Non-Dual denials', that is, when one starts to imply that there is nothing to do, that one cannot do anything about Enlightenment, that one is not responsible for one's own actions, that one's physical body is not real, etc.

There are many Zen stories about how a Zen master would take a stick and slap a 'Non-Dual' student to awaken them from these most significant denials, from Non-Duality

---

[7] See Chapter 4 on Level of Consciousness Non-Duality (Pre-Enlightenment)

Consciousness to Awareness[8] of the IS-ness of NOW.

You simply cannot deny that you are here, that everything is here, that this experience is here, and that everything appears as it appears. Of course, the absolute thing is consciousness itself. This pure light of Awareness is the most real thing, the unmoving absolute reality upon which there is also the present relative changing experience.

How can one see things more clearly?

Irrespective of the level of consciousness, it is good to keep things simple. If you deny something, there is a problem. You are limiting yourself. No matter how beautiful Non-Dual explanations and justifications one may come up with, it is still denial because All is inseparable.

All are included in this present moment, exactly as it is. Any denial, no matter how glorified and wrapped up it may be in spirituality, Non-Dualism, and mysticism, is still separation. Therefore, I want all of you to know that denial is denial, and judgment is judgment. That is what they are. This is why it is important to simplify things.

When you keep it simple, any sort of glorified philosophy, spirituality, and mysticism can be easily seen through. Therefore, no matter how beautiful or glorified something looks, as Buddha once said, it is essential to keep one's discernment and inquiry into a deeper essence behind any appearance; thus, healthy discernment is required.

Is Full Consciousness full or empty?

Full Consciousness is not fragmented. It is not limited, but it

---

[8] See Chapter 4 on Level of Consciousness Awareness (First Step of Enlightenment)

is open and whole. It does not, however, imply fullness that you get 'more full' of something, while it does not mean that you are empty, without anything.

You get emptied of your limitations as an empty Consciousness. Your awareness permeates every object. It penetrates every energy and substance – that is the real meaning of emptiness.

It is consciousness that penetrates all. It is not limited by any appearance, name, form, or shape. Therefore, you should not think in terms of fullness or emptiness because the real meaning of Full Consciousness is openness, penetrating all, and seeing all as the present Self.

Are Seeing and Awareness the same?

Awareness is recognizing that you already see with your eyes; hence, even if you close your eyes, you still know that you have your eyes closed, and now, you see darkness and emptiness.

Even if you turn off all the lights in your room, you still see the darkness, and even if you say that you do not see anything, or you see nothing, you still see 'the Nothing'. That seeing is the Primordial seeing. In other words, that is your own Consciousness.

You are always Aware. How do you know that you see nothing in the darkness? Because you are Aware. How do you know that you see something when you open your eyes? Because you are Aware – this seeing is called Full Consciousness – it is the present open Consciousness itself.

Seeing is the most natural thing. It is always instant, always present, always direct, and always here. When you see with your eyes and look at objects, you have a limited seeing because you are contracting your infinite seeing, which is your Consciousness itself.

How would your body feel in Full Consciousness?

You feel very good and relaxed, and you are no longer interested in being stressed. Your body feels pretty good because you are not keeping any emotions inside. If something arises, you feel it, and it passes away. You are not keeping any emotions in your body, and you are not attaching to any emotions.

Your body is not struggling with emotions anymore. When it is not struggling with feelings, it feels balanced, harmonious, and well.

Being in Full Consciousness does not mean that you become healed from physical diseases. No, it depends on your lifestyle. However, you would feel much healthier because emotions are not blocking your body, and they are not dragging it down.

Mental and psychological issues are not pressing or 'deep pressing' your body. The body feels more at ease, more relaxed, and more harmonious.

Being healthy depends on how you take care of your body. It does not mean that you do not get any disease anymore. If you have not taken care of your body for 20 or 30 years, do not expect miracles. You would be healthier, but your previous unhealthy lifestyle would still take a certain toll on your body.

Ideas that, if you are enlightened, you have no diseases, no health issues, and the body lasts forever – well, they are simply an illusion.

You do not have to attach to your body, and try to be super healthy, thinking that being super healthy makes you more Self-Realized. No, it does not. If you are physically very yogic, or are living a super healthy lifestyle, it does not mean that you are going to be more Self-Realized.

If you work on your consciousness, you do that, but if you engage only in physical yoga asanas, that does not make you more Self-Realized. The real meaning of yoga is union with God, or in other words, Self-Realization.

Nor does being enlightened mean that you will live forever. As Nisargadatta Maharaj puts it, living long is not important. Becoming free and liberated – that is important.

This is what I mean when referring to naturalness, that is, you are not attached to your health or longevity. Being vegetarian is a healthier and more conscious way of life. It is more aligned with the universe, not harming other life forms. It is a much better way of life overall, but it has nothing to do with Enlightenment, Self-Realization, or freedom.

Naturalness means non-attachment, that is, you are not attached to anything.

Self-Realization and freedom do not mean that you become a saint, that you sit on a cloud and get rid of all your habits, that you have transcended and no longer have to eat, that you are no longer human, and all that stuff.

If you want to be freer, become 'more free' from your thinking, ideas, and concepts of what something is supposed to be.

Is it necessary to live in a spiritual environment to be more Self-Realized?

If you want to be free, do not get attached to anything, nor should you attach to spirituality.

Many people on this journey become spiritual. You start to become very spiritual, your whole life becomes very spiritual, your whole house becomes like a temple, and Buddha statues are in every corner of your house.

It is OK, there is nothing wrong with that. However, do not get attached to it, and do not think that having a more beautiful space makes you freer. Creating a higher vibrational space is supportive for energetics, but it does not make you more Self-Realized.

Many known teachers lived in shacks, caves and simple houses. Living without attachment to spaces and environments is freedom.

Does being in Full Consciousness mean seeing auras, being a healer, having psychic abilities, and being able to do channeling?

Being a healer is being a healer. In other words, it is a gift of healing. It is a certain gift, practice, hobby, or profession.

Receiving messages from higher dimensional beings is called 'channeling', but it is not the same as being liberated.

Being a lightworker is also a certain service. Being psychic and having extrasensory perception is also a gift, and working with that gift brings a certain responsibility. You must work with your gifts, and you must develop them.

All these extrasensory perceptions, psychic abilities, and so on are gifts. Every human being has a telepathic and empathic ability. You need to work on it. It takes practice, just like becoming a good swimmer, tennis player, or anything in sports – you must train for it.

These gifts have nothing to do with liberation and Self-Realization as that has nothing to do with that. Self-Realization is liberating yourself from attachment to any activities and objects.

That is what I mean by Full Consciousness being natural because it is not limited by anything. There is no attachment to anything.

You have this wonder akin to a baby, but it also has intelligence. You are no longer a child or an adult. This wonder is beyond age. You are not as naive or immature as a child, and you are not as stuck and rigid as a grown-up. You are awake, full of wonder moment by moment, and there is a certain directness in this wonder too.

I need to clarify that I have psychic abilities, and I have been working on them for more than a decade. It is just a gift that I have, and that's it. However, my psychic gifts are not the reason for Self-Realization.

I want to clarify that you do not need any psychic gifts to be enlightened. That is surely not the case.

How do Chakras relate to Awakening?

It is good to work on your chakras to purify their dross thereby becoming more open energetically, while assisting in general openness.

Present awareness is the most fundamental thing you need to know and recognize. After recognizing awareness, you have the foundational and essential support for your energy work.

You recognize that you are not your chakras, your kundalini energy, and you are not any kind of energy. You are the present Consciousness itself, thus opening a space for energy work to be more supported.

Recognizing Awareness does not necessarily mean that you have already become Self-Realized. The journey is to clear the path, your mind, your energy system, any obstacles, and your chakras of any blockages too so that this present natural Consciousness becomes open and boundless, and you recognize that this is the essence of who you are.

How come you can explain everything so easily?

My ability to explain things is a gift that is natural to me because I have been insightful from birth.

Some Self-Realized teachers remain quiet because they are unable to explain something. You meet them, stay silent, they exchange a few words, and hopefully, that helps if it touches you deeply.

For example, after his awakening, Eckhart Tolle would sit on a bench in a London park for two years, trying to grasp what was happening to him.

"I spent almost two years sitting on park benches in a state of the most intense joy. But even the most beautiful experiences come and go." (Eckhart Tolle)

He did not know how to explain the nature of Presence. Consequently, he approached a Buddhist monk, who helped him to realize what was happening to him. Now, with decades of teaching experience, Eckhart Tolle can explain very well what Presence and the present moment are about.

I would like you to recognize that freedom is about openness and freedom from any concepts, limitations, or idealizations. Consequently, you can easily live as you are, and do not need to push yourself and demand much from yourself.

Go beyond any attachments and judgments, see what keeps any separation within you, and meet everything in your present moment, in your Awareness. Gain more clarity of any limitations within, and the truth will set you free.

Non-Dual Way of Life: Becoming a Spiritual Adult

"Once Buddha asked a musician how he tuned his instrument before playing. The musician said 'If I tune the strings too tight, they break. If I tune them too loose, no sound will come out. So not too tight and not too loose works best'. To which the Buddha replied, 'This is how you should hold your mind in meditation'."

What does it mean to be in Non-Duality[9]?

Non-Duality is living from a deeper space of Being, beyond opposing inner energies and feelings. Therefore, the same can be applied to one's inner state, neither too loose nor too tight. This is how 'The Middle Way' approach became one of the fundamental teachings of Buddhism.

Another saying in Non-Duality is that there is a state beyond effort and effortlessness. There is a place beyond happiness and sadness, and there is a way to be beyond that, called the Natural state. It is the Openness, where sadness or happiness arises, the Natural Open Aware Spaciousness for all.

Over the years, I have witnessed some people who have what I call 'luxury' problems, that is, at some point on their journey, too much excitement becomes their obstacle, and too much fascination, or too much desire for freedom, becomes their obstacle.

Eventually, the time comes to become more Present, to

---

[9] See Chapter 4 on Level of Consciousness Non-Duality (Pre-Enlightenment)

ground more in the Here and Now. The foundation of Non-Duality and a way of life beyond opposition is to understand that every feeling has an opposite feeling. Every emotion has an opposite emotion, such as anger and joy, happiness and sadness, and bliss and misery. Therefore, every feeling, emotion, and energy has the opposite.

What commonly happens is that people tend to cling to positive feelings and avoid negative ones. That is how one derails from natural balance, from the middle way.

What are feelings and emotions?

There is no such thing as positive or negative, only energy. That energy in human terminology is usually called feelings, emotions, or thoughts. In reality though, there is only energy. The problem arises when a person is attached to the energy when they like it, and then, they try to get rid of the energy when they do not like it.

When people try to attach to happiness and keep it, they lose their Presence and ground in the Here and Now. The expression that a person has their head in the clouds is rather apt. Meanwhile, when a person has sunk into deep sadness, we say that they are depressed (deep pressure of energy).

Looking at humanity, we can see that there is a big problem with attaching, avoiding, trying to keep, and trying to get rid of feelings, emotions, and thoughts, while there is only energy.

The saying, 'to let what comes come, and to let what goes go' implies trying not to hold on to or avoid whatever is in the present. You can welcome it, allow it, be with it, and let it pass on its own accord. You are the Space for Energy!

You are your own Home. All your feelings are your guests within You. You are the sky, and all these feelings are the clouds within you. Essentially, you are thus This Present Space, this present Awareness, where guests come. A sense of love comes, followed by a negative feeling, and both come into your home, within you, in your Space, your Aware and Open Space.

We can all understand what is supporting and what is loving. The opposition, on the other hand, is what you are trying to avoid and thus resist. This resistance is usually an instant internal reaction; sometimes, it is instinctual. However, if there is no resistance, there is no opposition. Everything comes and goes as quickly as the flow of air.

What are some of the most challenging dualities?

The most challenging dual forces are self-opposition, self-judgment, self-destructiveness, and self-suppression. These are some of the biggest troublemakers in human experience. They are unconscious resistances that are difficult to deal with in a waking conscious state because you cannot do much about them. Only when you go deeper into your subconscious can you gain the power to deal with these automatically self-opposing energies and feelings.

You have probably experienced feeling happy, when suddenly, something happens, plunging you into helplessness. These opposite emotions create instant resistance. However, it is your resistance to your reactions; therefore, they are your responsibility. They come up from your subconscious and unconscious mind. They have already been there in the shadows.

How do we deal with them? How do we come to this Non-Dual way of life, where we are not controlled by opposing feelings?

Let us lay down some foundations and ground rules. The foundation of Non-Dual living is to feel the feelings and be with the energies you feel. You are the Space for them. This is rule number one.

* * *

Feel your Feelings Practice

I sometimes ask people in a challenging moment, such as fear, to show me how big the fear is. They usually want to tell me their stories, but I want to see the actual size of the feeling. Is it half a meter in diameter, one meter, two meters, or even five meters big?

Most people would say that the feeling is about a meter in diameter, but the most enormous energies that people carry can sometimes feel several meters wide, like a big cloud. Then, I usually say, okay, so there is a five-meter feeling like a big cloud, but you are the sky; you are thus bigger, much bigger. This feeling is just a cloud in Your Space.

This exercise brings an instant Shift in Power, hence returning the power to you.

Therefore, in every meditation, you always start with your breath, then feel your breath and the space around your breath. When you go deeper, feel the Space around your feeling, your emotion, and around the cloud energy. There is a reason why I always say that. This is because one of the ground rules of Non-Duality, Presence, and mature or awakened being is to feel your feelings and be present with them.

Be with your clouds of energies and be fully responsible for that. That is your responsibility. If you blame someone for how you feel, you instantly start giving your power away. If you judge somebody, you start giving your power away. It is not wise to do that.

You are always bigger than the feeling. You are the Home, you are Space, and you are the sky. You are the emptiness, as Buddha said. Therefore, Buddha can welcome anything because he is the home for all. Everything happens in your Space.

It would help if you were with your fear, dealt with your own energy, and only later dealt with other people because that is more complicated. If you are not Present, you cannot do much about others.

The Non-Dual perspective is to be present and centered in yourself, to understand that this is your feeling, your energy. You are experiencing this now, and you will take care of that.

The other important ground rule is not to be in the feeling, in the energy, and thus, not to be lost in it. Nonetheless, when people are in a good mood, they experience happiness in the energy of love, and they are 'in the flow', and just 'love it', claiming to be so happy. Everybody forgets the ground rule; thus, they get lost in their feelings and energies. People love to be in good energies and those friendly feelings, but those do not serve in the long run. They do not make you more Present, and do not serve your true awakening.

Being Present is not residing in the bubble, in the river, in the energy. Even when the good times come, you still need to be

Present Here and Now, rather than lost in those pleasant feelings and energies. Various justifications arise: 'I just want to enjoy myself; I just want to have fun, I need this.'

However, what happens is that you are lost in the energy and feeling, and you have no power. You are not awakened. You are merely semi-veiled. Enjoying semi-sleepiness is a lovely feeling, but you are only half awake now, and half asleep, because you are in the energy, in the bubble.

How do my thoughts relate to my feelings?

To feel the feeling sounds very simple, but it is a difficult practice because, what usually happens when people have challenges is that they think about their sadness and anger, and they project things onto other people – you did this, I am sad because of you, and I am angry because of this. They think and that is a problem.

You cannot solve emotions through thinking.

People have only created strategies for prevention so that, next time they face a similar situation, they know that they should not do this or say that. Forget about it since it never works. It never truly worked! You are wasting your time strategizing about your feelings.

A staggering 95% of the thoughts that every average person has are related to feelings. A more mature way of being is to feel your feelings. If people did this, their communication with others would improve. Instead of making up stories and associations, you tell another person how you feel. I feel this, I feel sad, and so on. The other person may be shocked and

63

may answer by saying `Wow! That is honest. ´

There is no blame or judgment, just honesty. You can thus see how it immediately improves relationships with others.

It is your responsibility to feel your feelings. That is how you can open up to Presence and come into Non-Duality and other higher levels of consciousness. This is called self-responsibility. That is why Presence is called spiritual maturity.

It is no longer some 'being-in-the-flow' hippie kind of thing. Presence is growing spiritually, becoming present, mature, and responsible. You are not denying or escaping anything.

How can I return power back to my deeper Self from my thoughts and feelings?

When I meet a person for a private session, they usually start talking about their stories. I then ask them what they feel. That is how we find out what is here. Sometimes, people are unaware of what they feel, and that's okay. Just stay with it, not knowing what it is. You do not need to know precisely what it is. You can also feel it, whatever it is, and be with it.

You are much more connected to yourself when you go into the feeling. You are using many more bodily senses in comparison to thinking. This is because thought is like a small stream, but feeling is like a big river, like the river Ganga. Feelings are very rich.

People have come up with many terms and labels for what they feel. They call the very slow and deep energy in the heart 'sadness', for instance. There is additionally the fiery, active energy they call 'anger'. Rather than labeling this energy, just feel it. Feel the actual raw energy itself.

64

I often meet people who have significant challenges, and they say that they are unable to manage these challenges, that it is just too much. My reply is to wait a moment, slow down, come to the feeling, and eventually feel the raw energy.

Do not label it fear, hopelessness, loneliness, or something else. Do not even put a label on it. Let us stay with the raw energy. How does that feel? They obviously say that it feels uncomfortable like something is grinding, but the raw energy is not as bad as thinking that it is the fear of survival or hopelessness, for instance.

Raw energy is not as bad as associations or labels in the mind. Again, associations and labels have NO Power in them. You have given your power away to labels, to associations.

How does the process of going into my feelings heal me?

When you feel the feeling, it is unnecessary to label what you feel. Just feel the raw energy, and you would always see that it is very doable. Feeling the energy is just something uncomfortable, and it may feel like something is grinding in the stomach, solar plexus, or the heart, but it is doable, and that's it. It is not so bad.

Associations, justifications, meanings, and stories have no power in them. However, when you come back to the feeling and raw energy, that is where your power comes back to you.

As you spend time doing this practice, you find that you are healing deeply. You are healing from the things that forced you not to be present. You are healing from the things that took your power away.

In the Presence consciousness, you start to heal deeply. There is deep subconscious healing happening. It is not just changing beliefs. It is much deeper than that. It is not making new habits, which is a subconscious playground. In Presence, you are healing deeply from all the things that took your power away, those that were never healthy, and never helped you to be Present and Alive.

When you are present with your energies and feelings, you are healing them, and when a certain number of emotions get processed, you become lighter and healthier. The breakthrough into that initial lightness is called Non-Duality, where you can be present with energies without reacting to the conditions in your life or avoiding them. That is the entrance to Non-Duality. It is called Transcendence, which goes beyond the dual conditions of feelings.

"All sorrow is due to the fact that many are seen where there is only One. Duality is pain. So long as man does not wake up to his identity with the One, the cycle of birth and death continues for him." (Anandamayi Ma)

At one point in my journey, I wondered if it would ever end as I faced one difficult energy after another to process, but then, I realized that I was becoming lighter, and my Non-Dual space was strengthening, which was a sign of progress.

Therefore, transcendence means growing above. It is not escaping but going through and then growing above. It is hard work, and that is the real meaning of the word transcendence, living beyond any position.

Now, you know what living beyond duality is because you went through duality and felt the feelings and raw energies.

You felt how you were pulled to the left and right and pushed up and down.

At first, you were like a kite in the wind, blown in one direction and the other. First, humans are like kites in the wind regarding consciousness maturity. However, you then grab the string firmly to bring it down. Afterwards, you put the seeds in the soil, and they grow into a beautiful big tree over time. This is what transcending duality means.

How can I grow in my transcendence of experiences?

In a larger sense, in terms of Full Consciousness, this experience is not only in you, but it is You. This whole thing here and now is not only your guest. It is you, in you as you – and that is the Absolute, when Awareness and experiences are ONE.

This experience is yours. Every experience is precisely for you. Sometimes, it is good, and at times, challenging, but it is for you. There is no more distance, no resistance, no avoidance, and that is what unlimited means – being inclusive. It is indeed all included, all integrated. It is All Absolutely you, not only for you, but it is you.

There is nobody else here. There is no more distinction, separation, distance, or any entity behind it. That is called a complete Non-Dual realization, but there is a path to that Absolute Non-Duality and openness.

"As long as I am this or that, I am not all things." (Meister Eckhart)

As we have discussed, the ground rule is to feel the feeling. That is how it starts, that is how it goes, and the more you spend time feeling, being with the energy, being the space for the feeling and energy, the more you mature.

That is how I can identify and know, like a laser, what is presently there because I spent time maturing, being with feelings, energy, and space for them. Many good teachers can do that because they spend time truly being with what is here and now, and it is a very integrative process. Therefore, you do not need to wait. Some of you might think that you are not yet present and should thus stick with your stories. However, you can start practicing from childhood to feel your feelings, to be with your own energies. This is self-responsibility. Everyone should practice it.

Children should start learning how to feel. You can teach your children how to feel, to stay with what they are feeling right now. It is not so difficult. Ask them to slow down, and then, just feel it. This creates a very integrated being, a very responsible, mature, and honest person. You can start practicing at whichever level of consciousness you are because that is how you arrive at Non-Duality.

How do I enquire into what or who I am?

You should realize that it is not only the feeling and energy that is present, but ask, who is myself? Who is present? Who is the identity?

I am a happy person. I am an enthusiastic person. I am in love, and so forth. You always identify with feeling or energy, and then, in Non-Duality, you just reflect on that. Am I really this feeling only, or this energy only? No, I am not. You just notice that you are just here, and that there is no more identity of myself. There is no more somebody here, just the present, aware space, where feeling or energy arises.

These are thus the fundamentals of Non-Duality, and now, you can understand that you can practice it from childhood or wherever you are now. Feeling the feelings without labeling thereby reclaiming the power back to yourself. That is how you become a mature and self-responsible being who can be present here and who no longer reacts to feelings. Consequently, you no longer act out and say what you did not mean.

Sometimes, we get too involved in being human in the way humans take feelings for granted and in taking experiences and labelling them as good and bad because that is where suffering lies.

Suffering is taking reality in a distorted way.

That is where opposition lies. As we relax these thought patterns, labeling, defining, and assigning meanings, we can come to a deeper Presence and experience life more clearly. Clarity of now is another term for Consciousness.

I feel like I am trying to be present. I start noticing my mind dipping in and out of the feelings. It is like the mind is waiting for something to transcend, to move.

You are waiting. Isn't it a certain feeling that you are waiting? It has an expectation. Are you feeling anticipation, or waiting? Just stay waiting. Just stay with expectation more deeply. There is confusion, so stay with that. Besides, do not try to run away from it. Do not let it slip away from you.

Bring the power back to yourself and say, okay, I am just going to be here with exactly what it is now. There is waiting, expecting, and then, becoming confused. There is a duality somewhere there. Just stay right in the middle of it.

If you go left, you slip. If you go right, you slip. Stay right here in the middle. This is what happens. You may fall to one side or the other more deeply. You must thus stay right here in the middle, and do not move. This is very beautiful and deep, and sometimes, it can go deep, deep, deep. Then, it just releases. Stay as long as you need.

I can surely stay with a rough feeling when I concentrate on it, but how do you keep in touch in everyday life? Do you always stay in touch with your emotions while doing something else?

Yes, it comes with practice. First, practice in times of meditation. If you are going on a stage of life, first, you need many rehearsals before a live show. It would help if you had much practice in a meditative way. You are not as present usually in everyday life. It is indeed much more challenging to feel the raw feelings and energies. So, please, do not blame yourself for it. Okay, I went out in life, and it hit me. Okay, I am going back to my practice. After some good practice, you go out and gain some more courage. You say, okay, I am not reacting like this anymore. I am not doing this anymore.

You soon get your confirmation that your practice is now paying off. You are bearing the fruits of a certain amount of practice. If you are trying and something happens, it is okay. If you have no bad intentions, do not worry about it. You get karma only when you have bad intentions. So, if you still get into the same argument with the same person, do not worry about it. You can say, well, I am human. You do not need to pretend to be so spiritual when you are human.

Everybody has spent 20, 30, 40, or 50 years being conditioned to avoid emotions. Now, in just a few months or years, you need to catch up with the last few decades of what you have been accumulating, storing, or avoiding. The good thing is that it does not take that long.

When you reach that way of feeling and being with feelings and energies as they are, without any other mental associations and supported justifications, a huge inner detox process happens, and you detox yourself very deeply.

As you sit in practice and do it, you start seeing results, and then, you get those confirmations that you are no longer reacting in this way, no longer doing that, and no longer resonating with this and that. These are all your confirmations that you are on the right path and are steadily maturing.

In Inner Love[10], people tend to escape reality for a while. It is the honeymoon phase of spirituality. However, real life begins in Presence, and you return to life. You go back to the feelings and raw energies, you emerge from the clouds and bubbles, and then, you just start sitting with them. There, a significant transformation occurs, and much power returns to you.

By returning to real life, you grow into maturity in life, and then, you go back into real love, into love with your experience, whatever it is.

---

[10] See Chapter 4 on Level of Consciousness Inner Love (Second Awakening)

CHAPTER TWO

Full Consciousness

In Full Consciousness, no filter is in the way of the Pure Light of Being. It is the Absolute Self, God Self, the Source of All that is.

Clarity of Full Consciousness

What is consciousness?

It is neither a concept nor a word. It is the present existence in all totality. It is the present existence of all that is seen, unseen, known, unknown, material, or immaterial.

You may be familiar with the concept of the universal mind, universal consciousness. Full Consciousness is not only universal energy, frequency, or vibration but also the source from which it all originates.

Full Consciousness is not somewhere else. It is right here. It encompasses this whole present experience and in which the experience is happening. I like to refer to it as a transparent existence.

You most likely notice what is right in front of you and what is in your room, but you fail to notice the transparent space in which you are. This transparent space is not separate from you because it is your own pure Consciousness.

The simple fact, the simple obvious-ness that you are aware and conscious is usually overlooked by the entertainment of the mind.

The mind is tied to objectivity, to what it can see and think about. The mind thus skips the context. The space is akin to reading a book. In other words, when you are reading text on white paper, you are looking at the black letters, you are reading the sentences, and your eyes are somehow ignoring the white paper on which the black ink appears.

Consciousness is that white paper and black ink is not separate from white paper. It is, in fact, on white paper. Any story can be written on white paper, any complex mathematical equation can be solved on the white paper, any simple drawing by a child can be seen on the white paper. This white paper is the consciousness that we refer to, and, in reality, it is not even white, it is transparent.

Therefore, consciousness is transparent, it is here and present, upon which your life is being lived.

"You are the unchangeable Awareness in which all activity takes place." (Papaji)

Any thought in your mind appears in this transparent space. Even emotions, pleasant or intense, are all experienced in this transparent space.

Separation is a thought, separation is a program, it is a feeling that 'I am separate', being experienced in the transparent space of your own pure Consciousness. Separation is nothing more than just a feeling. It can also be a thought, a sense, a feeling, or a sensation that you are somehow separate.

When you are resting peacefully in the evening, you are not feeling separated. You are resting peacefully. When you are happy, you are not thinking about separation. You are enjoying happiness, and thus, all emotions, happiness, peace, and separation are what I call 'experiences.'

Freedom or liberation is freedom from all experiences, good and bad. This freedom that I speak of is this transparent space, conscious space, also called the Self.

A thought of you arises in this transparent space, and you think that you are different, unique, and separate. It is just a thought, a feeling, a sense.

This conscious space has no fixed identity, and that is your real identity, your real essence, the source of all.

This conscious space, transparent space, is the ultimate home. It is the only home. It is the home of all experiences, always here and now.

It is a home of wholeness, a home of happiness and peace because all is experienced in this transparent, conscious space.

When you pause for a moment, when you pause any thought, you are already aware, here and now.

It is so simple. There is nothing more to add to that. Anything that the mind adds to this simple awareness is an addition of the mind.

Seeking happiness

The mind seeks happiness, first of all, in knowledge. Then, the mind seeks happiness in feelings, to feel happiness, to feel love, to feel peace, and then, it realizes that spirituality or consciousness work is the path to happiness.

The mind starts looking away from materialism into the internalization of the inner self, of inner dimensions, and of inner experiences.

Spirituality is that which is inside, materialism is that which is outside, but Liberation is neither inside nor outside because inside or outside is just an experience. The outer experience or the inner experience.

Previously, you would not have imagined living without thoughts, without your personal story. You would not have imagined living without the feeling of 'I', myself, or having a very strong sense of boundaries in your skin and bones.

As the mind matures, it relaxes more into this emptiness. Those rigid conditions, rigid beliefs, and rigid ideas soften and become healed and transcended.

Consequently, you are no longer interested in them, consciously or subconsciously. You become more interested in the transparent emptiness, in the transparent conscious and open space.

This transparent conscious aware space becomes more interesting than any other experience, inside or outside. Whatever the mind can think of becomes less interesting than the actual awareness in which those thoughts arise.

Your interests, conscious or subconscious, willing or unwilling, by choice or by condition, are what we call 'resonance'.

That which resonates with you, resonates with life experiences that are needed on your Soul's journey, however unpleasant they might be.

This interest is actually a resonance of all good and bad, and eventually, you stop resonating, and you resonate increasingly less with the duality of good and bad.

You start enjoying increasingly more the transparent, open, pure aware space itself. It is called a shift in awareness, a shift in focus, and a shift in perception.

Before, you were fully focused on objectivity and materialism, and now, you suddenly shift into the transparent conscious space.

The transparency of all your interests has shifted, and your resonance shifts. This is called Awakening.

Self-Luminous Natural Consciousness

This transparent aware space is undeniably here. You only need to simply ask yourself a question: 'Am I Aware?' And that is an obvious 'yes'. It is undeniable.

Experiences are debatable and are subjective to the experiencer, but awareness itself is undeniably present. When you ask the question, 'Am I aware?', it is an obvious 'yes', and there is no separation at that moment.

Enlightenment is stabilization in your Natural Self (Sahaja Consciousness), it is a dis-identification from objectivity, outside and inside experiences.

There is no more need for a particular experience, no more condition or bondage of any particular experience. Therefore, whatever happens in the world, in your life, the only question is to whom it happens.

At a lower state of consciousness, the answer is that things happen to me, to 'I', in relation to your personal story. However, at a higher level of consciousness, it is obvious that all happens in awareness. You are not the energies or experiences that are subject to change.

Your identity shifts into Awareness itself which becomes self-evident. You start to realize that it is the most stable identity there is, the most fundamental Being, fundamental reality, fundamental truth, and existence itself.

As you recognize Awareness, you can see that it is always shining, self-luminous, and transparent.

At night, when you look at the darkness, you observe, 'I see nothing'. You see the darkness at night, and there are no lights. When you see the light, you say, 'I see the light'.

Therefore, Awareness itself is a transparency that is shining through the whole universe and all dimensions.

Wherever your focus is, Awareness is shining, just like the sun is shining by itself. Awareness is obvious to itself, just like the sun knows itself that it is a Sun, and it is shining.

In Awareness, all experiences are welcomed exactly as they are, and resistance is no longer needed.

Resistance of 'I'

The core of resistance is the 'I', myself, the position of the Lower self. It is like a stick in a wheel that hinders the wheel from spinning freely.

When you remove the 'I', the experience is allowed as it is. However, it does not necessarily mean that your experiences always become full of bliss, love, and peace. That depends on your vibrational resonance and the evolution of your Soul. That is the evolution of your point of sustainable Awareness.

No matter how big we may perceive and refer to these things, they are all experiences.

Developing wisdom of the transient nature of experiences, inquiry, and realization of every experience that happens in you is also necessary. You must inquire diligently and observe closely what is actually here.

Recognize your attachments, repeating cycles, your interests, and your resonances so that you clearly, fully, and absolutely understand objectivity, how the search for happiness works, and the transient nature of experiences.

In meditation, feelings of love, peace, or bliss are amazing experiences, but they are merely transient. You need to start clearly distinguishing what you are truly searching for.

What are your ideas about Enlightenment? What are your ideas about liberation? What do you assume this liberation to be?

What is your motivation? To have fun? What is Real freedom?

Many people think that Enlightenment solves all their life and personal problems, problems with children, problems with finances, problems with health, and circumstances in their lives.

What is your motivation? Trying to prove something to someone? Trying to achieve something? Trying to prove something to yourself that you can do it? Trying to achieve the next highest height?

What is the motivation behind it all?

I invite you to inquire within you.

And is 'being for the sake of being' enough?

Is being 'aware for the sake of being aware' sufficient?

Inquire into your resonances and motivation because there is no one else other than you holding that.

You are your own obstacle, your own boss, and your own time, telling yourself, 'I might need a couple of years for this'. You create your own time within yourself.

Your resonance and motivation are the mirror appearing in Awareness.

That is the experience appearing in Awareness, and it is only you who decides moment by moment, second by second.

You may wish to simply have more peace in your life, not be bothered by someone, not want to feel in a particular way anymore, etc. It is none other than you who has come to this conclusion or holding, this seeking, or needing one more thing.

As for the questions, 'Is being for the sake of being enough?' and 'Is being aware for the sake of being aware sufficient?', when it is enough, that means that the ultimate liberation is close by.

When the mind expires, when the mind exhausts all options, all strategies, and all possibilities, something drops, and this becomes enough.

It is enough to be Aware, to be for the sake of Being Aware and to Be for the sake of Being. It is enough to be white paper, it is enough to be a transparent space for all experiences. That is true freedom and liberation from all dualities.

Awakened Emptiness

"All things are empty: Nothing is born, nothing dies, nothing is pure, nothing is stained, nothing increases, and nothing decreases." (The Heart Sutra)

How can one become a vehicle or empty vessel for consciousness to operate through?

When you look for something, such as a sense of your 'I' or

'myself', you find nothingness, emptiness, and transparency. You may start with arising thoughts in order to look at them and inquire: 'What are these thoughts? What are they?' They seem to be bubbling up and then disappearing. They want your engagement, and if you engage, then you interact with them.

When you recognize the thoughts as bubbling energies, you also recognize that you are not your thoughts. They are merely bubbling energies that you were interacting with. When you find out that you are not the thoughts, you feel slightly more open and more spacious because you recognize that they simply appear in Awareness then disappear from your Awareness. Your head is not going to disappear when thoughts go away. Your head is thus this space for thoughts to come and go. Similarly, your body is a space for feelings to come and go.

Let's look at this emptiness, familiarizing ourselves with emptiness instead of content. Most life one is constantly engaged with content, thoughts, and emotions. For most spiritual people, nothing much changes, as they are still busy engaging with energies, with content. They are now spiritual thoughts, spiritual feelings, and spiritual energies. It is an upgraded version, but still engagement with content.

Emptiness is usually overlooked even by spiritual people because all these emotions and feelings of peace and love are more tangible than emptiness. Emptiness is indeed still overlooked because one typically asks: 'What's the value of emptiness? If there is nothing, then what should I do there? What's the point of it if there is nothing there?'

Many people go to a spiritual teacher who gives them a wonderful and heightened experience – love, bliss, joy, or ecstasy. When the time comes to leave, they contemplate this fantastic experience: 'Now, I can go home and keep the experience alive in my memory, and I have enough 'food' for the next three months, six months, or even a whole year.' In other words, they feel 'replenished' until the mind becomes unsatisfied again, the food bank expires, and there is a need for another great experience.

Many years ago, I recognized that the law of abundance is always accurate. I realized that I had so much stuff that I did not need. For instance, thoughts, I didn't really need them since most of them disturbed my peace. Energies were entertaining, wonderful, challenging, and difficult. I was grateful to the universe for too much abundance.

In the Western world, we always feel a lack of this and that, and I realized that the universe gave me too much, just too much, and then, I realized the law of abundance – I just had too much stuff that I did not need.

Consequently, I began looking for a way to become emptier and more willing to let go. Indeed, we have to arrive at that point of realization, where we acknowledge that we do not need all that stuff. Some minds would argue and justify that they actually do need things. While taking this and that away, they would still keep something. It is akin to negotiating at the market with the mind, and we must negotiate with our mind to understand what we need and what we do not. But I came to a point where I realized that emptiness is better than anything else that comes and goes.

Is the feeling of emptiness the same as the feeling of 'I AM'?

Can I lose emptiness? Well, that is more difficult to lose

because it is always here. Therefore, I should probably get to know emptiness better because it does not come and go. And it made complete sense for me to realize that I am probably that emptiness because it is fundamental. A feeling of 'I' arises in the emptiness – oh, that's 'I' – and the feeling of 'I AM'.

The 'I AM' feeling arises. It feels like there is an assumption that it is me. The mind confirms it. However, after 20 minutes, or one hour, it goes away. This feeling of 'I AM' also lingers, but simply disappears after a while. And then, it struck me: 'Oh! If this 'I AM' feeling goes, then, it's not me either, or what stays is awake emptiness.'

In this emptiness, this feeling of 'I AM' comes up, and then, it dances the Leela, the play of life. It expresses its forms, shapes, and bountiful expressions, like a whole theater. And then, of course, when the 'I AM' feeling meets another sense of 'I AM', there is another person with a feeling. It then comes to, 'let's dance together now'. Let us see what we can produce together because there are now two of us.

Subsequently, it gets a bit more complicated when one feeling of 'I AM' meets another sense of 'I AM' since the possibilities of what may happen are endless. If both feelings of 'I AM' came back to emptiness and recognized that it is just a game, a play of 'I AM' arising in emptiness, they would wake up and see awake emptiness.

How many 'emptinesses' are there?

One, the same, and only ONE. Therefore, those two 'I AM' feelings would awaken to the one emptiness and recognize that is the true ground of all experience, the true place of all expressions and diversity. It is the same with every one of you here, now, having this sense of your 'Are-ness' – that you Are, that you are this female or male over here, having this sense, and feeling that you are. For a moment, if we pause those natural assumptions, we may awaken to recognize the Emptiness present here, the space of mutual experience in which all these separate 'I AM' reside.

Would I lose my identity or sense of self in emptiness?

The goal is to familiarize yourself with this emptiness, to start to affirm to your mind that it is okay not to play the game of 'myself' for a moment. It is okay, for the moment, not to have a fixed and rigid identity. You are not going to lose anything. What you might lose are the fears, anxieties, uncertainties, worries, doubts, and confusions because that is what the mind is wrapped up in. Familiarizing yourself with emptiness alleviates all these anxieties and fears. It clears the content, enabling you to relax in this emptiness in order to get to know it.

It is very healthy for everyone to familiarize themselves with emptiness and the unknown, even at higher levels of consciousness. 'If I had an idea of my identity, I would be limited by it.' Therefore, the awakened person enjoys emptiness. It is liberating to be empty. It is the most peaceful thing there ever is. In this peace of unknowingness and emptiness, there is nothing for the mind to do.

It simply falls back into this unknown, and then, you find it so light. It has no density, no substance, no name, no form, no concept, and no limiting perception. This emptiness is so light. It is the light of awareness, not the energy of light, which can be quantified by speed, length, and weight.

This emptiness is rather lighter than the energy of light and brighter than the sun because the sun shines in emptiness.

Therefore, which one is lighter, the sun or aware emptiness? Emptiness can host billions of suns – emptiness is indeed home to billions of suns. Emptiness is hence the lightest thing there is since there is no effort in it. The effort is only to let go of holding on.

Emptiness does not have any effort. It is openness, nothing holding, no substance, no need, and no form. This emptiness is shining through your eyes, your whole being. Your entire being is in this emptiness. Awakening means recognizing what is real, how things actually are, and what is fundamental as your nature. Consciousness is another word for this emptiness.

Everything happens in it. You are happening in it, you are in it, and if you remove any resistance, you will open up to it and recognize: 'Oh! I'm empty! Amazing! This is beautiful. I don't need to know anything. I'm delighted to be in this unknowingness.

In this unknown, I'm awake. I can see all the stuff. I can see these energies here, now. I can see this sense of 'I AM' arising, another kind of energy that is very assertive. I can see how stuff arises in me and then, it pretends to be me. But I know that that's not really me.'

When you relax, relax, and relax, you can see that 'I am' emptiness. You are free. You do not need to play the game. You do not need to pretend to be spiritual or enlightened. Meanwhile, you do not need to pretend to be anything because it would all just appear.

These appearances emerge in awakened emptiness. Any subtle substance, as you go deeper, deeper, and deeper into consciousness, is revealed to be assumed to be you. You clear your conscious mind, then, your subconscious mind. Subsequently, you clear your unconscious mind. And then, you meet all these divine lights, souls, and gods and goddesses atop the subtlest realms. You might think that you are divine, love, bliss, and light, and, of course, if you identify with all of that, you become limited.

You soon realize that those concepts and assumptions become a limitation, only to appear and disappear later. Therefore, in awakened emptiness, you can recognize how increasingly subtler things arise from deeper within because there is a whole universe in you.

What is the difference between the conscious, subconscious, and unconscious mind?

The conscious mind, holding all your knowledge, books, and stuff, is a tiny container. Meanwhile, the subconscious mind is a bigger container as it registers what you consciously perceive in your life and everything in your life. Say, you went for a walk and saw a trash can. Your conscious mind gives no importance to it, but it is still registered in your subconscious mind because you saw it or experienced it. Therefore, it is just registered and recorded.

Unconsciousness is even deeper, even more buried. It is even vaster, a doorway to that emptiness. As you start experiencing fields of peace, love, happiness, and bliss, it can get increasingly subtler and higher in vibration and frequency. That part is infinite. The subtleness of the universe is infinite. It has infinite frequencies rising in more nuanced and subtler and blissful vibrations.

86

You still have to realize that it all happens in awakened emptiness. Those subtleties occur in awakened emptiness, and if you identify even with the most beautiful, divine perfection, the light which is called sattva, sattvic quality, the most beautiful, divine, harmonious and peaceful vibration, and pure light, if you identify even with that, you would still be limited.

Therefore, awakened emptiness is the purest thing there is because it is the place where purity happens. This most subtle, blissful vibration arises in awakened emptiness. The densest and heaviest stuff also rises in this emptiness, and thus, there is much familiarization to be done with emptiness. The more you familiarize yourself with the nature of emptiness, the more you familiarize with the nature of the content with what appears in emptiness and assumes identity.

You are okay in the higher realm, and have no more assumptions about yourself, but then, there is still 'the world'. You can thus observe: 'Oh, I'm in my lovely bliss, but there's this trouble. Why are these people causing me trouble? Why don't I have peace? Everybody's constantly disturbing my lovely peace.' Consequently, while there is no 'me', there is everybody else. You are spiritually awake, but everyone else is not, and they are giving you trouble. That is thus a higher-level challenge.

The absolute awakened emptiness recognizes that even otherness, the world, and other identities also appear right here, right now, in this awakened emptiness. If you transcend your current appearance of identity, there are other higher appearances of different identities.

What does the awakened person care about?

They do not bother too much about other egos and identities. The whole game drops. It stops having a hook on them. The world does not disappear as such. It is not that this body suddenly no longer exists, or you do not exist anymore. No, your body is here, and everything is as it is.

But in this emptiness, there is no hope that this or that would change. This hope dissipates, and you recognize that it was a hook. And if you take this hook seriously, you may be in trouble if you take yourself seriously. If you start defending this and that, problems might arise. If you take other people's hooks seriously, more trouble may arise.

In an awakened emptiness, as life requires, you can still be a daughter, son, mother, husband, wife, lover, friend, or colleague. Indeed, you can still play all these roles and perform your duties and responsibilities. You are not hooked on them. You do not identify with them. You do not derive a sense of reality from them, the sense of realness and your identity. You are not hooked by it.

You are consequently a better person when you are not hooked up. You are a better friend, colleague, and partner because you are no longer pretending and defending, assuming, and getting confused about what is what, who you are, and who the other is. Those confusions dissolve, and what you are left with is – clarity.

Clarity is not about knowing everything. That is not clarity. If you say that you have all your goals set up in front of you, and that you know exactly what you are doing, that is simply your smart brain talking. That is your brilliant mind and your intelligence talking. Clarity is the purity of Consciousness.

You are bothered by neither unknown, nor known, and that is clarity.

The nature of emptiness is your own nature, and the word Awareness becomes obvious because you need no effort to be aware since you are open Now. This emptiness, consciousness, or Awareness is naturally effortless here, and you do not even think about it because you are just conscious and open – that's it. No effort. Because you are empty, you are not hooked.

It is the most beautiful thing because you can truly appreciate everything as it is. The flower's attractive appearance, you appreciate all of it as it is.

How do I know I'm making progress?

We realize that there is a lot to release and that many things are held inside. Once you release these resistances, there is a natural release of suppressed energy that can bubble up as ecstasy or bliss. This suppressed energy can bubble up as something deeper in psychology and unconsciousness, but either way, it liberates you more.

Essentially, it is all about releasing, becoming more open, light, empty, and aware, one way or another. I would suggest not putting any expectations on this, and to just sense whether you have become lighter and if things are more open. If you allow more and hold less, these are good signs of awakening. If you are less entangled and less focused on objects, you can allow things to be lighter.

That is an excellent way to measure your progress. You do some work and then you observe that nothing is happening. However, after a week or two, you meet the usual people, and you notice that you were no longer hooked on their story, that you did not respond as you used to. That is where the fruits can be seen. The fruits of your work become obvious.

Transforming Mind into Full Consciousness

Real freedom is liberating your fixation on experience into the boundlessness of open pure Consciousness.

Let's examine all spiritual traditions and religions. Interestingly, they all point to the underlying Source behind all experiences that are here, and that is your own pure Full Consciousness. Your own Consciousness is right here, not in the sky, not somewhere out there in the universe, or some divine realm. It is very easy to verify the presence of Consciousness with the question, 'Am I aware and conscious?'. The answer is obviously 'yes'.

You are not separate from Consciousness, but only your mind ignores it. It is too obvious for the mind to pay attention to Consciousness until it realizes that everything arises from Consciousness since it is the Source of All. All are within this boundless pure Consciousness. Upon deeper inquiry, we can find that Consciousness IS All.

The ego-knot is a fixed position, a fixed identity. When you argue with someone, you are standing very firm in your fixed position. Therefore, everybody has a good sense of the nature of a fixated ego.

From the fixed position, the goal is to relax fixation into open

Consciousness. Relaxing is one word, while deconditioning is another word for that relaxation, as fixation needs to be exposed in the Light, to be seen, met, and healed. Consequently, a person's attention can relax from that fixation, and more open Consciousness can be present in their experience.

Where is Full Consciousness?

In spirituality, it is very common to seek and search for Consciousness. Different paths help in different ways. While a variety of approaches can be helpful, the goal is the same.

There is a path of energetic purification, healing, deconditioning, Self-Enquiry, a devotional (Bhakti) path, etc. These are the paths that help to relax mind structures and unite with the ever-present Consciousness, to release and let go of the structures that veil this pure and simple light of Consciousness that is already here.

Even the word Light is not entirely correct because Consciousness is just here. It is transparent, and you cannot put a color on it. It is transparent, empty, despite not being a void or empty space, without anything, since it includes everything as well. Your whole experience is included already.

How do I get rid of mind structures?

The first thing to know about mind structures is that you are holding them. The universe is supporting you, and it is helping you to hold your mind structures since that is what you know.

If you release your mind fully for a second, you may feel so light that you might have nowhere to hang on to, and you may feel as though you are losing everything you have ever known.

That is where fear kicks in, along with safety mechanisms that say: 'I need to feel safe. I need to feel secure. I need to feel grounded. I need to feel stable. I need to know what's going on. I need to understand what is happening fully.' That is why you are holding onto the mind.

Spiritual paths help you warm up thereby enabling you to let go of ego-knot and that you do not need these dense and heavy mind structures. You do not need these defense mechanisms, thinking that your ego would help you survive.

So, what stays when the mind is gone?

You are still here when you are Self-Realized. The only thing that you do not hold, and which is holding you is pure Consciousness. Your mind cannot have that Consciousness. Consciousness is keeping your mind. You can also say that Consciousness is holding all of it. Therefore, the only thing that stays in Consciousness itself is your own Self, your True ever-present Natural Self.

You can ask yourself the following question without defensiveness: 'Who am I?' Without thinking about it, or trying to understand it, ask yourself: 'Who am I? Am I still here without understanding?' Of course, the answer is 'yes'. Are you still Aware without understanding? Of course, you are.

As a backup, it would be good to know that you are always aware because, if you are not familiar with the source Awareness, your mind may become anxious and feel insecure. Therefore, two things are necessary, namely, to decondition the mind and let go of holding, and the second, which is even more important, to know who you are. Do not imagine God, angels, and fairies, and do not imagine being in love all the time. It would be better not to imagine anything at all.

Being aware of who you are is very simple and natural. Being aware, or Consciousness itself, because there is no Being who is aware, apart from Awareness itself. Therefore, Self-Awareness is who you are. For example, even if you are reading right now, you are aware that you are reading right now. Awareness is so immediate that it is much quicker than any process. Even if your mind turns blank and you observe that there is nothing in your mind, you are aware of that nothingness too.

What makes me Know something?

The mind is a process. Understanding is a process. The same applies to realization that somewhat implies 'getting it', but even that is a process because, when you get it, you keep it. However, what is fresh and alive? Even if you know what it is, you might say: 'I know consciousness, or I know God.' Still, how do you Know that? You see that there is a certain Awareness before even Knowing. It is not separate from you.

How can I be satisfied with Awareness when I want Happiness, Freedom, and Love?

We need to simplify our end goal. Our goal is to be aware as Consciousness, openly, effortlessly, and naturally. We should notice if something obscures it, like a certain mind mechanism.

Awareness itself, which is evident here, is so simple that it is usually overlooked. The mind overlooks Enlightenment.

Those on the path seek this freedom, happiness, and love, but if we look a little closer, we might still most likely overlook the source of freedom, happiness, and love.

If you are honest with yourself, you might most likely really seek not the Source of happiness itself, but the experience of happiness.

Probably, you seek freedom, love, divinity, or a feeling of being pure, good, and divine. Therefore, what you are looking for is that image or feeling you keep in your mind or heart.

That is how you overlook the Source itself, the fulfiller of all qualities, feelings, and experiences.

If you are honest, most likely, you are looking for something else, for a certain feeling, quality, energy, or experience. That is what 99.9% of people are seeking in spirituality.

If people were seeking Awareness, they would realize that Awareness is already here. It is open, untouchable, and transparent. It is what illuminates this experience.

If you are honest, you might acknowledge that you have experienced bliss before. There was no single problem in your mind, and you wanted that forever. Let's examine this statement for a while.

A person has a particular experience and wants all other

experiences to be like that; however, somehow, it is not possible. Of course, that person soon feels disappointed, and wonders how to get that experience back.

Consciousness is the Self-Luminous Source for All experiences. It is independent of experiences and yet inseparable from any experience.

The mind seems to be tricky. How can I have more clarity?

Self-honesty is very important in inquiry, enabling you to look in the mirror of Awareness and see a mental structure, mental image, or imprint.

Seeking a particular experience is an obstacle. Natural Self is freedom. It is not the freedom you feel when traveling or climbing a mountain, as those are temporary, transitional feelings of freedom. The freedom is in liberating your fixation on experience into the boundlessness of open Consciousness.

What is veiling it? It is a certain imprint, fixation, position, and a certain holding onto something in you. I invite you to slow down and connect with what is being held here. You may relax and let it go, stop holding it, and release it. If you are unable to do that, at least, just notice it and become aware of it. That is an excellent beginning to gaining more clarity.

My mind appears to be so real. What can I do?

You can use the 'As If' technique to inquire into yourself. You can use it when you feel a problem or have a challenge.

You can say: 'I feel so stuck as if it is real.' It helps soften the assumption of real-ness that the mind is struggling with.

Morning Meditation is needed to relax and balance your mind and energy, thus helping you to come into a more open space, where you can inquire into the truth. That is the purpose of meditation.

While in that place, you can ask: 'Am I aware?' The answer is 'yes', and you can stay in this simple Awareness for a while. There is nothing complicated to do as it is always present. Consequently, the mind emerges and grabs your attention, veiling Awareness, making you feel a certain sense of separateness.

This is uncomfortable, and thus, you search for a way to come back and feel comfortable once again, becoming openly aware. When the mind intrudes, you can always observe: 'The mind appears to be as if it is real. This fear or anxiety seems as if it is real.'

What is the relationship between emotions, feelings, and Awareness?

In reality, none of the emotions are yours. They are just fleeting. What is truly you is your Consciousness in this present moment. All these assumptions are transitory. What is truly permanent is pure and natural Consciousness.

The changing experience and the ever-changing present moment in Awareness are not separate. It would help to recognize that anything you feel is not separate from Awareness. Every feeling, emotion, and thought is not separate from Awareness.

When you are watching a movie on a screen, the movie is not

separate from the screen. It is on the screen. That is how you are able to see the movie. Likewise, all thoughts, emotions, feelings, and energies are not separate from Awareness; however, Awareness is free from them, just like the movie screen is free from the movie. It does not get wet or damaged by the ravaging fire in the movie.

What if I feel separate? How can I collapse the subject-object distance?

The layer of separation can collapse when you recognize that this feeling, this energy that is here, is just a feeling, and is not separate from Consciousness. That is how you remove that layer, that distance. You might hold it because of protection. You do not want to be fully in this experience only.

The way to collapse this distance, separation, or tension of otherness is to allow it to be here, to recognize that it is just a feeling in Awareness and verify why you are holding it. What benefit does it give you? Most likely, you were seeking something loving, pure, and beautiful, or perhaps, you were avoiding something, to have that little bit of protection, or a little space from something, or maybe a little afraid of being lost in the experience, or nothingness, or being lost in Awareness.

You do not get lost in Awareness or experience of nothingness. That holding was making you feel stressed, tense, and uncomfortable. It felt like something was bugging you. Therefore, the way is to go deep within and meet that which is unwanted or denied, where that distance of separation is held.

97

What is real? What can I be sure of?

You may recognize that there is only this moment, this present aliveness and aware experience. Everything else is an assumption, memory, imagination, projection, wish, hope, or desire. Avoiding and seeking anything else are the mechanisms of the mind. Therefore, they are assumed to be real. They are experienced as if they are real. For example, your life, what do you mean by life? What is your life? Your life is here and now. The present moment, breathing this present air is LIFE.

Regarding the World – what is the World? How do you know there is a world? You only see this moment. Only this moment is certain, undoubtedly. Do you need to recall your memory to breathe the present air? Believe me, I know what you know, I know that you believe yourself to be this person, that there is a world in your experience, that there is what you call life, but I want to tell you something more profound.

The question is, how do you know all that? You might simply say: 'Because I know.' What is Knowing? What is that? Isn't it holding? Yes, knowing is holding. You are aware of holding the knowledge and knowing.

If you relax that knowing, there is no more 'I' position. You have left the knowing, your fixation on knowing, and ultimately, when you relax the fixation on knowing, there is only pure Consciousness left at this moment, just like this.

You can be sure that there is pure Consciousness, being aware of this moment, openly as it is, and that's it. Everything else is 'in-between' stuff. If you really sink into this, it is a Highway to freedom. It is a highway to undoubted certainty of reality, of absolute reality.

It is thus healthy to brush off all your assumptions, wishes, desires, ideas, what you know and do not know, what you want and do not want, what you seek, and what you avoid. These ideas are subject to belief, argument, uncertainty, and doubt. Upon closer inspection, you find that they have no real validity. You can be sure that you are aware and that this present moment is like this. Exactly like this, all of it. You do not need to think about it. It is here already.

As soon as you start thinking about it, you divert into the river of the mind, into what you know and can analyze. You do not need to think to believe that the moment is here, that this experience is here, that there is a body sitting here, apparently seeing something happening. There is light. Apparently, this room is present. It is all like this already.

It is all happening here like this, but as soon as you start thinking about it, your experience contracts into what you know, and you lose that openness. That is why absolute is absolute. It is open and clear. When you start thinking, it gets complicated.

This openness, simplicity, and Consciousness are simple. It is all so simple that you do not need to think about it. You do not even need to understand it. If your mind is holding you and wants to understand it all, in that case, you need to train and prepare yourself, meditate, and learn to be open until you can be open without the need to think and understand anymore. Consequently, Consciousness is experienced, and you open the doors for Consciousness to reveal itself to you as you. This is my invitation home, here and now, to be aware.

CHAPTER THREE

Awareness & Experiences

"A diamond was laying in the street covered with dirt. Many fools passed by. Someone who knew diamonds picked it up."
(Kabir)

Am I Aware? Bringing Awareness to the Mind

Your True Self must be here, in the present moment. Your deepest Self and the truth of who you are must be here. As an analogy, many clouds are veiling the truth. There are many layers of conditioning, degrees of identification, and fixations of the mind and ego. All these are veiling the true nature of who you are.

However, that which is in-between is simply just in-between. You should not exaggerate the conditioning and identifications. You should not be afraid of the number of clouds, and you should not be discouraged by the seeming distance or separation. We can say that all of that is simply in-between. In the present moment, true nature is here, present, and alive, and then, there is the in-between, the veiling.

I invite you to very slowly ask the question, 'Am I aware?'

100

The immediate answer is 'yes'. It is a confirmation that you know that there is a knowing that you are aware of.

There is a knowing that you can see that Awareness sees that you are aware. This knowing is immediate. It might have taken you just half a second to verify, maybe one second, with a little pause. It is a very immediate verification that, 'Am I aware?' yields the answer, 'Yes'.

Perhaps, at this point, Awareness may seem slightly alien. It is rather unknown. We may say it is a bit difficult to grasp or hard to understand. It might even seem too simple. The mind may wander and continue wondering, 'Yes, I am aware'. What is the point? What is the meaning of it? What is the value in that?

The mind may not recognize the value or importance of this fact, this truth, the importance of the most fundamental essence. The mind is more familiar with whatever it is interested in. Therefore, the mind skips to the next thing it knows best or is most familiar with. The invitation is to slow down, slow down the mind, and slow down your usual interests and familiarities. Whether physical or multi-dimensional, slow down even the experience of this physicality or multi-dimensionality and even rest from energy.

Yes, we rest from energy because some of us are so familiar with energy that it feels like a full-time job. Today is a short holiday to rest from the mind and energy. We can rest even from experiences and any activities within the experience. The invitation is to slow down, soften, and relax into the essence, while bringing awareness into the mind, enabling it to better see, understand, and recognize Awareness itself.

The mind is like a cloud, or a combination of clouds, and Awareness is like the sky, open and transparent sky. Can clouds exist without the sky? No. Can the mind exist without Awareness? No.

How do you even know that there is a mind? The correct answer is that you are aware of the mind. Yes, you notice the mind because you are aware of the mind. How do you even know that there is this body? Because you are aware of the body. How do you even know that there are these thoughts? Because you are aware of them. How do you even know that there are your struggles? Because you are aware of the struggles. How do you even know that there are energies for those sensitive to energetics? Because you are aware of these energies. How do you know that you are resting? Because you are aware of your rest.

Now, let us delve a bit deeper. How can you recognize peace? How can you recognize love? How do you recognize happiness? How do you recognize bliss? How can you recognize that there is no bliss? The only answer to these questions is because you are Aware.

Therefore, love, happiness, peace, bliss, or any opposite, and lower experiences are only known within your Awareness and because of your Awareness, and are only known because they are known. They are only experienced because they are known and because they are recognized. When you experience something, you know that you are experiencing it. There is a knowing of this present moment.

There is a knowing here of this present moment that you

exist, that you are sitting here, that this body is yours, and these thoughts are passing within you. There is a knowing, and this knowing is essential. You are aware of even the space of Presence. The fact that you are aware precedes any objective or subjective experience – objective, being identified with objectivity, this body, for example, or subjective, being identified with the observer.

You are aware even of the observation process or the mind trying to understand. However, how do you know that the mind is trying to understand? Because you are aware. So, the invitation is to slow down. When you slow down, it is easier to manage your experience, whatever it may be. When you slow down, it is easier to access Awareness that is present and here. When you slow down, it is easier to bring Awareness consciously into the present experience. It is easier to notice Awareness, to stay in Awareness, and to be aware as Awareness. Awareness is not foreign to you. I want to emphasize that. It is not a concept or a new idea.

You are aware that you are here, that you exist, that you are alive. It is so fundamental that it is even beyond this bodily experience. It is closer than understanding or unknowingness.

For example, peace is a certain feeling in your chest that everything is good, perfect, and balanced. Love is a feeling of being supported, cared for, nurtured, intimate, and close, and it is an energy of the heart. They are all qualities, and Awareness goes beyond all qualities in our universe. It is transparent, and in some ways, it is untouchable by experience, and yet, it is experienced too. Now, this is where some dualities and non-dualities come in.

I am slowly guiding you to recognize increasingly more the nature of Awareness, which is undoubtedly present. I am inviting you to relax your mind, to relax from searching and from understanding, thereby bringing you much closer to Awareness itself.

Relax, be aware – that you already are. Relax any effort, relax any understanding, looking, or searching, and relax your focus. This is how Awareness reveals itself.

Everything that has ever happened has taken place in Awareness. Everything that has ever happened in your life has been in understanding, like the fish analogy. The wise fish would claim that fish live in the water, but the young fish would always seek it. Similarly, human beings have always lived in Awareness, always, ever, from birth, to the last breath and even in-between. Even before and after, we have always lived in Awareness. That is where all these mind paradoxes come up, all the contradictions and dualities of experience.

It is a unique situation here for any being who has realized Awareness. Humanity is so unique that it is probably a very rare situation, even in the whole universe. Now, in a practical sense, the first step is to recognize, 'Am I aware? Yes'. The second step is to understand that Awareness is Self.

The third step is to understand that it is you, that this Self is you, and that has been the case in every single experience you have ever had. Meanwhile, the fourth step is to clear what is in between: confusion, uncertainties, or knowingness. As Buddha said, to clear the ignorance, to illuminate the ignorance, to illuminate the mind with Awareness, to bring the light to the darkness, to the truth. Dissolve ignorance to bring Awareness to the mind.

The iceberg of the mind melts in soft Awareness, in the ocean of quiet Awareness, in the ocean of the present, alive, transparent, softness of Self.

The mind has questions. It has doubts and uncertainties. The mind has unknowingness, and wants something tangible, practical, understandable, and graspable, something that it can keep and hold. To attach to, possess, attain, and achieve, and in the end, to get it – this is what the mind wants. This is how the mind functions. Then, in the end, one day, everything finishes, and all is 'happy ever after', like the ending of a movie or story.

However, life is not like that. There is no journey, really. That is a big paradox since there is no journey and no end.

Awareness is Now, and the apparent journey is your journey back to the Now, back to Awareness, back here, right now.

It is the apparent journey in eliminating and removing all doubts, worries, confusions, and misidentifications. It is a messy journey, and a relative one, albeit not a journey per se because there is no journey as such.

Nonetheless, to the mind, coming back is a journey. There is a process, there is progress, and there is a continuation from A to B to C, and eventually, arriving at D. This is how the mind functions. Please recognize that Awareness is not that complicated. It does not have to be long. It does not have to be far because it is here, now. It is obvious. What is not apparent is everything that you believe.

Anything that you believe in is food for confusion. It is food for doubts, worries, and unknowns; therefore, the healthy way to live is to let go of all beliefs, including the belief that God is this or Source is that, and the Self is like this. It is only like this, or it is all like that. The belief that it is so far away, in another galaxy, is beyond 3D, and is only for the mountain Yogi and cave dwellers. It is only for the lucky ones, for some extraordinary souls who have descended from heaven, and only angels can get there. And you know, only Jesus can do this, or only Buddha has achieved it.

Anything that creates more distance from your own Awareness is not serving you. No matter how beautifully a book is wrapped, regardless of the billions of copies printed, no matter how beautiful it may be, if something is distancing you further away from your Awareness, it is not helping you.

Therefore, television, well, you know what that does already, and all dogmas, philosophies, complex analysis, and scientific validations. You know, when you think of it, what sort of instrument can validate Awareness? What kind of mechanical or electrical instrument can validate it?

Nowadays, scientists are investigating the quantum field, but that is as far as they can go in a sense because they can never contain Awareness. It truly cannot be contained. It's impossible. No device can hold Awareness. Similarly, Awareness is the most obvious thing, but it is untouchable and ungraspable. No device can keep and hold it. You can only harness energy. You can only harness atomic, quantum, and zero-point, renewable energy.

106

Science can only deal with universal energies, which are necessary and needed to advance technologically. But for yourself, a simple question, 'Am I aware?', gives you the ultimate answer in the whole universe. This one question answers it all, and further looking into this question, inquiring further, bringing Awareness back to the mind, dissolves it. The mind dissolves like an iceberg melting in the warm ocean in soft Awareness.

3 Key Steps of Enlightenment

Enlightenment is awakening to this present moment's Awareness, noticing, and seeing objects without being mixed up in any phenomena.

There is always a deeper place of Seeing, even amid confusion, doubts, and worries. This indeed explains why one has a certain Awareness even when one is worried about something. Awareness is actually the source behind any experience.

One of the key questions is, how do we awaken to Enlightenment?

Deconditioning the mind

There are three key parts to this. One is Deconditioning the mind, especially the mechanical parts of the mind, its habits – the habitual way of thinking, patterns, and responding to situations, people, and environment.

The conditioned mind is like a mechanical clock. It is interconnected and wounded together in many layers. Like an onion, it has layer upon layer, and they are all connected.

Sometimes, I give an example of noodle soup when explaining the mind. When you take one noodle out, it becomes slightly loose, and then, you take another noodle out, and it becomes even looser. Taking more noodles out becomes quite transparent, and you can already see through it.

Deconditioning allows the light of consciousness to come through. One does not need to decondition or solve all the issues to come to Full Consciousness. Some assume that all their problems would be solved, but that would take longer and more work.

However, for consciousness to shine through, and for one to recognize oneself as Consciousness itself, a highway approach is to decondition the key points that are blocking Consciousness. By finding and addressing those key points, we can work through them more easily and open our Consciousness much more quickly.

Disidentification from what you are not

The second part of the three parts of Enlightenment is disidentification. At the lowest state of consciousness, there might be a tendency to identify with constantly being angry and always thinking that he or she is right and everybody else is wrong, and so on.

At a slightly higher state of consciousness, people are identified with their body, with the ideas of 'I am the body' and 'you are the body'. That is the body identity, where people are exploring their physicality.

Then, there is a mental identity regarding knowledge and what one knows. It is accumulated knowledge, and identity is formed with that, and once we clear that out, a person can come to recognize that he or she maybe is the knower, and not what is known.

Consequently, that opens the possibility of Self-Realization, going into oneself and realizing increasingly more who one is at a deeper fundamental level, and equally important, who one is not.

Disidentification is the second major part. Nonetheless, a common pitfall in this second step is when a person sits back and asks, 'Who am I?', 'Who am I?', and claims, 'I am this', 'I am that', 'I'm not this', and 'I'm not that'. However, this is mental exercise. People typically get stuck because they need to do all three steps of Enlightenment in synchronicity, in combination.

A person cannot just do one thing and expect everything is going to progress forward. Similarly, one cannot continue healing only because one would get stuck in healing and would not go higher.

A person can only do so much at a certain level, and then, the tendency is to go round and round in circles. We need to see consciousness opening as a multi-layered approach because, as I have mentioned, there are many layers of the mind, layers of identity, and layers of stuck points.

Familiarizing with the higher states of consciousness

The third part is familiarizing yourself with the higher states of consciousness, especially in the company of that individual, commonly called a teacher, a guru, or a guide. A being who has already reached that place can help to familiarize with higher consciousness and then, show the next step.

Why is this necessary? It is because the mind does not know the higher states of consciousness. The mind has never experienced them before. So, how can it become familiar with something that it does not know? On the other hand, people read a lot of books, and then they start making up all sorts of assumptions to try to familiarize themselves in that way, but reading is not going to get one far, compared to the actual experience.

A teacher or guide would always help to familiarize yourself with the most optimal place that a seeker can ascend to or open up to easily. A teacher who truly sees another person would know that this place is the next step that is doable for that person.

If I were to speak from my place only and where I am at, nobody would understand me because Absolute Self is all there is. For most people, it is not so practical to know that because it is way too far for them, they cannot relate to it in any helpful way.

Therefore, familiarizing with a higher level of consciousness (in most cases, gradually) is essential. During this process, the spiritual guide envelops fellow spiritual explorers in this higher field, allowing them to experience that directly, familiarize themselves, and get to know higher consciousness.

Additionally, Consciousness Transmissions[11] are a highway to familiarize, dis-identify, and de-condition. Consciousness

---

[11] See `About Full Consciousness Transmissions´ at the end of book for more information

110

transmissions do not support a false identity. They enhance and support the Natural Sahaja Self.

Heart on the Right Side (Amrita Nadi)

"Your heart is the size of an ocean. Go find yourself in its hidden depths." (Rumi)

The inner Sun (Amrita Nadi) is the channel of Bliss, the seat of Consciousness within the human energetic body. It emanates from the Heart on the Right, two fingers wide on the right side. The energy channel itself looks like a coiled shape, "S," which curves forward from the chest on the right. It goes up through the throat and then curves up the back of the head, towards the crown and above. It is not within the spinal column or part of the kundalini mechanism.

Sri Ramana Maharshi has, on many occasions, referred to the heart as being on the right side:

"(Heart on the Right) Heart is the seat of Jnanam as well as of the granthi (the knot of ignorance). It is represented in the physical body by a hole smaller than the smallest pinpoint, which is always shut. When the mind drops down in kevala nirvikalpa, it opens, but shuts again after it. When sahaja is attained, it opens for good."

"That the physical heart is on the left cannot be denied. But the heart of which I speak is not physical and is only on the right side. It is my experience; no authority is required by

111

me. Still, you can find confirmation of it in a Malayali Ayurvedic book and in Sita Upanishad."

This channel is also where the ego-know, the sense of 'I' arises. If we trace attention back to its source, we will see that it arises in the heart, not the head and specifically, it arises on the right side of the heart, just a little to the right of the breastbone.

Returning to Consciousness is a process of softening our attention and focus. In this process, we realize that our attention and focus on normal circumstances are outwardly focused. In spiritual practice, it becomes increasingly inwardly focused. Consciousness is neither outward nor inward. Consciousness is right Here, right Now, and Open, Unbounded, and Unlimited. It is an experience of no limitation, contraction, or separation. It is very natural to be in Consciousness. It feels very naturally you, yourself, simply Open.

To remove Separation, the primal cause of bondage, and the primal cause of contraction, we must journey back into the seat of Consciousness within our energetic body. When the ego-knot

is opened, the Amrita Nadi rises and goes up to the crown of the head, up and above to reunite with the Absolute Self.

The primary tool for opening the ego-know is our attention and focus. It can be connected with the practice of Self-Enquiry, where the person examines, 'Who am I?', 'Who is this separate self?', hence trying to trace the source of this 'I-ness', of this sense of separation.

We come to find that it is the heart on the right where the I-sense arises, and thus, if we draw ourselves within and relax into it, the healing process starts, and the Self can begin to shine, increasing its capacity to shine through the body and the veils of the mind.

We will now explore a practice of relaxing our attention and focus. The more you explore how your attention works, the more you gain control over it, and the more you gain strength and the ability to surrender it or direct it to the Source from where it arises. Since your attention is constantly Here and Now, the practice can be done anytime, anywhere, simply here and now. You may first notice that your attention is always focused on something. It always needs an object.

Therefore, as you relax your attention and focus on things or spaces or energies, it gradually softens. You might notice how many tensions are created because of that focus on objectivity. That is where everything gets crammed, blocked, contracted, and tensed up. Indeed, 99% of all the pains in the physical body are related to tension arising from attention constraints. They are all energetic pains.

If you are too involved in objects, energies, or spaces, another practice is to recognize that there is involvement, but you can perhaps zoom out, or you can withdraw and retreat into the background openness. You can also try to notice the space around your attention. What happens when you feel the space around your attention? The boundary within it collapses.

However, there is always the next thing that your attention immediately focuses on. You collapse a boundary for two or three seconds, and then, something else appears and captivates your attention again, but step by step, it is a softening process. It is a process of detachment from objectivity. It is not that objects disappear since everything is still here the way it is but your involvement, focus, and inner constriction start to soften and dissolve.

Your body also needs time to heal from many decades of tension. Many fresh energies may open up, and both your Awareness and inner space may expand. You may become aware of so much more you have never noticed before.

You can gain control of your attention by surrendering it, dropping it, bringing it back to the origin from where it came, from the heart on the right.

Every time you drop your attention into the heart on the right, the Self gains more strength in your experience. The Self becomes stronger and more evident until Consciousness starts to overshine the mind, and it becomes much simpler and more natural to keep on dropping the contractions. It becomes nearly automatic. You see it, drop it, see it, drop it, and surrender it, until everything gets absorbed into Consciousness, and all contractions disappear.

In quantum physics, it is already known that the observer can collapse a quantum field being observed. Therefore, each one of you can now experience that. You can simply collapse the energy field in which your attention was contracted. Suddenly, Openness unfolds, or natural healing occurs.

This is a very direct way to return to the Self. You may sometimes feel that you get stuck somewhere, and you do not know how to progress forward. That is where a deeper inquiry or additional support is needed. That is where a teacher comes in and advises you on how to overcome a particular obstacle, go deeper, or simply help you amplify the Self, the radiance of Consciousness, so that it is easier recognized, more supported, and quicker integrated.

* * *

Inner Sun (Heart on the Right Side) Meditation[12]

Step 1: Take a few moments to slow down. Feel your breath. Feel more space around your Breath.

Step 2: Imagine there is a beautiful Sun behind your body, shining into the Heart on the Right, on the right side of the chest. This Sun is shining through and emanating from your chest forward.

Step 3: You can bring your right hand closer to the Heart on the Right. You can sense that there is some vibration or warmth, a sense of more space, and an inner brightness. Or perhaps any tension, pressure, or little heaviness.

Step 4: You can make circular movements clockwise or anticlockwise to feel more into the Heart on the Right, where there could be a small cloud. But remember that there is a beautiful Sun on the back shining into the Heart on the Right, shining forward. Therefore, if there is any cloud in front of your chest, it's okay. You can let it be.

---

[12] This is an introductory meditation, more advanced meditation is given in person. This meditation works best in the company of a guide, while receiving a Consciousness Transmission.

Lighthouse of Your Focus & Attention

Unbounded Awareness is the freedom that is already here; it is who you are beyond duality.

However, your focus is usually on your thoughts, feelings, or energy. Unbounded freedom, unbounded Awareness, is already here, just like the air or the space all around us.

But who is noticing the air all around us? How many people are noticing this space all around us? There is a tendency to look at objects, to look at things, to look at thoughts, and to look at feelings and energies. There is a tendency to look at everything, which is a passing phenomenon. To look at that which is changing, thus forgetting where all phenomena are happening.

What is the deepest groundedness of Being? Where is that freedom while everything is changing? The tendency to place one's focus and attention on that which is objective and changing is even deeper than instinctive tendencies, one's habits, than one's beliefs and thoughts. To discover how things work, one must go right to the core, where it all began.

What is the actual cause of people's involvement in the thinking process, of being entangled and mixed up in the mind? For those who are more advanced in meditation, it is being mixed up with energies, chakras, kundalini, or various energetic fields and spaces.

There is a constant involvement and mixing between who we are, our identity, and that which is experienced. To return to boundless freedom, we need to examine how it works. We may recognize that our attention and focus are the keys. Our attention and focus are always keeping us occupied with what is happening. Usually, the night is the only time when we are exhausted from daytime activities when our attention and focus drop while resting. People experience a sense of peace and homeness as nothing else is interesting during that restful moment. Everything of the day is done. There is nowhere else to go, just resting in the Now.

On average, a human being has about 90,000 thoughts per day. Most of humanity is identified with the mind and with what they know. However, it does not feel right, it does not feel fulfilling. A little closer to the present moment is the feeling of one's body. In order to feel the body, one must focus on that which is present, here and now.

When one starts to feel the body, one's attention and focus get involved either with physical sensations or with the inner stuff, that is, emotions, feelings, energies and perceptions. There are a myriad of different emotions, feelings, and energies that can be experienced. The inner world is much bigger than the outer world.

In the inner world, we may discover the whole universe. The inner world is the world of energy, spaces, and access to higher dimensions. Going inside expands our experience with much subtler dimensions and energies. How many experiences can one experience? The possibility is indeed endless, as big and as diverse as the whole universe. One can meditate on experiences for decades, and still, experience something new. There is always something more, and more, and more. Where is the end? Where is the real home, which is not a changing experience?

Coming back to attention, one may recognize that one's

attention is traveling. One's attention is in fact being involved in these experiences, energies, and different spaces. This realization alone that one's attention is constantly traveling everywhere is already a huge realization in itself. One may recognize the real cause of the feeling of longing. One may further realize the real cause of the feeling of searching for inner completion. This is because a person's attention is always searching, looking, trying to find something, and the sense that there is always more, and it is never enough.

To solve this issue, we need to ask: 'Where is the root of Attention itself? From where attention arises?' It seems that attention and focus arise from our head, right? We may thus say from our head, particularly our third eye (pineal gland). This is because we would mostly look outside from our head.

However, if we shift our focus to the spiritual heart, we may see that the heart space holds the inner world, that of searching again. The search from the spiritual heart is closer to home than searching from the mind. As we settle more into meditation, we may perceive our attention dropping from the mind into the heart, feeling more at home. A certain inward movement occurs. It already starts to find something.

Being in the heart becomes more satisfying, but it is not the ultimate satisfaction as one cannot stay in the heart chakra forever. One may say that one's attention and focus arise from the heart, but by going even deeper, one may find that it arises not from the heart chakra, but from the heart on the right side (Amrita Nadi).

"'I' is the body-mind, the fraction of the Whole that is now appearing and will soon disappear. 'I' must be surrendered to the Heart, to the Whole, which is Infinity, Wonder, and Love." (Adi Da Samraj)

The heart on the right, the Amrita Nadi, is the seat of the Self, the seat of Consciousness. Attention and focus actually arise from the heart on the right, just about two to five centimeters on the right side, from the center of one's chest. You may put your hand close to the heart on the right and try to feel it. You might feel a slight tingling sensation or a slight energetic feeling, or you might start feeling some slight pressure. It can take a little while to sense into it, but it slowly becomes increasingly evident.

The heart on the right side is also where the original problem lies. Attention arises and veils this heart on the right side. From this place, attention and focus twist in the heart on the right, becoming a small narrow stream of light that shoots up into the head. This explains why attention and focus are like a lighthouse, a beam of light, not boundless Awareness. It is from this place that attention and focus twist as a slight vortex, which is a reverse vortex. It twists unbounded Consciousness into a small stream of light. The whole ocean becomes a river.

We have realized, and even measured, that the average human has only 4% of the heart on the right side (the Amrita Nadi) open. In other words, 96% of this ocean is veiled. I call it the solar eclipse, where the sun is the heart on the right, the channel of bliss, the source, the Self, and 96% is eclipsed for the average human being. Therefore, open and boundless

Consciousness narrows down into a personal subject-object experience.

Even though the reality is completely open, completely here and now, the average human being perceives a duality of inside and outside – the river now recognizes that it is separate from the ocean. This is where the sense of separation arises. This is where the sense of the 'I' feeling arises, that it is me, myself, or 'I', as a separate individual, a personal identity. Since this 'I' has been within everyone for decades, people have made it home. They have made that little 'I' feeling their home.

Of course, everyone tries to make the best out of their situation, but it is rather strenuous keeping that separate 'I' identity happy. Indeed, it is very rarely happy. That little 'I', that small and separate self, is more of a trouble bag. It is usually confused, anxious, doubtful, and worried. It is sometimes peaceful, albeit rarely, not fully knowing what is happening, how it came to be, and why it is not free.

Because of that small stream of attention, energies became interlocked. Consequently, everything got limited and locked up from infancy. This is how the mind, or the energies, became interlocked with the identification of the 'I', the small self. The mental framework became structured because of this interlocking. Hence, the mind became mechanical and densified as a mental/emotional/psychological complex.

In reality, there is no mind, but rather, there is energy. It is indeed the energy that gets interlocked, and because of these interlockings, thoughts are constantly trying to remind one that one's energy is locked up, that something is wrong. Thoughts are only the consequence of interlocked energies.

Because of these interlocked energies, people experience a lot of tensions, thus stress, fears, anxieties, and a sense of inner discomfort, a feeling that something is wrong. A feeling of longing or searching is present because one knows intrinsically that something is missing. That intrinsic knowledge is correct, and it reminds one that something is not as it should be. Freedom, boundlessness, and the naturally aware Self are missing in one's apparent experience.

This knowledge alone, what you have just read, is already a major step towards Self-Realization. However, with the conscious mind, you can only understand the problem, which is already a big step, but then, the actual locks are energetic and are in the subconscious and unconscious. You might need some help from someone who has already 'been there and done that' and who is already free and liberated. There is a need for assistance to help to open those specific locks for you to become freer and freer, enabling your awareness to become boundless in your experience.

Knowing the root problem is immensely important because this already points to the solution. How many people on Earth know the actual problem, the root cause of all suffering on Earth? In Buddhism, it is said that the root problem is Ignorance, Desire, and Attachment. However, how did Ignorance, Desire, and Attachment come to be in the first place?

There are only a few examples, usually offered by some Eastern gurus, about the nature of Enlightenment. Nonetheless, even more misconceptions and assumptions are also formed about Enlightenment. Most gurus do not point to the root cause but usually discuss side effects. One thus asks whether the teacher is helping others to awaken, or whether they are focused on improving their students' lives. It is good to know how many of their students have awakened. Indeed, checking how many students have awakened into Self-Realization is a good measuring stick.

How would you feel once the inner tension is resolved?

Once this root problem is resolved, you may no longer feel that anything is missing. You may feel that you no longer need to look for anything because you already found your home, here and now. You might feel that there is no more longing, and no more longing for love, peace, happiness, or anything else. You may feel no inner bondage of limitation inside. You may feel that there is no one opposing you within anymore. The inner conflict is resolved, while the good inner voice and the destructive inner voice that constantly conflict in your head are at peace.

So, in essence, there is no internal opposition, no inner judgment that you are not good enough, that you cannot do this or that. There is no more inner victimization and inner abusiveness because you may sometimes want to do things right, but things do not happen that way, and you cause even more trouble for yourself. There is no more inner suffering since your body relaxes. It is a very relaxed way of being, but very aware, very alert, very much here and now, very present.

Here, now, aware, alert, very much like a cat. One moment you cuddle a cat, and the next, the cat leaps and runs due to some noise behind a table. Cats are very relaxed and aware beings. A huge awareness of the now is experienced, and you are completely aware of what is going on in a very relaxed way. There is not much effort. The inner struggle is released, and the internal struggle is gone. The inner opponent is gone, inner resistance is also dissolved, and resistance to what happens and to what dissipates.

So, now tell me, how would you feel? Amazing, free, and liberated. All this trouble is gone. It's a celebration, isn't it? And then, depending on your energetic configuration, you may feel nice feelings too. If you are more heart-centered, you might feel more intimacy, acceptance, and unconditional love, and it can be very natural to you. You may feel peaceful, clear, and content if you are more mind centered. Nothing is opposing you in your head, nothing is contradicting itself.

Depending on your energy configuration, you would feel many things in a much purer way.

The avatars, ascended masters, and many gurus are great souls who have gone through countless lifetimes of energetic purification. But the actual awakening, enlightenment, and full consciousness are realizing who you already are – it is possible for everyone! There is considerable confusion between energy purification and who you really are.

To become a sage, an avatar, or ascended master, well, that's a big job. It is also what I bring forward, but that is a path of self-mastery and ascension, and a path of becoming a teacher and master.

However, to awaken into who we already are, as the boundless freedom of natural and pure Consciousness, is the first task at hand because we first need to tackle the real problems that everybody is facing in order to become free of those problems. Only then can we speak about the path of self-mastery and ascension. Sometimes, they happen together, but first things first.

So, let's be clear that awakening is available, but some problems must be dealt with, namely, attention being contracted on the right side of the heart, and then, the head, and then, the whole thing of interlocking of energies makes the conditional reality seem real. It becomes a conditional reality experience. It seems real and feels real, but it is not. It is conditional. The true real reality is unconditional. It is unbounded and free.

Power of Your Focus & Attention

The present moment is like a painting. It is already painted the way it is. When you start thinking about something, you start painting the image of the present moment, but luckily, pure Now is not affected by that.

Thoughts are quite chaotic. They are disorganized like jumping monkeys. Therefore, the mind needs to be trained so that you can stay in the present for at least a few moments. Staying in the present moment is not easy since your focus and attention are rarely ever present with what is truly here and now.

Unfortunately, for the majority, this is how life is lived. The average human being is only 4% fully conscious, fully here and now with what IS. That means that 96% of the time, the average person is not here and now with what IS. Once the mind becomes more trained to be here and now, it starts to discover what it has been missing all along.

The mind has sought love, joy, peace, bliss, and freedom.

Love, joy, happiness, and bliss are not in the mind, yet the mind is looking in the mind itself. Joy, happiness, bliss, and freedom can only be found here and now, in the present. When the mind is trained, when the mind is brought to the present moment, that is called 'stillness'. That stillness is not a pause because a pause is just the entrance. That stillness is the entrance to a larger here and now of open natural and pure Consciousness.

"To a mind that is still the whole universe surrenders." (Lao Tzu, Tao Te Ching)

The problem is that your focus is constantly engaged with mental activities. It is in some cloud, in some kind of personal bubble, which you call your world, or more precisely, your personal worldview.

My duty here is not to fill your mind with more stuff, but rather, to empty your mind, clear your mind, and empty you from stuff that is cluttering you, and from that which is cluttering the space of stillness and natural Consciousness. It is better to understand less, but to Feel more, to be here more, to be more in the present.

My duty is to help you to re-discover what is real. Happiness is here, joy is here, peace, bliss, you name it – all can only be experienced in the present Awareness. But the mind has many fields of coverings, clouds, and veils of other concepts, ideas, and beliefs.

The mind and your focus are your biggest traveler! They are rarely ever Here and Now. That is the nature of the mind and your attention and focus. You do not have much power over your mind, but you have power over your attention and focus, and over whether to allow your mind to follow or not.

Your power IS your attention and focus – right now. That is where power resides – seeing and choosing what you want to focus on and what you want to experience. You do not need to engage too much with certain thoughts, feelings, or stories.

You have that power, and I want to show you that you have it. I can show it to you, but I cannot give it to you because you already have it. It is yours to learn to control. However, I can share with you how to use it so that you hold that power. Your attention and focus are the first steps to utilizing your power.

Consequently, you may find that you can start changing some of the things you focus on, like whether to follow (or otherwise) those things popping up in your Awareness. What is popping up in your mind? 'Look at this', or 'I forgot that', your mind says. 'I shouldn't do this or that', or 'There is a problem', and 'This is important'. Your focus usually is 96% automated to focus on what pops up. You can realize now that you have the power to engage or otherwise, to follow or not whatever appears.

However, this power does not come instantaneously, and you might not be able to immediately take control of your reality and become a superhero. You see, you have spent the last 20,

30, or more years following whatever popped up in your head or appeared in front of you – this habit became an addiction. It is a habit, and you have lost your power time and again over the last years, and now, you can start to reclaim it!

Advice: When you are consciously in control of your focus, if you start to feel overwhelmed if you start to feel confused or anxious, it is time to let go of control, it is time to give it a little break and allow things to happen as they happen.

This training is best done slowly, but more often, during the day, rather than in prolonged durations in one go. It would be good to come back to your previous comfort zone and relax from control. By consciously controlling your focus and then relaxing, you can push yourself closer to the new you, to the next level, to higher consciousness. And then, you have to love yourself, heal, let go, and integrate. It works in cycles with every new opening. You push yourself, and then, you heal and love yourself. Today, you discovered your power. Use it wisely.

What Is the Essence of Experience?

One of the most critical components of being you is that you are aware.

You notice this present moment. Somehow, you see whatever is happening, and you see that you understand something now. When you put thoughts together, you see that there is a mind, you see what you like or do not like, depending on what is in the mind. You see that you are aware, that you are meditating in a beautiful and peaceful meditative space, and that you are enjoying it.

How do you know that you are having these experiences? How do you know that you meditate in that peaceful and loving space? And when you come out of this meditation, you exclaim: 'Ah, that was an amazing meditation! I wish I had more time. I'm going to try to come back to it tomorrow.' How do you know that? What was before this amazing experience? How did you even know that you had this fantastic experience? So, can we say that you witnessed yourself having this amazing experience? Isn't it that you are witnessing your whole life happening? Could it be that you are witnessing any experience unfolding?

The obvious question is how or who is witnessing that. The answer is that there is a certain sense that you are somehow aware that you are present, that you somehow know that you are experiencing this, and somehow, everything fits in your experience.

Let's examine how much you can fit in yourself. You can read books, enjoy these concepts, and fit them in your mind. You can play and dance, practice sports, and everything fits in your experience. You can be in a deep meditative state and have an infinite cosmic experience fitting your experience. You can meet a Divine being, God or Goddess, and they fit in your experience.

You can meet Jesus or Krishna and all the saints and sages, gurus, and avatars, and they all fit in your experience. Did you ever understand the obvious fact that everything fits in your experience? Therefore, the question is: What is experienced, and what is You in which it is all fitting?

What is happening NOW is something amazing, extraordinary, profound, and special while still ordinary and simple.

What does awakening mean?

A very common saying is that humanity is like sleeping Gods, more like baby Gods, in reality. Indeed, the name 'Buddha' means awakening, awakening to the truth, and seeing the reality of IS-ness of what is really happening.

In this instant, you can realize that all is fitting in your experience and your whole experience, whatever it contains in your whole life. Any possibilities that you could ever think of and experience in any dimensions would fit in your experience.

You are aware of that somehow. All of it is in you. You are witnessing that there was no single moment when you were not witnessing your experience. That is how big you are. That is who you really are. You are that in which any possible infinite experiences fit in you. You are That. Therefore, you need to investigate further: Who is this 'myself'? What are the associated qualities so I can start sensing more of it and familiarizing myself with my real Self?

What are the qualities of my Being?

I mentioned aware space as an associated quality with your being because all experiences fit within it. It is transparent, and thus, anything can fit in it – any object, tree, mountain, river, earth, galaxy, black hole, supernova – anything can fit in the aware space.

We can thus say that it is transparent. We can also say that it is infinite since you can fit anything in your experience. Whether looking at the night sky or through a telescope, it all fits in your experience.

We can further say that it is alive. It has always been alive. No matter what you have experienced, it has always been alive. Even those who die for a moment and have out-of-body experiences come back with amazing stories. Some of these people who experienced NDEs (near-death experiences) were doctors. They have written fantastic books about how they died for a few moments and experienced something exciting. They were alive, and then, they came back to the body, and their whole perspective on life has changed. They experienced a certain awakening, realizing that they are a spirit that cannot die.

That is an intermediate spirituality. Your being is always alive. That is obvious. It is always in the presence of NOW. Even if the future fits your mind, whatever you can think of, you can also recall the past, and in memory, it also fits in your mind. So, the past, present, and future all fit in your experience. Can I ask you what color is your being? Now, that is where it can be funny. Some of you may say pink, while others might say black, white, and so on. These are just your experiences.

Your Being is colorless. It is transparent. Buddha named it emptiness, perceiving this word to be the most convenient. To him, the Self, or awakened state, is empty. It is empty, but you are in it, you are That, and it is everything – the whole universe is in your Awake Emptiness.

I prefer the words transparent, awake, and alive. Even the vacuum fits your experience – if you suck all the air out of some container, the vacuum is still there within the experience, and thus, awareness is still alive. Transparent lightless light, because all the rainbow colors and millions of variations of color tones, fits in it too.

Sound and soundlessness are other qualities. Being self-illuminating also means that you are always seeing, always aware, and constantly noticing in your transparent lightless light. Even in the darkness, when you close your eyes, you see the darkness, and when you open your eyes, you see all the colors, shapes, and forms. You see the sun too. So, you are this lightless, transparent, alive light that always notices everything.

"Light is also in you, since its essence is light."
(Anandamayi Ma)

In Non-Duality, it is called the Self. In other words, you see yourself, you are self-aware, the deepest Self of all, the I-I, the Absolute Self of all. It would help if you kept your mind open as you read this. If you say, 'Oh! It's space', you would put your finger on it thereby limiting it.

Familiarize yourself with the nature of the Self and its associated aspects. They might seem far away, or you cannot fully experience them, but if you are listening, it is undeniable that they are here, and this is the nature of being.

You only need to familiarize yourself and investigate what your mind tells you otherwise because your mind might object. It might say: 'No, no, I'm much smaller. I'm just this

131

personal self or the body.' The mind might object or identify with something else.

Some would say that they may be the Spirit only, but what is that spirit? Have you ever really investigated what that Spirit is? So, you need to listen to your mind and see what identifications or objections it may have. It is essential because these objections are held in your system.

They are the programs of limitation, or rather, suppressive programs that are functioning, and now, they can surface. Consequently, these suppressions might say that you now cannot be this infinite, open, transparent being because you are much safer being a Spirit or a body, or what you already know. So, it is 'the Knower' who says so. Therefore, the identity of the knower is saying so.

Other mature beings may say: 'Okay, I understand that I'm this infinite, open, self-luminous, always aware being, but I'm having trouble since I'm always focused on this point of experience.' That would be 'the Perceiver' identity.

You might not identify with 'the Knower' anymore, that you are this knowing or knowledge. Still, you might remember that you are this limited perceiver, a certain focused point of perception – also an identity.

Therefore, you need to look closer at your experience and investigate it. Do not resist your experience but simply explore it. What is it? What are you experiencing? How are you feeling? What is your mind telling you? It is a feedback loop.

What is experience?

I am pointing to who you really are, but then, you are looking at the mirror of your mind and getting feedback on something more limited.

Therefore, there is a reason. There is a certain program, identity, and belief behind it. Or, if you are lucky, you simply did not know that you are this infinite, open, transparent, luminous, constantly aware, conscious being, undeniably always present. You thus say: 'I just didn't know; nobody told me this.' If you have no objections to that, that's amazing. It is going to be easier to be That.

Your current experience is certain feedback. How do you know that something is suppressed? You know it because there is something bigger behind it. How would you know that something is smaller? Because there is something much bigger behind it.

How would you know that you are blocked? How would you know that you have conditioning, or that you have an identity? Or how do you even know that you do not know? You might thus claim: 'I don't know anything. I'm just here.' How do you know that? Because you are seeing it. Simple. You are seeing it, noticing it, and aware of it. Because you already Are. This is how you are illuminated. I am reminding you of who you are.

If you were unaware of that, then, this is the most important thing you need to hear. If you know, to a certain extent, then, you need to know much more about who you already are and continue enlightening yourself about your own nature.

If you have doubts about who you are, they need to be clarified. If you have anxieties and fears, they need to be clarified and illuminated. Then, you say: 'Okay, now I can understand it. Now, I am much safer, more comfortable, and now, I can open up to myself.' If you are objecting to your infinity and self-radiance, that is something that you need to look at because there is a suppressive program. So, every experience has certain feedback on your Awareness.

You can notice your experience, and simply allow it to be as it is, without resisting it. If something is limited, let it be because you are not trying to change how you think and feel, or the circumstances in your life. Let it be as it is and recognize that your experience is more expansive in allowing it. You are more in touch with the wholeness of your experience, including something limited and uncomfortable. Simply recognize, just for a moment, that this experience is like this. It is incredible because there is a certain wholeness to it.

It has a certain unconditional aspect because it is unconditionally like this. Even if you try to resist anything, anytime, anywhere, it is part of the experience. It is hence very unconditional. The Self and the Universe are very unconditional.

If you do not harm someone intentionally, then it's okay. The problem lies only if there is intentional harm because you would 'pay karma' for that. Causing harm can also be unconscious, but it still creates karma. Whether you had a good intention or not, you would still have to resolve the unconsciousness of that action.

There is a law of balance, but if you do not harm anybody intentionally, you are good. Nobody is judging you. God is not judging you. Angels are not judging you. Nobody is judging you. Are you maybe judging yourself? But as long as you are not wishing anybody for intentional harm, you are good.

So, whatever happens, good or bad, it's okay. The universe is unconditional. It is all as the experience is. My invitation is now to bridge this gap of experience and Awareness.

How can I increase my Awareness in my day-to-day life?

If you pause any activity for a moment, you can recognize your noticing. You are noticing everything. All this is in this instant. That is an awakening experience. It is both simple and ordinary experience. The most important thing for you is to recognize that it is possible to experience that. In that instant, you are your Awakened Self. The mind might conjure up some veils, and some energy might appear and conceal it, but that's okay because you now know how to access your Awakened Self.

In the deepest sense, everything objective is just an experience, and since you are noticing, you are beyond it. Noticing means that you are before the experience.

As you develop a relationship with your experience, there is a closer connection between Awareness and experience. It becomes an intimate relationship, a more unconditionally loving relationship.

All is inseparable from this experience. This lightless light of Awareness, seeing, and noticing penetrates and burns out all separation. Therefore, the light of being is called the Self, in which the whole experience is already included.

How can I be free from my experience?

Anything that life manifests in your life, in your now, is a resonated state, a purification of karma, and an accumulation of merits of past lifetimes. Essentially, it is as it is. This Experience is a combination of all factors, known and unknown.

Freedom lies in not trying to improve your experience, although everybody is working on it since it is humanly natural to want to improve your experience.

Instead, freedom is to see that every experience is in Consciousness, is seen in You. It is seen. You see every experience, and that seeing itself is You.

You can shift your focus from this bounded 'me' into the boundless 'me', who sees all of it now, the whole experience.

Whatever your experience is, all are secondary to your consciousness. Your Consciousness is number one. What is happening is number two because what is happening is a highly complex process of many things, merits, karma, circumstances, planetary needs, service to humanity, and so on.

It is indeed all connected in a very complex way. The most important thing is, however, to recognize that all that happens is in your consciousness. That is how you are assured that, whatever happens, it happens for a certain reason, it is playing itself out.

Shortening the Distance Between Your Focus & Awareness

Everyone is used to looking through this tunnel of focus and having comfortable boundaries and distances. If this distance comes closer, it just collapses, or the inflated bubble pops. If the distance between Focus and Awareness collapsed, the mind would be shocked. Indeed, it would not know what to do.

When the distance collapses, everything is so close that everything is immediately here.

There is nothing to focus on anymore. Suddenly, there are no objects to grasp, and suddenly, everything is so close that you are everything, and the mind cannot be in that state for long. What is enough then? What is enough is what is now, what is already here. Is that sufficient? Or do you need something more? The mind has specific ideas of satisfaction and what would bring fulfillment. There are certain hopes and ideas of what ultimate fulfillment is. Probably, one has assumed that it must be something more than what is here, that this ultimate Enlightenment, fulfillment, or consciousness is more than what is here.

It is when the mind 'sugar coats' things and assumes that Enlightenment is the ultimate fulfillment. The mind functions in terms of, for instance, going out for dinner, feeling hunger, and getting food. The first course, second course, third course, and dessert at the end, and then, it is so full that it cannot take it anymore. Now, there is a need to lie down, rest, and process it all since it is too full. However, the mind cannot be fulfilled because it needs to process it all when it is full.

The mind comes up with ideas, associations, and goals. Something got stuck in your mind some years ago, a few months ago, or just recently. Perhaps, you saw something, and it got stuck in your mind about what things must be like. People have a certain projection, a certain image in their mind of how it must be, and they try to match their present reality to that image. People are trying to clone the Now to that image or projection. Is that even possible?

We know the truth from human history that this is not quite possible. The last few 1000 years have proved it already. People have tried to conform reality to their mental projection, and it did not go well.

Therefore, you need to clarify what you are looking for, the search, the projection, the yearning, and the desire. What gap are you trying to close? Is it feasible? Is it realistic to mold the present moment according to your desire? If you drop this gap, this distance, what is left, is what is here. You can start by accepting it, by allowing it, even just for a few moments, just allowing and accepting what is here. Then, you may feel that there is some tension, some yearning arising. Something is arising, taking you out of the Now, back into the mind and desire. You have expressed your desire for your home to be comfortable, acceptable, livable, and bearable, just to be ok.

This is how this desire takes you out of the Now, with great strength, blowing you out, or with great resistance not to be here. Then, the mind would say: 'Well, there's nothing left. I have no more hopes, no more exciting desires to chase, no more fuel. If all is gone, I have nothing exciting anymore.'

However, the only thing that would be gone is desire or fear itself, but you can still be sitting here, and all would be well. Desire is gone, yearning, searching, looking are gone, and all the inner troublemakers are gone, but are you willing to give it up? Does it feel more comfortable chasing things?

This gap, this distance, is this strong pull outwards, and you need to know that it is very safe to be in The Now. It is only fear itself that is afraid. It has some imagination, or it is scared of the unknown. But what is unknown here? Everything is right here. There is still a chair and table, floor, ceiling, and body, and you are still sitting here. Nothing is gone. Fear itself, aloneness, and desire are gone, while the distance and gap close.

So now, perhaps the mind may be more cooperative since you have cleared the core uncertainties. We may say that it is a huge surrender. We may say that it is a great disillusion, a great stopping, the end of this whole search and projection. What you need to know is that nothing is going to change in your life immediately. It is all going to be the same as it is right now.

If you were aiming to do away with all your problems, that is also not the case. You still have to sort them out if you have relationship problems. If you have work, financial, or health issues, they can still be there, and you must work through them. You must still eat, sleep and function. Therefore, rest assured that life continues, and nothing much changes. You are, however, no longer yearning, searching, looking, missing, and needing. What changes in your every moment experience? How are you experiencing this NOW?

* * *

Awareness - Mini Meditations[13]

Sometimes, the busyness of our everyday lives prevents us from maintaining regular meditation practice. The good news is that we do not need to sit in meditation for an hour a day in order to progress spiritually. There are effective practices that we can engage in when we have even just a few minutes here and there.

The following short practices can easily be incorporated into the day. Their aim is to bring our attention to our Awareness that is always there. This attention to our Awareness slowly dissolves the conditionings of the mind, thereby enabling our true Self to shine through.

Freedom Here and Now
1. Acknowledge what you See and Sense Externally
2. Acknowledge what you See and Sense Inside you (e.g., emotion, feeling, thought, or energy)
3. Acknowledge that you are Aware of emotion, feeling, thought or energy – is that a 'yes'? – Pause
4. Who is Aware? – Pause, do not answer, do not move
5. Awareness is Already Always Aware
6. Practice Awareness Anytime and Anywhere as Freedom from all that is externally and internally

Lose Yourself in Bliss
1. Notice your Attention or your Focus
2. Focus Externally or Internally on anything
3. Expand the boundary of Attention or your Focus
4. Drop your Attention into Boundless Present Space

---

[13] These meditations work best once you are at the Awareness Level of Consciousness or above. However, you may try them out, but it's important to be gentle with yourself.

5. You are that Boundless Present Aware Open Space Here and Now
6. It is Warm and Shining Aware Self-Illuminating Light as Bliss
7. Practice Awareness Anytime and Anywhere as Boundless Shining, Seeing Awareness

Melting in Love
1. What are you Focusing on Now?
2. Soften your Focus or Attention
3. Relax your Heart Space
4. Drop your Attention into the Heart Space
5. Love is Softness in your Heart, Love is surrounding your Heart
6. Breathe into the Heart from behind and soften
7. Melt in Love Anytime and Anywhere

Awareness Is Freedom from the Mind
1. Notice the I-Feeling, remove all thoughts
2. Stay with the I-Feeling, without thinking, just feeling
3. Are you Aware of the I-Feeling? Yes? Confirm
4. Who is Having the I-Feeling?
5. Awareness is Already Aware of the I-Feeling
6. Stay Aware of the I-Feeling as Awareness
7. Awareness is freedom

Freedom from the 'I' Function
1. Pause for a moment
2. From where do the thoughts emanate?
3. From the 'I'
4. Slowly repeat to yourself I-I (twice 'I') and again I-I...I-I...I-I...
5. Continue repeating until you see that ALL thoughts come from this 'I'
6. That is clearly the case

7. That is the source of your Identity
8. You are Aware of the I, you are free as Awareness

Hard Truth Will Set You Free
1. Pause for a moment, do not think
2. Are you Aware already of this present moment? Yes? Confirm
3. Awareness is the Boundless Light
4. Why do you need to think? Isn't it slow?
5. It is easier to think because there is weakness
6. It is hard to stay as Boundless Awareness
7. The Mind is holding you in its grip!
8. But the Mind is seen in your Awareness
9. So, stay in Awareness, just seeing...
10. Witness your limitations being burned out
11. Be Free!

Short meditations are highly beneficial since, focusing even a few minutes on your boundless Being increases the strength of your Awareness. These meditations may bring increased clarity, relaxation, and groundedness to your everyday life.

CHAPTER FOUR

Levels of Consciousness

Levels of Consciousness©

A Map to Full Consciousness www.NewHumanityLife.com

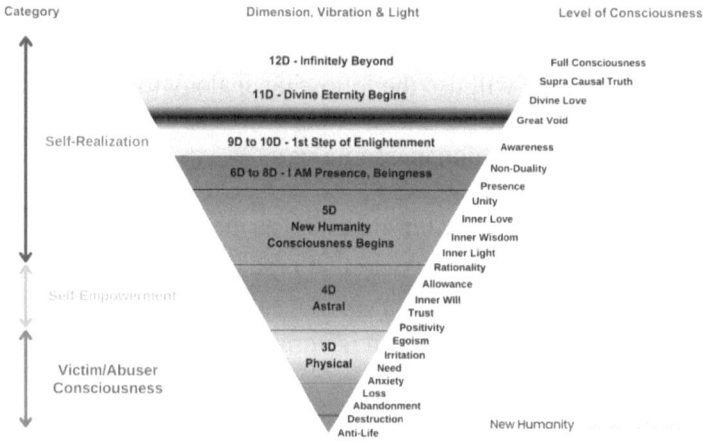

Category	Dimension, Vibration & Light	Level of Consciousness
	12D - Infinitely Beyond	Full Consciousness
	11D - Divine Eternity Begins	Supra Causal Truth
Self-Realization		Divine Love
		Great Void
	9D to 10D - 1st Step of Enlightenment	Awareness
	6D to 8D - I AM Presence, Beingness	Non-Duality
		Presence
	5D	Unity
	New Humanity	Inner Love
	Consciousness Begins	Inner Wisdom
		Inner Light
		Rationality
Self-Empowerment	4D	Allowance
	Astral	Inner Will
		Trust
		Positivity
	3D	Egoism
Victim/Abuser	Physical	Irritation
Consciousness		Need
		Anxiety
		Loss
		Abandonment
		Destruction
		Anti-Life

New Humanity

"Wherever you are, that's the entry point." (Kabir)

What Are the Levels of Consciousness?

The Levels of Consciousness (LOCs) represent the density of the mind. At the lowest LOCs, the mind is very dense, and this density is reduced at higher LOCs. The less dense the mind is, the easier it is to experience the natural Being, known as the Self, or Full Consciousness.

The Levels of Consciousness (LOCs) can be hard to grasp, unless one has had first-hand experience, moving through a significant part of the scale, or having experienced big jumps up the scale.

Since many people misunderstand what it means to progress up the scale, we will use the following analogy to describe it.

The ocean of consciousness analogy

Imagine all Levels of Consciousness as the layers of the ocean. Below is LOC Anxiety that is so deep that no sunlight reaches down to that level. People residing at this level permanently may think that it is normal to be in the dark.

However, people born at higher levels who have gradually descended to these low levels would have an inkling that 'something is not right', and they would know deep within that something else is possible.

Right above LOC Anxiety is a different world that is still dim. However, enough sunlight at least comes through so that shadows and silhouettes are visible.

Furthermore, it is now possible to navigate towards the light. Meanwhile, life is still hard and full of struggle in LOC Need to Positivity, but, at least, one can now move towards the sunlight. Contrastively, at LOC Anxiety, one would hardly remember that there is even such a thing as sunlight. It all seems hopeless and unchangeable.

Moving up the Levels of Consciousness has little to do with reading books or intellectual knowledge. It has, however, everything to do with removing core conditioning and creating space for more of the Light of Consciousness to shine through unfiltered.

For example, if you go around expecting a lot from other people, you would be constantly disappointed and angry. You would be caught up in all sorts of dramas on the surface 'story level' of what is happening.

However, if you remove the 'core belief' of having expectations, all the anger, disappointment, and drama on the surface would suddenly disappear. You would live in a different world because you have just shifted your perception of the world and others.

As the core conditioning is resolved, it is automatically replaced by inherent correct clarity. Some density of the mind has been released, and things become much clearer.

As you move into LOC Inner Will, Allowance, and even LOC Rationality, you start to see things more clearly and in detail. It is still well below the surface of the ocean, but much more light comes through here, and life feels much more supported and enjoyable than at the lower levels.

When you reach LOC Inner Light through LOC Non-Duality, you would swim around right below the surface in almost full daylight. This is where the real mystery can start to happen.

At intervals, you would no longer identify with the body, but rather, with the ocean of consciousness itself. As you progress even higher and breach the surface in LOC Awareness to Full Consciousness, you would paradoxically realize that you were the ocean all along. Indeed, all the levels were contained within you.

Changing the TV channel

Progressing up the scale is not about how much you 'know', but rather, about removing ingrained 'knowledge' that distorts your vision and blocks your light of consciousness.

Each main level of consciousness is like a different TV channel. When you change your level of consciousness, it feels akin to changing the 'TV channel' that is playing out your life.

If you like horror movies, stay below LOC Anxiety. If you prefer drama, LOC Need through LOC Allowance is good for that, but if you like adventure movies, I recommend the higher LOC Inner Light through LOC Unity.

For those interested in being present with real life, here and now, having clarity of paradoxes of the dual nature of the mind, LOC Presence and LOC Non-Duality are great. Meanwhile, if you want true fulfillment, bliss, and freedom of being, move into the bandwidth of LOC Awareness through LOC Full Consciousness.

Each level contains certain 'lessons' that keep repeating until you have worked through them. This is called karmic or cycles of mind's conditioning. You then move out of that level and into the next one.

146

It is like a school of life, with different classes and levels. The lower-level lessons are usually more gross and dramatic than the higher-level lessons. To progress as quickly as possible, you need to re-prioritize your life, where movement up the scale becomes your number one priority.

You may realize that you can grow and learn spiritually, rather than having to manifest additional challenges in your life in order to grow in consciousness.

Three Categories of Consciousness

"We are here to awaken from our illusion of separateness."
(Thich Nhat Hahn)

---

1) Victim/Abuser Ego

In the lowest levels of consciousness, the human mind is dense and filled with repressed and hidden negativity. People at these levels are close-minded, rigid in their belief systems, and quite abusive to others in their actions or speech.

However, people at a higher level of consciousness can also experience some of these negative feelings due to trauma, a lot of negative influences, or social conditioning. In such cases, it is just temporary, as they know that something is not right, and they are not supposed to feel so bad.

These low consciousness levels range from Anti-Life to Egoism. They are a 'survival mode existence', where everything is perceived as a struggle, and those who 'give up' are dragged down in the whirlpool of self-destructiveness.

Perceived weakness is singled out and preyed upon, either mentally or physically, or both. Herd or gang mentality is typical, and the lack of compassion and mercy at these levels, even in young children, can be shocking.

People in this consciousness range would identify mainly as either 'victim' or 'abuser', which, in reality, are two sides of the same coin. A victim's ego projects most of their repressed negativity onto their own self, while the abuser's ego projects this repressed negativity onto others, like perceived enemies and the world and society in general. In between are a myriad of combinations of these two extremes.

The native inhabitants of LOC Anti-Life to Egoism

People native to sub-LOC Positivity levels are typically born into environments and families that match their low birth level. This can be anything from war zones to extreme poverty and abusive environments in the lower half, to gang territory and rough neighborhoods in the middle.

People native to sub-LOC Positivity levels would usually spend their entire life below this level, and they would not be inclined to evolve much. Meanwhile, people native to LOC Anti-Life to Egoism are typically dominated by one or several chronic negative emotions, like depression, anxiety, or anger.

Anything below LOC Positivity is energy-draining, lacks integrity, and is destructive and essentially harmful in influence.

People in higher levels who are temporarily experiencing the lower levels would usually have a more conscious and reflective relationship with their problems. Conversely, people born at these levels do not even know that they have problems.

Lost and trapped people from higher levels

Most people who eventually find themselves interested in personal development and spirituality are typically born at the higher levels of consciousness of LOC Inner Will or Allowance, the levels at which spiritual curiosity emerges.

However, consciousness tends to drop throughout life as a person gradually absorbs negativity and programming from parents, peers, school, society, and mass consciousness. During the teen years, it may even drop below LOC Positivity. However, individuals would not experience these lower emotions the same way as those born at these levels.

People originating from higher levels might have a knowingness and remembrance deep inside that something is 'not right', and that they do not really 'belong there'. They may typically feel a deep calling as young adults to regain what has been lost, to de-program themselves and heal.

They would often find themselves victimized in the field of lower consciousness as the natural compassion of those born at higher LOCs is taken for weakness in sub-LOC Positivity. Therefore, they would usually search for a way to reach the lighter LOCs from where they came.

Many evolved souls choose to have experiences in the lower realm of consciousness to gain strength. In fact, the ability to do so is a sign of inner potential. By stretching the rubber band as far into negativity as they can handle, individuals can be catapulted into higher levels at a much faster rate than would be possible otherwise.

2) Self-Empowerment: Overcoming the Ego (LOC Positivity to Rationality)

Breaching the crucial threshold of LOC Positivity might feel like an internal pole shift. Your head is suddenly above water, and you can see the sun again. Above LOC Positivity starts the journey of true self-empowerment and the ability to change your life for the better.

LOC Positivity to Rationality is where the dense and compressed mind starts to melt and decompress its rigid beliefs. Life and living conditions are significantly better here than in sub-Positivity levels.

While sub-Positivity levels would correspond to the yogic term 'Tamas' (i.e., darkness, imbalance, disorder, chaos, anxiety, impurity, destruction, delusion, negativity, dull or inactive, apathy, inertia or lethargy, violence, viciousness, ignorance, and entropy), the levels between LOC Positivity and above are all about 'Rajas' (i.e., activity, passion, transition, individualization, drive, move, dynamism, and ambition).

In LOCs Positivity and Trust (especially the lower part of this range), one is still circling the circle of the sub-Positivity levels, and one would feel the pull strongly. It still takes much energy to 'keep afloat' here. This changes in LOC Inner Will and Allowance.

People become increasingly more positive and optimistic in LOCs Inner Will and Allowance, which are, once again, reflected by increased positive support from Life itself and the occurrence of seemingly 'miraculous' synchronicities, ranging from simple things, like a book we needed to read falling into our lap, or meeting just the right person at the right time.

However, this is also a level full of traps and pitfalls as the ego would often try to stop its own unraveling.

The release of compressed emotions

Emotionality and sensitivity increase at this level as repressed negative emotions from the lower levels are released and processed out of the system. This is usually known as learning to 'Let it go…' and can be a bumpy ride of emotional ups and downs.

Restlessness and excess of unbalanced energy are common. Longing for peace and harmony, and the words and concepts in spiritual teachings would start to resonate at the medium/higher end of LOC Inner Will to Rationality. The downside is that it is also easy for the innocently naïve seeker to be effortlessly fooled by wishful thinking or mistaken intellectual understanding with true Beingness, Non-Duality, and Self-Realization.

As much negativity is cleaned out, the Inner Space begins to open, becoming an increasingly dominating influence from LOC Allowance upwards. The person is no longer functioning merely from the three lower chakras but has now started to awaken the all-important 'motor' of the heart chakra. Unbalanced and exaggerated empathy is common, and there is usually a lot of crying and releasing as the heart keeps expanding and opening more and more.

'Non-spiritual' inhabitants of LOC Positivity – Rationality

Non-spiritual people 'native' to LOCs Positivity and Trust

are usually regular worldly people oriented towards pleasures, security, survival, materialism, and distractions from 'negativity'.

In LOCs Inner Will and Allowance, there are many artists, creative people, and educated and successful or career-minded people. Meanwhile, LOC Rationality is a level where people start to reach excellence in whatever field of interest they pursue. Indeed, the corporate world includes successful and influential businesspeople, individuals with strong leadership abilities, who have already mastered their employees' emotional states.

Since most of the intense emotional cleansing has been taken care of in LOCs Inner Will and Allowance, LOC Rationality is a level dominated by intellect, inner understanding, and reason. Many genius scientists, inventors, and artists are found in LOC Rationality.

This is truly the level of 'worldly excellence' and success, albeit Only the Beginning of the actual spiritual knowledge. Spirituality is not about knowledge and understanding, but about actual experience, real connectedness, 'living the talk', and finally, about real Love, Presence, Awareness, and pure Consciousness itself.

3) Self-Realization – From Awakening to Full Consciousness (LOC Inner Light to Full Consciousness)

"Your own Self-Realization is the greatest service you can render the world." (Ramana Maharshi, Abide as the Self)

The awakening of the Inner Light and Inner Wisdom opens

the path of Self-Realization. Inner Love and Unity consciousnesses are the most common spiritually awakened states of humanity, leading to the more advanced Presence consciousness. Non-Duality is considered a pre-Enlightened consciousness. Thereafter, there are the four steps of the actual Enlightenment, from Awareness awakening to Full Consciousness realization as the Absolute God Self.

Level of Consciousness Inner Light and Inner Wisdom is the life-changing first stage of spiritual awakening, where the Inner Light penetrates the densest part of a person's energy field to allow greater emotional healing. As fears and heavy emotions are transcended, objectivity and clarity of one's life increase. One can practice being the observer of life 'from above' in order to gain wisdom and higher intelligence. Synchronicities become apparent, the senses sharpen, DNA begins repairing, and one feels more alive. However, in this early awakening, the mind's energies remain predominant. Eventually, a natural calling to Love may arise to transcend the mind's limitations.

Level of Consciousness Inner Love and Unity is the honeymoon phase in the spiritual journey due to a greater sense of openness and oneness. This love beyond intellect guides us to return to our heart and soul. It is not oriented to relationships, but instead, to all of life. The mind's energy softens and drops into the heart, where we commonly realize that love is the way, and all is love. Courageous exploration of our feelings and life circumstances becomes common as the drive to heal increases. As this love matures, it expands into Unity Consciousness, creating a feeling of connectedness to all life. Unconditional love and compassion naturally arise in this feeling of unity.

LOCs Inner Light, Inner Wisdom, Inner Love, and Unity are

153

the states of realization, where 90% of all spiritually awakened humans reside because the next step, LOC Presence, is more advanced, and is usually quite challenging to open.

In LOC Inner Love and Unity, we can use the analogy, where a person is at the most beautiful tropical paradise beach enjoying the sunshine, dipping into the ocean for a swim from time to time. LOC Presence is the ocean itself. There is no more person. There is no one in heaven or at the beach. It is a complete surrender of the spiritual ego-self and all energies to the field of Presence itself.

Level of Consciousness Presence is the level of spiritual adulthood as we begin to stay present with what IS, and we can sustain difficult spiritual energies. The sense of being a separate 'I' slowly dissolves in Presence, allowing deeper aspects of our conditioning to surface, thus enabling a deeper healing of the distortions and unhealed memories that have shaped our life. A sense of 'being', rather than 'doing', arises, bringing great expansion and peace. Presence also has an aspect of the mighty 'I AM Presence' in Ascension Teachings.

Level of Consciousness Non-Duality is the natural outcome of the work of transcending the dual energies in Presence. This is the fruit of the efforts that come with overcoming the biggest dualities and we are rewarded with a sense of relief and an expanded sense of cosmic consciousness. This is the stage often referred to as 'non-doer ship' as the realization that all is happening to No One becomes evident. It is easier to be present with what is here and now.

Level of Consciousness Awareness is the first stage of Enlightenment. There is a sense of oneself as the Universal

Self, where consciousness is now expanded to encompass the whole Universe as 'I AM All' or 'All-ness'. Awareness is much lighter than Presence or Non-Duality because a sense of larger openness greatly dissolves the sense of separation from others. The brain and nervous system increase in coherence as we further heal blockages in the nervous system thereby enabling a greater sense of lightness as the brain is lit up to a large degree, hence 'Enlightenment'.

Level of Consciousness Great Void is a surrender to THE Great Void, neither a cosmic space, nor a single black hole. At this level, we surrender to the great unknown of the unmanifested. The void is a place of resting from needing to know, comprehend, or to be aware. This Level of Consciousness also allows access to the unconscious, unseen, and not experienced, except in deep sleep. A great healing of previously unconscious patterns in consciousness is available here as disturbing psychological patterns are seen and released.

Level of Consciousness Divine Love is the second step of Enlightenment. This transcendence of the causality of all creation experienced in the Great Void is attributed to Divine Grace as no one can transcend all creation alone. Pure Consciousness is experienced more directly as the Divine light helps to transform, transmute, uplift, and melt into a higher level of bliss. The sense of 'I' further melts into the Divine Love.

Level of Consciousness Supra Causal Truth (Divine Truth) is the third level of Enlightenment that is the awakening of the Divine Truth. The light of Full Consciousness shines clearly like a diamond, with only a thin veil of mind separating us from Absolute Reality. The seed of the mind, known as 'I-Thought' or 'I-Sense', becomes visible. In order to remove this veil, we can watch the I-thought as it emerges in our field of consciousness or resides in the Heart on the Right until the last remaining vestige of the ego-self dissolves.

Level of Consciousness Full Consciousness is the highest stage of Enlightenment. It is known as the Natural Sahaja State, the Absolute Self, God Self, the Source of All Universes. With the veil of the mind removed, there is no more separation between us and the pure light of Consciousness. All is seen as Self. The Self is unborn, undying, undivided, and inseparable. It is all there, manifested and unmanifested, as the Source of both. It is the 'I AM THAT'. Full Consciousness feels very natural, open, restful, empty, and alive. It is the end of seeking as the seeker realizes that there is only ONE, and all sense of 'otherness' fades away.

Infinite Ascension, Soul Advancement[14] and Self-Mastery follows the Enlightenment of Full Consciousness. The level of Full Consciousness is not the End, but is actually an ever-alive, natural, and open God Self. Some beings choose to continue their work toward Ascension, Soul Advancement and Self-Mastery to the infinite levels above.

Ways of Opening Consciousness

In the process of opening consciousness, there are many paths that the seeker can take. Generally, in the lower levels of consciousness, there are a lot of programs and practices that the seeker can engage in to become familiar with

---

[14] More information at: https://www.divinemarga.com/locs-of-past-teachers

spirituality. There are major religions, whose various branches point to something higher and how to start the journey.

The Self-Empowerment category of consciousness offers the widest variety of choices since it is the consciousness level of most people.

The first spiritual awakening into the Inner Light is also quite common. Still, it usually happens via an encounter with the Light, either by meeting a group of people who practice meditation, with some of them already awakened to Inner Light, or through yogic lineage practices (e.g., Kriya yoga, Kundalini yoga, etc.), or meeting a spiritual teacher, or having an extraordinary spiritual experience via any other means.

Many people stay in the Inner Light. They absorb a lot of spiritual knowledge, read many books, and learn many general things about spirituality. There is a whole spiritual marketplace that fully supports this level of awakening, and from worldwide observation, we may say that there are over a hundred million people who have awakened to the Inner Light level of consciousness.

When it comes to opening to Inner Love, specific techniques are needed to cultivate the Spiritual Heart and enable Inner Love awakening. It requires a certain healing process of the heart for this Inner Love to awaken. This is also where the devotional path comes in.

Furthermore, this is where mantras and Bhakti Yoga practices become practical. It may be singing, or silent mantra recitations focused on the heart and devotion. The integrational part has to do much with knowing one's aim and cultivating the heart. Cultivation of compassion is also essential, as well as kindness.

It is still relatively easy to reach this awakening if the seeker is engaging in the correct practices, focusing on the spiritual heart. Inner Love is still common as, according to our research at New Humanity Divine Marga and observations of worldwide spiritual movements, there are tens of millions of people who are open in Inner Love Consciousness, albeit less than 0.2% of the global population.

Unity consciousness is also relatively easy as those who work on Inner Love usually progress and migrate to Unity consciousness over a period of time. There are a few million people open to Unity Consciousness, less than 0.02% of the global population.

However, with opening into Presence, the methods to get there are significantly reduced. This is an entirely different type of opening that requires a different approach. At this point, it is helpful to have a teacher or guide on the path to help awaken, while avoiding pitfalls or prolonged uncertainties.

Presence consciousness is where things shift drastically since this entails a 180-degree change, and options shrink suddenly. It is no longer about asanas, chakras, or kundalini energy. This is where a spiritual teacher comes in. Meeting with a spiritual teacher, it is possible to receive a Transmission of Presence. It would be the most common way as 99.9% of those who get into Presence experience awakening in this way. According to our research and observations, there are less than one hundred thousand people around the world awakened to the Presence level of consciousness at the time of writing this book.

Amongst the hundreds of thousands of yoga and meditation teachers, some of whom consider themselves to be spiritual teachers, only less than 1,000 known spiritual teachers worldwide currently teach about awakening to the real Presence and higher levels of consciousness.

Working through Presence is hard as it involves the subconscious and unconscious aspects and deeper psychological clearances. If the seeker is open to the Presence, psychotherapy can be supplemental and helpful because they have deeper access to healing. Almost all people in Presence usually hit a certain ceiling.

Assistance of a Guide

A spiritual teacher is essential due to their ability to surround people's psychological field and other surrounding energy fields, while providing more space for those energies to be released and relieved into the spaciousness of Presence. This is where transmissions are supportive in the dissolution of obstacles. During transmission, the whole psychological energy field is surrounded and assisted in being softened, unwound, and released. It cannot be accessed at this deep level in lower levels of consciousness.

There are many spiritual explorers who thought that they could do it themselves. When they came to me, we opened to Presence relatively quickly; consequently, some of them took a break, or thought they could get through the Presence themselves. When they returned two years later and asked to check their level of consciousness, they usually moved only 10-20% through the Presence level of consciousness. Indeed, they were shocked by the slow progress, and I emphasized that it would not be so easy.

The idea that 'I can do myself' starts hindering the process. I have also met many people who would try very hard, but I cannot recall a time when they moved into Non-Duality themselves, not in a short time anyway, or had encounters with other teachers open to Non-Duality and above.

With some practices, such as Bhakti (devotion), where one is surrendering to higher beings, it is possible to move into higher levels of consciousness. If we eagerly surrender to such beings as Krishna, or any other Gods and Goddesses, it might be possible.

Having a way of connecting with teachers or deities is a psychic gift. It is also possible to receive their grace 'from above' and move upwards. This is how it happened during my personal journey as I had an intentional connection with higher beings and worked consciously with them on a higher plane of existence.

Presence and Non-Duality are where spiritual adulthood is practiced. Meanwhile, to awaken all the way to Full Consciousness, 99.9% of the time it happens only with the assistance of a spiritual teacher.

At New Humanity Divine Marga, we researched many cases of awakening and looked at hundreds of famous spiritual teachers of the past and present from major traditions. It transpired that, one way or another, for a person to awaken to the highest levels of Self-Realization, an initiation into higher consciousness and consciousness transmission were necessary, either knowingly or otherwise.

Even those who say that they awakened spontaneously by themselves have received a transmission unknowingly from a being on a higher plane. In 0.01% of the cases, transmission came from their own 'guru from within', beyond their current comprehension. It simply means that a person's Soul was more advanced, and did the ripening work in their previous incarnations, where a spontaneous awakening occurred. Nonetheless, that is very rare, and normally, after that, a long period of integration takes place for the person to settle in and develop an ability to comprehend and be able to explain what happened.

Enlightenment cannot happen through an individual's own effort alone. Indeed, how can we overcome the mind with the mind, or ego with an ego? Higher power and grace are always needed, in one way or another, directly or indirectly.

Laying the foundations for Full Consciousness

Integration of Presence helps the seeker to transition to Non-Duality and to lay a solid foundation for working toward Full Consciousness. Transmissions and the grace of a teacher are a highway to Full Consciousness. Few teachers can assist in opening to Awareness, Divine Love, Supra Causal Truth, and Full Consciousness as there are less teachers who are at these higher levels of consciousness themselves.

In terms of integration, you can do it if you are open to these higher levels of consciousness. To a certain extent, you can do specific healings continuously because, when you open to higher LOCs, you open a bigger capacity to release previous limitations. Opening to a higher LOC assists us in releasing the limitations discussed below.

Integration has many components, including psychological and emotional, with the biggest being psychological. It entails the clearing of habitual patterns, such as, habits that are not healthy and not supportive for higher consciousness.

Many people have various habitual patterns, including self-sabotage, self-destruction, self-suppression, and self-limit. These are tough, and while you can clear several of them, having some help makes the whole journey more manageable.

Integration of psychology, emotions, clearing of conditioning, and all of that together are vital for maturity, while providing more opportunities for higher consciousness to settle in.

Asking for help is Wise

My suggestion to everyone is to keep your mind open and try different things, but when you hit your limit, ask for help. It does not matter whether it is me or someone else. What matters most is getting the help you need to move forward. Do what you can do yourself, then ask for help. It is the universal rule, ask, and you shall receive. If you do not ask, nobody will know that you need help, and even if they do, if you do not give permission to be helped, they cannot help you.

Ask higher beings, have faith, and trust that they will help you in their own way. Not how you want it, but in their way, because they are much wiser, they know you more deeply than what your mind knows. Higher beings have their way.

It is good to get into the habit of asking for help. You say, okay, I have reached my limit. I need help, and it's beautiful. There is nothing wrong with that, in any way, from anybody. Then, evaluate the results after getting help or doing what you can do yourself. Evaluate whether you have moved forward. Alternatively, you may ask for help from someone who cannot help you. Maybe they want to help and are trying

162

to help, but they are unable to help you to move into higher consciousness. You must thus evaluate whether you have moved forward following your efforts or somebody else's help.

You can go as many ways as you want to. It is nice to explore different options. I encourage people to get to know historical spiritual teachers, Gurus, Goddesses and Gods, traditional Hindu deities, Ascended Masters, Avatars, etc. I encourage all of you to get to know as many higher beings as possible, and to make friendships with them. It makes sense to have friendships with higher beings. You can have more help and friends on higher planes of existence.

Utilize all the options, do what you can, ask for help when you need it, and then, do not spend too much time assuming you can do it yourself as you will be disappointed. This happens to those with some ego in them, or those with a fixed mindset.

Those who work with me closely in opening higher levels of consciousness get recommendations to watch some videos from different teachers and to read their books, depending on where they are right now. So, do not get fixed on anything, or you will get stuck.

That's what the open path is. Everything moves harmoniously, like a universal spiral with all opportunities in front of you. You open your unique gifts to flower through you. Sometimes, you have to stick to certain things if instructed, and then, you can add to them. Furthermore, sometimes, I might say, now you've done this, it has worked for you this time, but now, we need to do something completely different, that is, to shift from Self-Enquiry into practices of Love.

I hope this clarifies the whole path in the broadest sense and how everything aligns: Yogic traditions, New Age practices, Ascension teachings, spiritual teachers, and gurus from all possible traditions. Keep your mind open, have options, and evaluate your progress now and then. If you are struggling, it means that something is no longer working for you.

Precautions of the Levels of Consciousness

Sometimes, the Levels of Consciousness can create misunderstandings, often in the fields of hierarchy, ego, and the difference between awakening and integration.

Therefore, we have drawn up a list of the most important aspects to avoid any false ideas, dreams, and judgements about the Levels of Consciousness, thus developing a deeper understanding.

- LOC does not mean being better than someone else;

- LOC does not mean that you cannot learn from people in lower LOCs;

- LOC moves up and down throughout the day; thus, it is good to be aware that you are not always in your measured average LOC (e.g., when something terrible happens or you get triggered);

- Any LOC level still contain blind spots, and any action from within these blind spots can be many levels lower within the LOC;

- Identifying with your LOC gives food for the ego;

- LOC is different from your level of Soul Advancement[15];

- There is a difference between Realization, Integration, and Soul Advancement; and

- LOC is not meant to create a hierarchy.

Do not judge anyone about their LOC as it says nothing about human behavior or being better or worse than others. It is a neutral statement, like a GPS on a map. You can get to another country by car, bus, train, or plane, and even on the same plane, people may have different experiences.

LOC precautions of teachers

LOC Full Consciousness is the realization of openness beyond any fixations, as the absolute reality, eternal existence, consciousness, bliss, pure intelligence, ultimate oneness, and emptiness. It is a natural state, and then, you need time to Integrate that into Experience, in your everyday life, and in usual life conditions, taking as much time as you need. It usually takes 4-7 years for integration after the opening.

Teachers at Full Consciousness can be very different due to their different personal characteristics, paths, and abilities, but primarily, because of their overall Soul Advancement and amount of integration into Full Consciousness.

Many beings can be at LOC Full Consciousness and still work on their integration through their life experiences.

---

[15] More information at: https://www.divinemarga.com/locs-of-past-teachers

Therefore, LOC Full Consciousness is the realization of one's Self, but then, further Soul Advancement and integration make a considerable difference to the expression of consciousness in practice.

These days, it is becoming more common to open into LOC Full Consciousness, while still being a relatively young Soul. This means that most teachers at Full Consciousness are not perfected beings and may not interpret Reality in the same way. Their expression of Reality can be quite different due to their experiences, level of refinement, integration, Soul Advancement, and experience itself.

A teacher's nervous system integration also plays a part in this. Nervous system integration refers to how one's nervous system operates and responds to ordinary life experiences.

Other teachers may measure LOCs from their point of reference; thus, the measurements may differ accordingly.

The Level of Consciousness DOES NOT compare how good two teachers are. It DOES NOT compare their teachings.

LOC only indicates the Level of Consciousness, and NOT what a person does with it or achieves in their life, or how they contribute to society.

Research of the Levels of Consciousness

David R. Hawkins (M.D., Ph.D.) (1927-2012) was the first to use Applied Kinesiology to measure the Levels of Consciousness on a scale from 1 to 1,000, thus compiling a 'Map of Consciousness'. His research has been published in the book *Power vs. Force: The Hidden Determinants of Human Behavior.*

At New Humanity Divine Marga, we have been researching the Levels of Consciousness for over a decade from a *practical perspective.* Our main focus is on the Self-Realization category of the Levels of Consciousness, from LOC Inner Light to LOC Full Consciousness, clearly explaining the path of Enlightenment with practical and effective approaches to awakening.

We have also done extensive research about Spiritual Teachers and Soul Advancement[16] beyond awakening to Full Consciousness.

Up to the time of writing this book, Sat Mindo Dev has helped over a thousand and five hundred people to awaken from the first step of spirituality at LOC Inner Light to the highest levels of Enlightenment of Full Consciousness.

Disclaimer: The two scales of David R. Hawkins's Map of Consciousness and the Levels of Consciousness of New Humanity Divine Marga are different in their approaches and practices.

---

[16] More information at: https://www.divinemarga.com/locs-of-past-teachers

Measuring Levels of Consciousness

Applied Kinesiology (AK), also known as 'muscle testing' or 'biomechanics', is a well-known and well-documented method to diagnose anything, from illness to food intolerances. This was the brainchild of chiropractor George J. Goodheart, who first invented AK in 1964, when he realized that beneficial stimuli increase the strength of certain indicator muscles, while harmful stimulation causes the same muscles to weaken suddenly. The method has since spread all over the world and is used by both medical doctors and alternative practitioners.

Dr. John Diamond took the research to a new level when he started to test muscle response to intellectual and emotional stimuli. He tested everything, from music to speeches and images, obtaining consistent universal results, indicating that certain intellectual and emotional stimuli strengthen or weaken the indicator muscle. His findings are described in detail in his classic book *The Body Doesn't Lie*.

Dr. David R. Hawkins (M.D., Ph.D.) was the first to use Applied Kinesiology to measure consciousness levels. As a high-level teacher, he saw the potential of muscle testing within the realm of spiritual growth and consciousness development. He used muscle testing to calibrate the first original scale of consciousness, and he published many books and delivered many lectures about consciousness calibration and development.

How does Applied Kinesiology (Muscle Testing) work?

Just like Hypnosis can bypass the conscious mind and obtain answers and information directly from the subconscious, the Muscle Testing method is a way of circumventing logic/reasoning to obtain answers directly from the body's connection to Source Intelligence. Muscle testing is simply using the body's innate connectedness to Source Intelligence to obtain a 'yes or no' signal about something our conscious mind does not know.

In practice, it is most common to perform muscle testing in pairs. The subject being used as an instrument would stand up with their arm stretched out to the side. The tester then makes an affirmative statement, like 'Person X calibrates higher than LOC Positivity' and presses the subject's arm down at the wrist. The subject is instructed beforehand to resist the push, and if the arm goes weak, it indicates a 'no' response, whereas a strong arm suggests a 'yes' response.

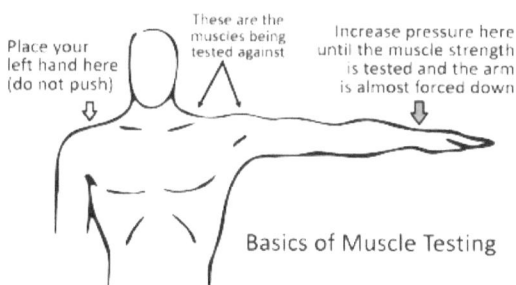

Basics of Muscle Testing

Other methods of Consciousness Calibration

While muscle testing is a great way to calibrate, its downside is that it takes two people to do it. Fortunately, alternative ways are just as accurate as you can do this on your own.

Dowsing can be done using a pendulum or dowsing rods. It is based on the same principle as regular Muscle Testing. Through practice and attunement, the 'yes or no' response is produced via the pendulum's movement or the crossing or no-crossing of the dowsing rods, as indicated by the image.

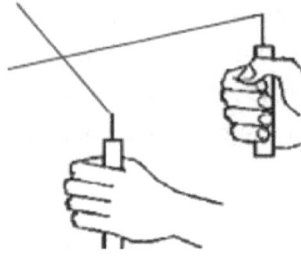

Intuition is not as accurate as muscle testing or dowsing.
Still, it can roughly estimate a person's Level of
Consciousness for high-level teachers and people with much
calibrating experience.

Accuracy – Can anyone do it?

Muscle testing or dowsing is something anyone can play
with, but just like anything else, it takes practice and
experience to master it. Ideally, being at least in LOC Inner
Love would help to obtain more accurate results. However, a
high level of Consciousness alone is not enough to ensure
accurate results. It would help to 'put yourself aside' and be
neutral to the results that are obtained thereby allowing the
signal to work through the body without interfering with it.

To calibrate a person's Level of Consciousness, you need to
know enough to pinpoint that person. If you have enough
information to do that (e.g., a picture, latest video or some
good research), you are good to go. Calibrating yourself is
also possible, but remaining neutral to the results becomes
more challenging the more personal you allow it to be.

First Awakening - Inner Light

Level of Consciousness Inner Light is the stepping-stone to spiritual awakening, where the Inner Light has penetrated the densest parts of the person's energy field. This is the first 'awakening' often spoken of in spirituality. In this awakening, life becomes brighter, lighter, and filled with continuous synchronicities. Everything takes on a deeper meaning, with insights into the inner workings of the mind, thoughts, and life.

"Don't you know yet? It is your light that lights the world."
(Kabir)

This state of consciousness allows emotional healing at a deeper level due to the greater objectivity that has been attained. This maturing process may lead to a natural calling for Love to further transcend the mind and emotions.

From this point onwards, you are on the spiritual path, on your soul journey, opening the whole ocean of Higher Consciousness and the entire universe.

Awakening into Higher Consciousness is the single most important first achievement of a human lifetime. Nothing else compares to the awakening to Higher Consciousness, no matter how much money we make, or any other personal achievements.

This awakening is not only for ourselves, but it also transforms humanity, while we become a carrier of Light and Higher Consciousness for humanity. Even if we do nothing, we are already emitting a higher vibration all around. We are already healing people around us to the degree and intensity of our awakening and advancement. This is thus the single most important transformative event in a person's lifetime that helps to change humanity.

"Whether you worship Christ, Krishna, Kali, or Allah, you actually worship the one Light that is also in you since It pervades all things." (Anandamayi Ma)

Common processes & realizations

- The densest emotional heaviness, energies, and fears are transcended.

- The inner space expands, giving a sense of inner peace and calmness.

- Intuition gets much clearer, louder, and stronger, making it easier to make decisions.

- A sense arises that you are not only the body.

- Although the opening to the Inner Light starts from LOC Allowance, complete awakening occurs at LOC Inner Light and integrates at LOC Inner Wisdom.

- Inner Light awakening feels like awakening from a deep sleep, where everything seems more enhanced, and you feel more focused and alert.

- The five senses become clearer and alive.

- Synchronicities become evident.

- Sometimes, to arrive at this stage, life circumstances and relationships change to match your vibration, which may take some time.

- The power of intention becomes much stronger.

- With the opening of the energy centers (chakras), the body starts functioning better, feeling younger, livelier, and more energetic. Meanwhile, health and well-being are enhanced.

- The ability to access 4D and 5D in meditation, seeing beyond 3-dimensional awareness.

Key Obstacles

Although it is already a spiritually awakened state, the person at this stage is still very focused on the mental energies of understanding spirituality. The heart is not yet the focus, and the mind can still be somewhat constricted, especially if the person stays at this LOC for a long time.

There can be a big interest in reading about spirituality, contemplating spiritual concepts, theories, philosophies, or specific paths and traditions. Individuals may have various experiences of light illuminating the mind, and may assume that they are already enlightened, which, of course, is not the case. Knowing it all is not the same as actual experience of higher consciousness. It is thus important to steer away from understanding and knowledge, focusing on an observation of the mind and its processes.

Life Force Energy Practice

Life Force Energy is called Prana or Chi. There is a way to attain more of this life force energy and use it for a higher purpose. It is indeed this energy that sustains life since it is everywhere. It is the foundation, the electricity that runs through the whole universe. Meditation is a very effective way to receive more life force energy.

Every day, we have a certain amount of life force energy, whether in the morning, full of energy, and in the evening, as we become tired. If we want to achieve more healing effects and higher states of consciousness, we need more life force energy. It is important to not only recover this energy, but also to charge more, thereby using it to raise our consciousness. It encourages physical, emotional, and mental well-being, helping to sustain a higher level of consciousness.

The combination of right posture, right breath, and right meditation makes this practice very effective. You only need 15-20 minutes to fully charge yourself and create a surplus of life force energy. The extra energy gained from this meditation can be used to raise your level of consciousness.

Life Force Energy gives overall health and penetrates your chakras to improve their health. The energy flows into the meridian points, then into the endocrine system and every organ of the body. It affects the whole being: mental, emotional states, and the physical body. It is needed to maintain good health.

Breathing Practice

Step 1: Interlock your hands by placing your left hand with the palm downwards on your right hand with your palm upwards, interlocking the fingers. Hold them in front of your solar plexus, where the prana energy is stored. This is the most effective way to store and keep the life force energy. It is like a battery. Consequently, the energy already starts to accumulate behind the solar plexus area.

Step 2: Breathe in through your nose for 4 seconds, hold it for 2 seconds, breathe out from your nose for 4 seconds, and hold it for 2 seconds. Repeat this sequence.

Step 3: As you breathe in, visualize the golden-yellow life force energy accumulating from everywhere and from the sun being drawn into your solar plexus area. Keep it for 2 seconds. As you breathe out, use a purification and energy cleansing method: you can visualize white light, scanning, and cleansing you from the top, right down to the feet and into the Earth.

As you do this, visualize yourself releasing any gray or black accumulated impurities or lower vibrational energies, letting them go into the earth beneath you.

Waterfall of Light Meditation[17]

Bringing the light blue light down in a waterfall is a rejuvenating practice that helps you feel cleansed and purified. Visualizing a white light is an excellent way to release heavy and dense energies. Connecting to the earth and nature grounds you, while the Inner Light increases and dissolves the darkness.

Step 1: Slow down, feel your breath, feel more space around the breath.

Step 2: Visualize yourself approaching a beautiful waterfall, a waterfall of light in a beautiful natural environment. Enter this waterfall of light. This light is pouring down on you from above like a waterfall, like a shower of light.

Step 3: While staying in the waterfall of light, you can feel the light pouring from above, washing away any heaviness into the earth.

This practice can also be combined with your breath.

Step 1: Breathe in for 4 seconds, visualizing the light pouring down from above.

Step 2: Hold your breath for 2 seconds, keeping the light inside.

Step 3: Breathe out for 4 seconds, letting go of any heaviness, any gray or black and darker energies into the earth.

---

[17]This meditation works best in the company of a guide and once you are familiar with meditation practices.

Step 4: Hold your breath for 2 seconds, staying clean and pure.

Inner Wisdom & Higher Self

Level of Consciousness Inner Wisdom and Higher Self is experienced in connection with inner spiritual wisdom and spirit, also known as Higher Consciousness.

This is an expansion of the awakening when you become increasingly able to observe your own thoughts, body, and emotions neutrally and more objectively. This space creates an opening for the Higher Self to come through. It can be felt like a higher intuitive sense, higher power, or even an internal voice that guides you through life, overriding the linear mind and limited sensory consciousness.

Inner Wisdom and Insight are gained, and a lot of knowledge starts to flow in. New realizations can be gained daily, and various spiritual and energetic experiences with the Higher Self become available, followed by a true exploration of the spiritual realms.

Your Higher Self is you, not some far-off entity hovering around and looking in on you occasionally.

The Higher Self is that fragment of your Soul that has never forgotten conscious oneness. It knows you inside and out because it is YOU.

Trust that it is constantly working to bring you experiences that best serve your evolutionary process.

The 'I am not this body, these thoughts, emotions, I am the Spirit itself' feeling arises at this level. Past experiences can be resolved to a certain degree here as the Higher Self pushes you towards healing and integration.

For those who are energy sensitive, connecting to the Higher Self also begins a gradual process of clearing and activation of the seven chakras and kundalini energy, and a process of centering into the Spiritual Heart and Inner Love.

Common processes & realizations

- An awakening of Inner Wisdom through inner spiritual understanding.

- Neutral Observation of your own body, emotions, and thoughts creates a space for the Higher Self to open.

- The Higher Self is you in a higher dimension: 4D Higher, 5D and above, often called your Spirit, Higher Consciousness, or Higher Spiritual Mind.

- This level is above the linear mind and limited sensory consciousness.

- Inner knowing and comfort to find the answer within. There is no need to search for answers outwardly.

- DNA repair starts here with the connection to Higher Consciousness.

- Multi-dimensional experiences are common.

- Feeling lighter in general, and an increased sense of freedom.

- There is the possibility of the awakening of spiritual psychic abilities.

- The Higher Self (not the Lower Self) remembers your past lives, knows all about this current lifetime, and has the key to future events.

- For energy-sensitive people, there can be an activation of the seven chakras, kundalini energy, and light body (Merkabah).

- The recognition that 'I am not this body, these thoughts, emotions, I am the Spirit itself' becomes stronger.

- The mind begins to soften and increasingly open.

- 8 months to 1 year is a good timeframe for the exploration of Inner Light and Higher Self.

- Working toward opening the Level of Inner Love/Spiritual Heart.

Key Obstacles

Connectedness to the Higher Self and observation of mental processes allow us to gain deeper inner insights and have greater intuition than before. The obstacle here is, just as in Inner Light, the concepts and theories of spirituality. We may even develop an identity of an old and wise man/woman, the inner wizard. There may also be too much focus on trying to understand, rather than trying to Feel.

To transcend this level, it is important to focus and center into the Heart, to Feel, rather than understand, and to start working on Inner Love because Love becomes the ultimate 'answer' to all spiritual understandings at this Level of Consciousness.

* * *

Higher Self - Observation Meditation[18]

The Higher Self is always connected to you but may not be noticed if you are in the stream of life. Bringing the Higher Self into your awareness connects you with your intuition and your soul. This happens by creating space for the Higher Self to make its presence known.

This meditation helps soften and open the mind, creating more space and peace around it, thereby making it easier to remain detached, as the observer, when difficult thoughts and emotions arise.

Step 1: Take a few moments to slow down, to bring your mind to the center, to the present.

Step 2: Feel more space around your breath and allow everything to be neutral.

Step 3: Feel more space above you and behind you.

Step 4: Feel that, from above and behind, you can observe your body sitting in front of you, and you can observe any

---

[18] This meditation works best in the company of a guide and once you are at the Inner Light Level of Consciousness.

activity of the body/mind.

Step 5: Continue observing the body/mind neutrally, feeling more space and lightness around.

Step 6: If you forget and come back into the mind, remember to come back to the neutral space behind and above your body, and keep observing.

Second Awakening - Inner Love

"Wherever you are, and whatever you do, be in love."
(Rumi)

Inner love is an intelligent and compassionate love. It is beyond intellect, and it is love that has a mutual attraction, and not necessarily towards a woman or man.

Love on a lower level of consciousness is emotional love. It is usually reflected through our relationship with our partner, but on a higher level of consciousness, intelligent love guides us within.

A mutual attraction can be with our heart, soul, and deepest heart. Our deeper heart calls us as an attraction. It gives us signals, and messages to our conscious mind to connect with something deeper.

The mind is saying: "What should I look for? What's going to make me happy? Shall I buy this, shall I go there, shall I travel, shall I meet someone?"

The conscious mind usually translates this into 'let me look for something', typically external. When we reach the higher consciousness of Inner Love, we realize that the calling is internal. It calls us to reach within and discover that the call is to find happiness and love inside.

This internal calling guides us to return into our heart, back to our soul. This is Intelligent Love.

In the subconscious and unconscious mind, there is a distance that needs to be worked through and healed, and Love is the greatest force, bringing us home as Love invites us to come back to Love.

Inner Love is when the mind drops and centers into the Heart. The mind surrenders all its knowledge to Love because Love is the Answer. Inner Love opens its doors to the Heavenly realms. It is the most beautiful spiritual honeymoon period, when fear noticeably decreases, and a sense of wonder becomes natural. A courageous spirit arises to confront everything in ourselves and our lives that is not a reflection of Love.

Inner Love is the consciousness level referred to as the 5th dimension in Ascension teachings. Inner Love can be opened by devoting ourselves to our Inner Spirit, our own Higher Self in the Heart. This Love further grows and matures to encompass others and to love 'thy neighbor', thus opening and expanding to the Unity Consciousness, where we feel at-oneness with everything.

Common processes & realizations

- Intelligent and compassionate Love.

- Love from within, which does not depend on outside

circumstances.

- Loving kindness as a state of being.

- Cultivating a compassionate heart starts here.

- This is a spiritual honeymoon time, being in love with all.

- The capacity to love all living beings arises.

- Love flows from inside the heart, and uplifts those around you.

- Love is accompanied by a sense of truthfulness and pure motives.

- Better discernment of the essence of people, situations, and issues.

- More accurate intuitive insights and holistic problem solving become possible.

- Inner Ascension to Heaven (5D consciousness).

- Connecting with Ascended Masters is common.

Key Obstacles

Limitations of the conscious mind, as well as your subconscious and unconscious mind, with its conditions, patterns, habits, and tendencies, and these conditionings are the actual distance from the Heart and Love.

Transcending, understanding, and surrendering to Love enables a shift from the mind to the heart.

Surrendering control, such as the realization that you cannot control your life, your relationships, and the world around you, thus surrendering to the Heart and Inner Love, creates a significant relief.

The inner old, wise man/woman identity needs to be disidentified because the Heart is not old. It is young and always fresh.

Healing fears that remain in the Heart or chest area. Many lower emotions and energies get transmuted and healed at this LOC.

Healing heartbreaks and the fear of heartbreaks are necessary as it strengthens the inner knowing that love is inside, no matter what happens.

Love is not to be found outside of yourself, but within, inside your own heart.

In Inner Love, it is essential to have higher energetic connections that assist you in feeling more connected and expanded, enabling a transition into Unity and higher consciousness.

* * *

Centering into the Spiritual Heart Meditation[19]

This meditation assists in surrounding you with loving, healing energy. The energy of Love melts pains of the heart, emotional disturbances, and chaotic feelings. The Goddess of

---

[19] This meditation works best in the company of a guide and once you are at the Inner Light or Inner Wisdom - Higher Self Level of Consciousness.

Love Kuan Yin is always available to offer loving energy to those who invite her. Pink is the color of Love energy and light. You can use this energy for your benefit and for that of others. This meditation can be repeated as often as needed to increase Love in your heart and to center into your spiritual heart (heart chakra).

Step 1: Take a few moments to slow down and connect with your breath.

Step 2: Have an intention to connect with beautiful, Loving Pink energy.

Step 3: You can invite the Goddess of Love Kuan Yin in this meditation to assist you.

Step 4: You can visualize her giving you a Pink Flower, which you can place in your heart.

Step 5: As you breathe in, Pink Loving Energy is flowing from the back side of the heart into your Heart and filling it up with Love.

Step 6: As you pause, Loving Pink Energy is surrounding your Heart.

Step 7: As you breathe out, you can send forward this Pink Love, and share it with anyone you know, with Mother Earth and all living beings.

Step 8: As you hold this intention of sharing Love, you increase your capacity to hold, give, and receive Love.

Step 9: You can allow everything to melt gently. There is no more need for protection because Love is the best protection and can heal all wounds. This love is Inner Love, and thus, it does not depend on anyone else.

Step 10: Gently melt further into the pink energy of Love, into the ocean of Pink energy.

Step 11: Allow everything to heal in the ocean of Loving Pink energy.

Step 12: You can give gratitude to Love, this healing energy, and hold an intention that this Pink Love is always in the background of your heart.

Unity & Oneness Consciousness

Level of Consciousness Unity is a more complete and holistic way of feeling yourself and one with others. Love becomes more unconditional, a natural sense of joy is common, and the heart opens to compassion for all sentient beings. Many people experience an evident, strong feeling and connection with the planet that we live on.

The degree of openness and sensitivity allows you to perceive that you are One with this conscious being, planet Earth, and you become aware that all living beings on this planet, including nature, animals, and the atmosphere, have a direct connection.

Native American/Shamanic tradition is a great example of the Oneness with Nature consciousness.

The feeling is of a Unified connection, that you are living in Oneness, and the flow of energy. The personal energy field is usually felt more unified as one whole field, rather than made of different parts (i.e., chakras only).

Unity Consciousness is an expansion of the Inner Love level, where the sense of love becomes unconditional. As the heart opens, there may be a purging of the lower emotional energy that has been part of the rigid mental and emotional conditioning.

The heart grows more as your connection expands, encompassing the planet, until the feeling of Separation merges into Oneness and Completion.

This field of consciousness affects others positively due to the compassionate and loving vibration emitted from a person at this level. Unity Consciousness increases the feeling of responsibility for others and the planet.

LOC Inner Light, Inner Wisdom, Inner Love, and Unity are the states of consciousness, where over 90% of all spiritually awakened people reside, including Yoga, Meditation Teachers, Healers, Light Workers, Channelers, etc. This is because the next level of LOC Presence is more advanced, and is usually quite challenging to open, generally requiring Consciousness Transmission and guidance from a spiritual teacher, who can impart this higher consciousness.

Common processes & realizations

- A strong feeling of oneness.

- A sense that all is connected.

- Inner completion of heavy emotional and mental energies.

- Natural joy from within arises.

- The level of spiritual healers, light workers, channelers, and meditation teachers.

- Love becomes more unconditional.

- Cultivation of compassion (love with wisdom).

- Overcoming the Pain of Separation.

- Your energy field feels more unified and whole (all parts being together).

- Integrates with the Divine Will of Planetary Consciousness.

- Shamanic tradition is a great example of Oneness with Nature.

- Increased feeling of responsibility for others.

- Unity Consciousness has a significant and positive effect on others.

Key Obstacles

In Unity consciousness, much of the fear inherent in the Inner Love stage is dissolved. The blockage here is the strong sense of the pain of separation that comes to the surface of awareness. This may feel like a separation from others, disappointment with romantic relationships, or feeling left alone on this earth.

Identifying with the collective pain of humanity, or feeling the pain of others in various ways, may paradoxically keep us feeling that pain too.

Intensities of imbalanced energies can cause challenges in normal life.

It is also where the 'spiritual ego' presents itself and dominates many people; for example, seeking ideals of unity and peace, while, in reality, creating problems for others.

It is also too easy to fall into the trap of 'feeling' more spiritual or enlightened than we truly are, based on wishful thinking, combined with intellectual understanding and meditative experiences.

* * *

Togetherness & Wholeness Meditation[20]

Unity consciousness is about feeling the wholeness of life as not separate from you. A feeling of completeness can be accessed any time by recognizing that everything together is wholeness. Unity is a great expansion of consciousness that can give you a sense of connection to others, animals, nature, and the planet. This is the beginning of true compassion. This meditation enables you to feel connected to all things. True compassion and natural joy arise as your energy field softens and harmonizes.

Step 1: Take a few moments to slow down and connect with your breath.

Step 2: Slowly bring your attention back to yourself, back to your breath.

Step 3: Recognize that your breath is here and now. Here are your chest and your upper body. Feel your lower body too, your legs, and feet.

Step 4: All things together are here and now, including any feelings or energy. They make a wholeness of your being. You can say: "I am everything together."

Step 5: This everythingness, or togetherness, is called oneness, completeness, and wholeness.

Step 6: You can recognize that you are all your chakras

---

[20] This meditation works best in the company of a guide and once you are at the Inner Love Level of Consciousness.

together. You are the togetherness. It feels more complete, whole, more like Home.

Step 7: You can also recognize that everything is connected together.

Step 8: Take a few moments to recognize the sense of larger completeness, larger wholeness. All the energies are flowing within you, and they are also part of the wholeness.

Step 9: Everything together is one, everything together is whole, everything together is completeness.

Third Awakening - Presence

"Simplicity, patience, compassion. These three are your greatest treasures. Simple in actions and thoughts, you return to the source of being. Patient with both friends and enemies, you accord with the way things are. Compassionate toward yourself, you reconcile all beings in the world." (Lao Tzu, Tao Te Ching)

In spiritual evolution, Level of Consciousness Presence is considered spiritual adulthood. This is the first sense of deeper peace and contentment, where it is possible to begin to taste one's deeper nature from the state of Presence. It is also the beginning of that time when deeper subconscious patterns can be healed.

Before Presence, there is emotional healing, but in Presence, the deeper aspects of the conditioning of Being can surface.

From here, one can start the journey of untangling oneself from the world, energies and their illusions.

This level of consciousness is relatively rare, and few people are awake at this level. Presence is very different from all previous energy work and practices. In Presence, the sense of being a separate 'I' starts to dissipate as the distortions and conditionings of the mind are seen and surrendered gradually.

This is a 'Being' consciousness, rather than 'Doing'. It is the 'I AM-ness', where Being is preferred, rather than interacting with energies in the chakras and objective phenomena. There is a realization that there is no 'doer' of activity because, upon a closer look, there is no one here as such. The present space is experienced. It was only an assumed identity. All thoughts and emotions are happening by themselves. One realizes that there is no doer, and there is no one doing something – it is all happening by itself.

At this level of consciousness, it is important to start familiarizing ourselves with the Unknown, surrendering to the Presence of one's Being, and laying down the foundation of Space and Openness for the journey to Full Consciousness.

Using the earlier example of the Beach and the Ocean: In LOCs Inner Love and Unity, a person is at the most beautiful tropical paradise beach enjoying the sunshine, dipping into the ocean for a swim from time to time. LOC Presence is the ocean itself. There is no more person. There is no one in heaven or at the beach. It is a surrender of the spiritual ego-self and all energies to the space-field of the Presence itself. It is a disidentification from your own energies. Therefore, opening to Presence usually happens with direct guidance and Consciousness Transmission from a spiritual teacher on a higher level of Consciousness.

Presence is also known as the mighty 'I AM Presence' in Ascended Masters Teachings. It is a direct connectedness to one's more perfected Self.

It is also called Cosmic Consciousness due to the exponential expansion of consciousness from the individual Higher Self to the Cosmic Christed Self. The meaning of the Christed Self is surrendering to the Cross of Time (horizontal dimension) and Space (vertical dimension), thereby transcending time and space to the Presence of the HERE and NOW as an actual Present Moment while being able to sustain not only Light and Love but all passing energies in the Present moment.

Common processes & realizations

- Considered as spiritual adulthood.

- A way of Being as I AM-ness.

- To Be for the sake of Being, without a need to search for anything or engage with energies.

- Simplicity is more restful than being engaged with complexities of energies.

- The field of being beyond the Chakras/Kundalini and energy.

- Beginning to Familiarize and become more comfortable with the Unknown.

- Being HERE in the Present Moment, nowhere else.

- Realizing that the Truth must be here. Where else would you find it?

- Allowing yourself to feel the deep feelings that were previously avoided.

- The ability to begin processing deeper subconscious distortions.

- The mighty 'I AM Presence' in Ascension teachings.

- Cosmic Consciousness expands to the Galactic level.

- Cosmic Christ Consciousness, where the ego dies on a cross of time and space.

Key Obstacles

Oneness and the cozy feelings of love are not so present anymore, as there can be a certain loss of individuality and personality.

Holding onto the energies of love, oneness, your chakras, and kundalini energy as an identity of the self.

An adopted habit of engaging with the complexities of energy gets in the way of the simplicity of Being.

A great obstacle is the Fear of losing yourself; thus, it is important to take time to familiarize yourself with the Unknown and the present Space of Being as your Home.

A lot of disillusionment of the Core Structures can occur, and many deeper subconscious patterns are brought to the surface in order to be met and worked out.

Deeper suppressed traumas may come to the surface to be

healed as you now have deeper access and greater strength to work through this challenge.

Energies may have a strong pull into conditional dualities and their expressions.

The seeker may assume that this is Enlightenment as there is nothing more (no more content, only space), but other people and the World can still be felt to be solid and separate from the seeker.

* * *

Beyond The Chakras Meditation[21]

Being infused and distracted in energies and sensations of experience is rather limiting due to being in energies only (content), thus lacking the Space where it all happens (context). Disengaging and withdrawing from the energy centers (chakras) are one way to recognize Being beyond Activities.

This meditation helps you familiarize yourself with the space of your Being. Once this space is experienced, it becomes easier to disengage from heavy energies when they appear in life. Emotions can finally heal when you rest in this peaceful space. This practice opens you to a deeper sense of your Being, calms your emotions, and brings a sense of peace.

Step 1: Take a few moments to slow down and settle in.

Step 2: Become aware of the activity and engagement present

---

[21] This meditation works best in the company of a guide, while receiving a Consciousness Transmission and once you are at the Unity & Oneness Level of Consciousness.

now.

Step 3: Take a step back behind the seven chakras and spine.

Step 4: Withdraw the energies back into the crown, third eye, throat, heart, solar plexus, and sacral, beneath the root. Disengage from the chakras step by step (from any energies, activities, and movements)

Step 5: Let go and rest in the Emptiness and Space of Home.

Step 6: Shift your focus 180 degrees deeper, into a deeper space, here and now.

Step 7: There is a force like a vacuum present, you can allow any content (energies, activities, movement) to clear and collapse into itself.

Step 8: Take some time to Familiarize yourself with the present emptiness, silence, and being.

Opening from Energy to Space of Presence[22]

Normally, we focus on our outer and inner environment. Our outer environment is what is going on around us. Meanwhile, our inner environment is our thoughts, feelings, and the energy sensations in our body. However, the space of our Being is not in any of these places.

---

[22] This meditation works best in the company of a guide, while receiving a Consciousness Transmission and once you are at the Unity & Oneness Level of Consciousness.

By bringing our attention to the space behind all of these energies, we find our natural Being in the present moment. It is in the present space that our energies harmonize and heal.

This process pulls our attention into the open space of Presence, enabling our energies to heal and harmonize. We learn how to work with our energies, rather than being taken over by them. Familiarizing ourselves with the open space helps us to settle into the present moment where all phenomena come and go. This healing practice is not only peaceful, but it also raises our consciousness.

Step 1: Take a few moments to slow down, slowing down all the energies, slowing down everything that is happening.

Step 2: As you slow down, take a few moments to invite your guides and your own I AM Presence.

Step 3: Gently collect your attention and focus back on yourself, back on your third eye, your head, and also back on your heart.

Step 4: As you collect your attention and focus back, some energies are also returning into your chakras.

Step 5: As your energies are returning, you can notice some more space around your chakras, around your chest, around your spine.

Step 6: The energies are starting to balance, complete, and harmonize. Now, you can recognize that all your energies together are your energy field.

Allow yourself very softly to expand yourself into that sense that all your energies are already here, and that is your Presence, your field of Presence.

Step 7: Familiarize yourself with the field of Presence, a way of Being, rather than Doing.

Step 8: You can also familiarize yourself with your energies being in your Space. Just like a home has its space, this is your space, where your energies are harmonizing and balancing.

Step 9: The aim is to familiarize yourself more and more with your space because this space is present, here and now. Meanwhile, the energies are doing whatever they are doing.

Non-Duality (Pre-Enlightenment)

Level of Consciousness Non-Duality is the next step of opening from Presence into Non-Dual realization, beyond the duality of energies, good and bad, Yin and Yang. This opening gives an opportunity to work through polarities, dualities, likes, and dislikes. This means that most of these limiting Polarities and dual energies are worked through and transcended.

Non-Dual life is spiritual adulthood, a capacity to be Present with what is here, now, and beyond entanglement with energies. You can say that this is a deepening of Presence, but an even lighter and more expanded way of Being.

The biggest dualities and key conditions are transcended, bringing a sense of relief and more liberation.

"Who is it that loves and who that suffers? He alone stages a play with Himself. The individual suffers because he perceives duality. Find the One everywhere and in everything and there will be an end to pain and suffering."
(Anandamayi Ma)

The evolutionary path becomes somewhat easier as there is a sense that nobody is here anymore, just the present Nothingness. No identity, no person, no position, only being in the Present Space of Nothingness. No-thing-ness is lighter than some-thing-ness. It is very relieving to know that the Personal I AM is no longer needed; thus, there is no fixed position, and nothingness feels lighter and more natural.

One trap in this level of consciousness is the tendency to deny that which is unwanted, that is, 'the world', due to the feeling of being disconnected from much of the mass collective heaviness and the drastically reduced sense of individuality. Some people here might say, "There's nothing you can do", or "There's no one to do anything". However, they may still have problems with other people and the world. The truth is that individual consciousness is being refined from karmic and collective conditionings, and the difficulties experienced indicate what conditionings are left within.

The deeper conditionings are still surfacing in Awareness for release, but these processes become subtler, lighter, and detached from energies and polarities. A feeling of increased liberation arises. Non-Duality is the Pre-Enlightenment phase of the journey.

Common processes & realizations

- Non-Duality is lighter and more expanded than Presence.

- Dual energies are being worked through for transcendence.

- Beyond Yin and Yang is wholeness; it is here and now.

- Seeing the whole thing from both sides, edges, and the imminent interconnectedness as a complete and whole picture (awareness of the two sides of the coin perspective).

- Realization of nothingness beyond polarities.

- No-thing-ness is lighter than some-thing-ness.

- Non-Dual Space is beyond the feeling of I AM or Beingness.

- In Non-Dual Space, there is no need to define anything or conclude anything.

- Disidentify from 'somebody-ness' and familiarize with 'nobody-ness'.

- From I AM, to Non-I AM. Non-I AM is lighter than I AM. From myself to no limited self.

- You might fall into the trap of denying the phenomenal world.

- The world still causes disturbances as there is inner refinement to work on.

- A feeling of greater relief and liberation arises.

- A Pre-Enlightenment phase.

Key Obstacles

A great obstacle is the Fear of losing yourself; thus, it is important to take time to familiarize yourself with the Unknown and the present Space as your Home.

Identifying with I AM, or Beingness, is no longer needed.

At this stage, usually, there is some degree of Negation, denial of the world, denial of others, and denial of your 'self'. Self-Realization can be seen as a denial of the individual ego-self.

A strong fixed identity of being nobody is another form of negation, including your feelings, and having a lack of compassion or coldness for others.

There might be strong pulls of energy contracting the attention into a fixed position.

Some people here might say, "There's nothing you can do", or "There's no one to do anything", or "It is what it is". However, they may still have problems with other people, the world, and themselves.

That negation is what keeps you at a distance from your Absolute Self, from a full merging and absorption into Full Consciousness.

The seeker may assume that it is the final Enlightenment as there is nothing more, but other people and the World are still disturbing them, troubling them.

Beyond Dualities Meditation[23]

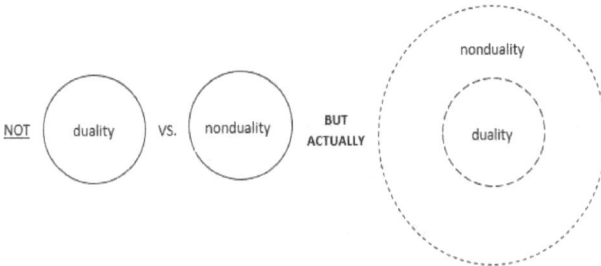

The Non-Dual Being is beyond any energies, and can stay present with whatever energies appear, despite still being beyond them. Once you have stabilized in Presence, it becomes easier to stay steady as the opposing ideas come into consciousness.

During this opening of consciousness, you may experience a merging of opposite energies. Dualities may no longer seem so separate. You would gain enough lightness to hold them in a lighter space of being. Allowing dual energies to rise in your larger space would dissipate them, releasing progressively the conditionings of the mind.

Step 1: Become more still and more present.

Step 2: Notice the activities in your present and see them for what they are – Activities.

Step 3: Shift your attention to the background of all activities

---

[23] This meditation works best in the company of a guide, while receiving a Consciousness Transmission and once you have spent a considerable time at the Presence Level of Consciousness.

and allow them to settle deeper.

Step 4: Observe whether there are any opposite energies, usually likes and dislikes, and allow them to merge in front of you and within your space.

Step 5: Familiarize yourself with the Space of no-thing, and practice disengaging from any substance and falling behind, thus allowing you to go deeper and beyond any-thing.

Step 6: A sense of lightness will become more apparent as you start liberating the dual energies that you hold in the space of no-thing-ness.

Step 7: Notice the sense of relief, a sense of liberation, and completion of dual energies.

Step 8: You are the Non-Dual Space beyond any-thing – lighter and more open than any energies.

Opening from I AM to Non-Dual Lightness[24]

Non-Dual consciousness can feel liberating as we dive into a lighter space of nothingness. In this state, deeper energies are allowed to surface. Meanwhile, difficult emotions and energies can dissolve, dissipating tension and contractions. Conditionings and rigid mental structures can be seen clearly, thus loosening them up for surrender. Going beyond the sense of I AM creates much ease and lightness, thus opening

---

[24] This meditation works best in the company of a guide, while receiving a Consciousness Transmission and once you have spent a considerable time at the Presence Level of Consciousness.

wider to the surrounding, more open Non-Dual consciousness.

Step 1: Take a few moments to slow down and connect with your breath.

Step 2: Now, take a moment to recognize that there is an assumption, or automated feeling, that there is 'my' feeling, 'my' energy, it is in me, and that there is a feeling of I AM.

Step 3: It might feel like you cannot do much about it, but you can start by acknowledging that, now giving more priority to the surrounding space of nothingness.

Step 4: Give more space around breath. Then, give more space around energy, gently settling into the space around the I AM.

Step 5: The Space around the I AM is lighter. It is a space of nothingness – the Non-Dual space.

Step 6: Recognize that the feeling of me, mine, or I AM is somewhat a contraction, and like a muscle, it is tense. When you relax, there is more space and openness.

Step 7: Familiarize a bit more with the space between everything.

First Step of Enlightenment - Awareness

"You are Awareness. Awareness is another name for you. Since you are Awareness there is no need to attain or cultivate it. All that you have to do is to give up being aware of other things, that is of the not-Self. If one gives up being aware of them then pure Awareness alone remains, and that is the Self." (Ramana Maharshi, Be as You Are, by David Goldman)

Level of Consciousness Awareness is the realization of Awareness as your own Self beyond duality. There is a considerable degree of lightness, compared to Non-Dual space. Being Awareness becomes the fundamental identity. The seeker's consciousness is felt as an all-pervading aware presence. A sense of larger openness arises as Awareness is beyond any space and nothingness.

The physical human brain lights up to the large degree of Enlightenment and brain-nervous system coherency. The conditionings and distortions unravel more quickly in Awareness, revealing a greater degree of clarity. An enlightened person can now change their perceptions and see what IS – the essence of IS-ness more directly.

In Awareness, the sense of separation from others is significantly decreased. The world seems less of a problem, and life seems to flow more smoothly. Meanwhile, the subconscious material is still surfacing to clear, but this material is increasingly subtler and easier to manage.

While problems still arise, the clarity of seeing and the sense of openness create a space for resolving issues. Some things that may have previously been perceived as problems dissolve as unimportant. A much greater degree of power and ability to meet life in a lighter way arises.

This degree of Enlightenment can be seen as the Universal Self, where consciousness now expands to encompass the whole Universe as 'I AM All' or 'All-ness'. This way of being 'All' with everything as the entire universe is called 'Universal Consciousness', the 'Universal Mind', or 'Unity Field'.

Common processes & realizations

- Realization of Awareness as your own Self beyond duality.

- Awareness of Awareness now becomes the fundamental identity.

- The Presence of Awareness is always here and now.

- Transcendence of objectivity, becoming the Pure Subject.

- I AM-ness becomes less tangible and feels more as All-ness.

- A greater degree of power and the ability to meet life in a lighter way arise.

- The Universal Self, that is, the previous Cosmic Self is now expanded to encompass the whole Universe.

- At this stage, an enlightened person can change their

perceptions (Emotions –> Thoughts –> Cognitions –> Perceptions) and their fundamental views on reality to see what IS from the perspective of enlightened clarity.

- The physical nervous system has been lit up or literally 'enlightened'. This is the first level of Enlightenment, leading to greater brain-nervous system coherence.

Key Obstacles

The subject-object duality is still present at this level of consciousness, and thus, Awareness is the subject, while everything else (the Universe) is an object.

Perceptions can hold particular views on reality and need to be seen clearly as only perceptions in Awareness.

Oftentimes, a person feels that s/he 'knows' everything, or that s/he IS All-ness, creating a certain fixation.

There might be strong pulls of energy contracting attention into the energy, no longer feeling as 'being as Awareness'.

The seeker may assume that it is the final Enlightenment, that Awareness is the final light of consciousness, but other people and the World are still disturbing them, troubling them.

From Experiences to the Light of Awareness Meditation[25]

Awareness is always there as it is the background of what is going on in life. Your Awareness is like a movie screen, with images passing on it in a regular flow. The screen never changes, irrespective of the image. Your Awareness can shine through when you finally see the screen. This can be done by constantly bringing your attention to the fact that you are already always aware, repeating this over and over, until it becomes natural.

"We see so much on a cinema screen, but it is not real. Nothing is real there except the screen. Knowledge of the waking state is knowledge of the knower of the waking state. Both go away in sleep." (Ramana Maharshi, The Power of the Presence, by David Godman)

This meditation familiarizes you with the light of Awareness. Energies dissolve in this light as you recognize the difference between energy and Awareness.

Step 1: Take a few moments to connect with your breath and slow down. Slow down any processes, any thoughts, any feelings.

Step 2: As you slow down, it becomes easier to meet your

---

[25] This meditation works best in the company of a guide, while receiving a Consciousness Transmission and once you are at the Non-Duality Level of Consciousness.

experience. Meet everything here, now.

Step 3: As you slow down, you can even pause your experience and recognize that you are already Aware. You may ask a question: "Am I Aware?"

Step 4: You can again relax back into experience and notice what is fresher and newer.

Step 5: Take some time to familiarize yourself with your experience with the fresher and newer. This is how you let more light of Awareness shine through.

Step 6: If you are going back to some river or something, you can then come out and see what feels best for you to do now.

You may choose to slow down further and go back into light Awareness, remembering that you already are Aware Now.

You can also allow experience to happen as it is and allow energies to process.

Step 7: If you start feeling confused, or want to avoid or change something, it would be good to slow down and recognize what arose.

As you shine some more light of Awareness, you may choose to process and heal it.

You do not need to demand anything from yourself. It is better to do this practice more frequently than to try to push yourself too far.

Column of Light of Awareness Meditation[26]

Awareness can be cultivated by bringing your focus and attention to it, while allowing the passing objects of the mind to soften. Awareness is a clear light that is not clouded by the activities of life. Using light to anchor Awareness is a technique that centers you in this space so that you can familiarize yourself with it.

This meditation strengthens your position as Awareness, harmonizes imbalanced energies, and heals blockages. Personal energies and identity untangle in the increased light of Awareness.

Step 1: Take a few moments to slow down and bring your attention to your breath.

Step 2: Slowly bring your attention back to your forehead and back to your heart.

Step 3: All around your body and energy field there is a gentle column of light of Awareness.

Step 4: You can notice that your attention is anchored somewhere, while, at the same time, behind it is the column of light of Awareness.

You can allow your attention to relax because it is supported by the column of light of Awareness.

Step 5: The column of light is present, here, now, and is your

---

[26] This meditation works best in the company of a guide, while receiving a Consciousness Transmission and once you are at the Non-Duality Level of Consciousness.

centering place. It is the light of Awareness.

Step 6: In this column of light, you can notice that there is your present energy, while some energies are pulling you left, right, up, and down.

Step 7: Take a few moments to be with your energies and allow them to soften and harmonize as you relax.

Step 8: As your energies begin to harmonize and the anchor of your attention softens, draw your attention from your energy to the column of light of Awareness.

Step 9: If your attention and focus go towards your energies, just return to the column of light of Awareness. The column of light is always here, now, present, and centered.

Great Void – The Unconsciousness

Level of Consciousness Great Void is a complete surrender to the great UNKNOWN. One must surrender the universal knowledge gained in the previous Awareness/Universal Self Consciousness. All that has been revealed must go back to the Emptiness of Void in order to be more liberated and relieved from knowing.

The Knower can now rest from knowing. It is such a light feeling, 'not to know'. Many teachers at this Level of Consciousness develop a mystical approach to their teachings since they no longer rely on knowing, and thus, enjoy the unknown.

Being in the Void is a very restful place. One can rest from the need to know, from comprehending the present experience, from the process of living, from feeling, sensing, or the need to have any general idea or definition of anything. One matures from any need to know, thus taking some time to rest from the mind as a whole.

This Level of Consciousness is also known as the Causal Plane of existence, from where the Law of Cause and Effect arises, governing all that happens in all creation and one's life. On a personal level, it is the Causal Body of one's own Unconsciousness.

This Level of Consciousness also allows access to the unconscious, unseen, and not experienced, except in deep sleep. With the strength of the Light of Awareness gained in the previous Level of Consciousness, a seeker can stay aware, even in an unconscious state, thereby enabling the deepest, unconscious, mental, and psychological patterns to be seen and released.

Here, one can access the core of some fundamental assumptions and things taken for granted, such as being a human being, being alive, etc. Awareness is brought to that which pulls one out of oneself and to the 'I' core, holding unconscious blind spots.

The Great Void is not a Cosmic Space like in Presence, a black hole, or a singularity experience. The Void precedes that. There are many black holes and singularities in the universe, but the Void is the Womb of all Universes. One may experience the Void as resting in the Divine Mother's womb before creation, beyond what is known.

Going beyond unconsciousness, the universal womb, into the Divine is the next step of Enlightenment. Usually, that happens via Grace. Grace pulls one out of the Great Void into the Divine. Grace is given either by Divine Beings, or by a Self-Realized/Enlightened teacher.

"The spirit of emptiness is immortal. It is called the Great Mother because it gives birth to Heaven and Earth. It is like vapor, barely seen but always present. Use it effortlessly."
(Lao Tzu, Tao Te Ching)

Common processes & realizations

- Unconsciousness and the state of deep sleep experienced while awake.

- Causal Place of Existence and a personal Causal Body of your own Unconsciousness.

- The Great Universal Void as a womb of all creation.

- A complete surrender to the great UNKNOWN. The Knower can now Rest from knowing.

- All the knowledge of the universe gained in Awareness needs to be surrendered.

- Freedom from the need to know or comprehend anything. Freedom and wisdom inherent in the words, 'I don't know'.

- Accessing fundamental assumptions and things taken for granted.

- The deepest unconscious, mental, and psychological patterns can be seen and released.

- The Light of Awareness needs to be strong enough to be able to step into the Great Void.

- It is surrendering to THE Great Void. It is not a cosmic space, black hole, or singularity.

Key Obstacles

While the Unknown can be very restful and wondrous in its mysteries, it is not a final Liberation. A feeling of missing something more Divine, Natural, closer to the Self, and ordinarily simple is still present.

The World cannot be denied and still disturbs our being. Therefore, we naturally begin to look for ways to get through that Great Void into the Divine and experience an even greater Bliss and Freedom.

Assuming mysticism can create a certain fixation. All the knowledge of the universe gained in Awareness needs to be surrendered.

The seeker may assume that it is final Enlightenment, that this Great Void or Emptiness is the final place as told by Buddha, but other people and the World are still disturbing, and cause some trouble.

Deepest unconscious, mental, and psychological patterns, fundamental assumptions, and things taken for granted cannot be ignored, and must be worked through.

Beyond Living Is the Great Void[27]

This meditation gives you a taste of resting in the Great Void, which is the great unknown. This space allows a deep Awareness that reveals what has previously been hidden in unconsciousness. The unconscious becomes available to heal while you rest in a state of not knowing. You are guided into a deep relaxation that is like a deep sleep for rejuvenation, surrender, and healing.

Step 1: Take a few moments to slow down and connect with your breath.

Step 2: Become softer as you slow down, feeling more space around your breath.

Step 3: You can recognize that there is no more need for energy, to understand, to feel.

You can rest in a deeper place, resting from feeling, resting from knowing, resting from comprehending.

Rest beyond any processes, in the restful void.

Step 4: You are already familiar with processes, and beyond the processes, there is this peaceful restful void.

Step 5: It is like the eternal void, where you rest at the end of your life. Life is finished, all the things you have done are finished, as well as all the things you have not done – you no

---

[27] This meditation works best in the company of a guide, while receiving a Consciousness Transmission and once you are at the Awareness Level of Consciousness.

longer care.

You are done with all the processes of life, and you just rest in space beyond all the processes of life.

Step 6: Life is that which is manifested, whereas the void is that which is unmanifested.

A baby in the mother's womb is not concerned about the world, has not yet met the world. All it cares about is being cozy in the womb. Similarly, you can rest in the womb of the Divine Mother. Before birth, or after death. Beyond the processes of life.

Step 7: You may experience moments when you blank out in deep sleep, although feeling nice and restful.

At first, the mind may need to adjust, but later, you will be able to stay conscious, even in this place, without blanking out.

Step 8: The beauty is that you are resting very deeply. You may feel a slight anxiousness about losing something, but actually, you are only using the attachment, the fear of the unknown.

Step 9: You are just going into a deep, restful state, like at night, when you look forward to this deep rest, knowing that you will feel very rejuvenated when you wake up.

Second Step of Enlightenment – Divine Grace & Love

"The man who is kind and who practices righteousness, who remains passive against the affairs of the world, who considers all creatures on earth as his own self, he attains the Immortal Being; the true God is ever with him." (Kabir)

Divine Love is the second step of Enlightenment, when one goes beyond the deepest unconsciousness, which is also the great womb, and comes 'out of creation' into the Divine, where Pure Consciousness can be experienced most directly.

The Unconsciousness or the Great Void is like the night, and the Divine Self is like the Eternal Light of the Sun that never sleeps.

Through Divine Grace, a person reaches the second step of Enlightenment as no person can transcend the Creation of all Universes on their own. Grace is usually received from the present Enlightened Beings, as well as from devotion to the Divine Beings.

The seeker realizes that their efforts to become enlightened, or to get rid of the remaining ego, would not suffice without the higher power of Grace. Therefore, true Devotion and Surrender to the Divine/God (in any higher forms) are a great way to remove obstacles on the path of Enlightenment.

It is a genuine unconditional Love and devotion: 'to love for the sake of love', becoming the ecstatic Lover of the Divine. Highest Bhakti (devotional) practices become truly fruitful at this stage, allowing an experience of the sweet Nectar and Bliss of the Divine.

Meanwhile, the seeker can melt into this Divine Love and may feel the 'I' sense beginning to dissolve into the Divine by giving themselves up to the Divine. The Divine light helps to transform, transmute, uplift, and melt into a higher level of Bliss (Maha Sahaja Samadhi).

"The eye through which I see God is the same eye through which God sees me; my eye and God's eye are one eye, one seeing, one knowing, one love." (Meister Eckhart, Sermons of Meister Eckhart)

Individuals can offer their personal and impersonal selves and their limited humanness to the Divine. The Divine helps to transcend the aspects of humanness of what is personal and impersonal as 'not myself'.

Common processes & realizations

- Grace helps to penetrate through the Great Void, the womb of unconsciousness and causality, coming 'out of creation' to the Divine and the Source of all creation.

- The Unconsciousness or the Great Void is like the night, and the Divine Self is like the Eternal Light of the Sun that never sleeps.

- It is through Divine Grace only that a person can rise to Divine Love consciousness, for no person on their own can transcend all universes.

218

- Grace is usually received from the present Enlightened Beings, as well as from devotion to Divine Deities.

- It is genuine unconditional Love and Devotion. Highest Bhakti (devotional) practices become truly fruitful at this stage.

- It is a recognition of the Divine, and in this recognition, you melt and surrender to it. You offer and give up your own 'I' to the Divine, melting into the Divine. It is an offering of personal and impersonal selves to the Divine. The Divine is beyond personal and impersonal.

- A higher level of Bliss (Maha Sahaja Samadhi) can be experienced.

Key Obstacles

Through Grace, a person reaches the second step of Enlightenment as no person on their own can transcend all Universes.

The seeker realizes that their efforts to become enlightened, or to get rid of the remaining ego, would not suffice without the higher power of Divine Grace.

Therefore, true Devotion and Surrender to the Divine/God (in any higher forms) are a great way to remove obstacles on the path of Enlightenment.

You need to offer your personal and impersonal self and limited humanness to the Divine. Meanwhile, the Divine helps to transcend the aspects of humanness of what is personal and impersonal as 'not myself'.

There are certain spiritual traditions where devotion, surrender, and love for the Divine are seen as the ultimate attainment. However, a subtle subject-object dual relationship can still exist between the devotee and the Divine.

Some people get stuck at this level of consciousness because of the sweetness and ecstasy of Divine Love, while trying to avoid the ordinary present world, which is also the Self and inseparable from the divine.

Learning about higher levels of consciousness enables the seeker to know that there are more steps to Full Consciousness. Therefore, more clarity, simplicity, naturalness, and freedom are possible.

* * *

Attuning to Divine Grace, Bliss & Blessings[28]

Through Divine Grace, we can enter the state of Divine Love, a blissful surrendered place of natural devotion and love. This meditation teaches surrender and devotion that melts the sense of 'I.' A blissful light fills the body, assisting in transmuting any persistent old energies, challenges, and issues that may come up, even from the past, allowing us to offer them to the Divine Light.

Step 1: Take a few moments to slow down and bring your attention to your breath.

---

[28] This meditation works best in the company of a guide, while receiving a Consciousness Transmission and once you are at the Great Void Level of Consciousness.

Step 2: Relax your attention and just feel that you are simply here.

Step 3: Behind the heart, on the right, there is a beautiful sun shining into your back, through the heart on the right, forward. It is like your chest is transparent, and if there are any clouds, it's okay.

Step 4: You can also see a bright star in the sky, shining from above, through your body, down into the ground.

Step 5: You can observe that your Divine Self is the bliss, the golden yellow white light. It also feels more centered and more present than before.

Step 6: The Unconsciousness or the Great Void is like the night, and the Divine Self is like the Sun that never sleeps, the eternal light.

Step 7: Some persistent old energies, challenges, and things may come up from the past. You can offer them to the Divine Light.

Step 8: First, meet your challenges as they are. Then, make an intention to offer them to the Divine, and then, surrender them to Grace.

Step 9: Take a few moments to familiarize yourself with this higher light that transforms, transmutes, and releases, this graceful light to which everything surrenders and melts into.

Step 10: You can receive Grace from any Divine Being that you feel connected with by surrendering your effort and yourself, thus being showered with their light and grace.

Step 11: You may repeat the devotional mantra 'SITA RAM'

to invoke Divine Love.

Step 12: As you relax your own efforts, you can allow yourself to be in this ocean of love, in this Divine blissful light.

Step 13: You are not seeking. You are allowing and surrendering to this Divine Grace. Seeking is an effort, and you can simply allow to receive Divine Grace.

Third Step of Enlightenment - Supra Causal Truth (Divine Truth)

On the Self-Realization path, Divine Truth Consciousness transcends causality, where the Absolute Self becomes more clearer and clearer. The light of Full Consciousness is now shining through the seeker like via a diamond or crystal, hence enabling much more clarity of Seeing. The seed of the mind and its way of birthing a sense of separation become also crystal clear.

This state of consciousness can lead to the desire to retreat from the world, where one can enjoy a deep sense of peace and fulfillment. The problem is that the sense of 'I' remains to be uprooted from its core. The I-Thought or I-Feeling is a very persistent and deceptive mechanism of self-preservation. It further enjoys hiding and staying at peace, as long as no one disturbs it.

There is a subtle, thin veil or distance kept from 'the World', from 'others', and a slight resistance from being fully submerged in the world, thus not yet being the Absolute Self, which fully Includes the whole Experience, the World, and

Others too.

This veil, once removed, also resolves the perceived Separation of humanity and the Divine. In reality, the physical and spiritual are ONE since there is only ONE, an all-inclusive and indivisible Absolute Self.

In Buddhist teachings, there is a saying that, at this stage of realization, if one sees the Buddha, one needs to 'kill' it since the true Buddha (Awakening) is openness itself, and not an image. Seeing any Deities and assuming a sense of 'them' and a sense of 'myself' thus need to be resolved.

The seed of the mind, known as, I-Thought or I-Sense, becomes visible. It was named by one of India's greatest sages, Bhagavan Sri Ramana Maharshi. The seed of separation is seen, and thus, it needs to be isolated from all other thoughts and eventually transcended by a continuous familiarization with the Absolute Self.

"The mind is only a bundle of thoughts. The thoughts have their root in the I-thought. Whoever investigates the True "I" enjoys the stillness of bliss." (Ramana Maharshi, Be as you are)

Abiding in the Heart on the Right, known as 'Amrita Nadi' or the Inner Sun, also helps in the final transcendence of the I-Thought or I-Feeling and any sense of separation.

Common processes & realizations

- The light of Full Consciousness is now shining 'crystal clear', hence with slight filtering via a crystal or diamond.

- Here, the famous I-Thought becomes visible, named by the greatest sage of India, Sri Ramana Maharshi.

- The I-Thought or I-Feeling is a very persistent and deceptive mechanism of self-preservation.

- The I-Thought or I-Feeling needs to be isolated from all other thoughts, and eventually eliminated by continuously familiarizing with the Absolute Self and abiding in the Heart on the Right, known as the Amrita Nadi or the Inner Sun.

- To enquire, isolate, and transcend the I-Thought/I-Sense, the assistance of a fully Self-Realized guide is usually necessary.

Key Obstacles

The Illusion that the seeker is already in Full Consciousness might be present due to the great clarity of Seeing.

The I-Thought or I-Feeling is a very deceptive mechanism of self-preservation. It enjoys hiding and staying at peace, as long as no one disturbs it.

It is important to see the seed of the mind, and thus, it needs to be isolated from all other thoughts and eventually transcended by a continuous familiarization with the Absolute Self.

There is still slight duality, a separation with the World and Experience, as well as an unwillingness to fully merge or engage with the World. The seeker may prefer to hide in a cave and enjoy their own inner peace and tranquility.

This veil, once removed, also resolves the perceived Separation of humanity and the Divine. In reality, the physical and spiritual are ONE since there is only ONE, an all-inclusive and indivisible Absolute Self.

Learning about a higher level of consciousness enables the seeker to know that there is one more step to Full Consciousness; thus, more clarity, simplicity, naturalness, and freedom are possible.

* * *

I-I - Opening to IS-ness & Openness[29]

The sense of 'I' is persistent, even at higher levels of consciousness. While you feel progressively freer from limiting emotions and assumptions, consciousness is still veiled from the Absolute reality, as long as this sense of 'I' is present. This meditation brings you into openness with what IS, with what is here, now. The focus is on relaxing the looking, searching, and wanting – the primary functions of the mind. In this relaxing mode, consciousness is opened, and the natural light of awareness strengthens to dissolve the sense of individual self.

Step 1: Take a few moments to slow down and bring your attention to your breath.

Step 2: Allow yourself to center and ground into the present moment.

Step 3: You are not looking for fulfillment as emotion, as

---

[29] This meditation works best in the company of a guide, while receiving a Consciousness Transmission and once you are at the Divine Grace & Love Level of Consciousness.

feeling. You are coming to the Oneness with what IS, with what is here. First, you can have appreciation as you notice and appreciate what is already here, leading you to greater satisfaction with whatever is here.

Step 4: You can start with the practice of 'I-I'.

Step 5: The 'I' is looking for happiness, freedom, joy, searching, and wanting. Relax this looking, searching, and wanting, thus enabling you to BE, without looking, searching, and wanting.

That is how you immediately close that gap, becoming ONE.

Step 6: We can further surround, slow down and contain this momentum of looking, searching, and wanting.

Step 7: The looking, searching, and wanting are an outpouring. You are emerging from yourself, leaving the screen, and entering the movie. The screen says, maybe I'll find myself in the movie, which does not work.

Step 8: The mantra 'I-I' allows the energy to come full circle and close the gap, and thus, what is, IS. There is no longer any distance to anything. That is Naturalness.

Step 9: You can appreciate this ISness, and this appreciation naturally transforms into satisfaction and contentment.

Step 10: One more time, you can gently use the mantra 'I-I', and then allow everything to relax, to be. There is this natural openness, here and now, which does not need anything. The openness is open.

Fourth Step of Enlightenment - Full Consciousness

Full Consciousness feels very Natural. It is called Sahaja, the Natural State of Consciousness. It is the end of seeking, the end of the search as natural openness is found – restful, empty, and alive. It is closer than the blink of an eye. The Self is even closer than the sense of closeness. Beyond closeness is the Natural you, here and now. This openness feels naturally like yourself as a true, unlimited identity. This is not the same as the sense of 'no self' that a person may feel in the higher states of Presence or Non-Duality as there would still be a sense of separation and many problems with the world and perceptions. In Full Consciousness, this separation is dissolved. There is only ONE, and all senses of 'otherness' fade away.

In Full Consciousness, no diamond, crystal, or any kind of filter is in the way of the Pure Light of Consciousness. It is the Absolute Self, God Self, the Source of All that is. It is the final state of Non-Dual Enlightenment, thus completing human consciousness. Divine and the ordinary become ONE. There is no more separation between physical and spiritual as all separations are dissolved. This whole Experience of NOW is fully included and is not separate from boundless Consciousness. The Absolute Self fully includes the whole Experience, the World, and Others too. There is only the Self.

All is seen as Self. All emanates from, and all IS, this Primordial Consciousness. The Self is unborn, undying, undivided, and inseparable. It is all there IS, manifested and unmanifested, as the Source of both. It is the 'I AM THAT'.

"Self is what gives breath to Life. You need not search for It, It is Here. You are That through which you would search. You are what you are looking for! And That is All it is."

(Papaji)

Common processes & realizations

- Full Consciousness feels very natural, and is called Sahaja, the Natural State.

- The Absolute Self, God Realization, Source Consciousness, Sat Chit Ananda, the IS-ness.

- An ordinary Openness, Lightness, Spontaneity.

- There is no more separation between physical or spiritual, human or divine, as all separations are dissolved.

- All is seen as Self. The Self is unborn, undying, and undivided.

- Without resistance, boundless, and radiant NOW.

- No self-contraction and self-opponent, nothing is excluded from the Allness of the NOW. It is the Underlying Equanimity and Inclusivity of All.

- Unmixed and Untethered Attention is Pure Consciousness.

- The Self is absolute reality, not relative, the Source of all manifested and unmanifested.

- Transcendent of form, name, vibration, frequency, energy, and space.

- Unmoving Reality beyond phenomena, self-luminous NOW, all is perfect in exquisite splendor.

- I AM THAT.

* * *

Liberation from Avoidance[30]

In Full Consciousness, the light of consciousness becomes very strong and capable of illuminating the recesses of the mind, where we often find unwanted feelings, thoughts, and energies. The Source allows all energies to exist in the light of consciousness, without avoiding or hiding them away. This meditation helps to illuminate the ties to these unwanted energies, enabling you to dissolve them in the pure light of consciousness.

Step 1: Take a few moments to slow down and bring your attention to your breath.

Step 2: Allow yourself to center and ground into the present moment.

Step 3: Notice that there is something unwanted, or avoided, and you already have the strength to step in it.

Like jumping in the river, at first, you stepped out of it, but now, take a few moments experiencing being in the river.

---

[30] This meditation works best in the company of a guide, while receiving a Consciousness Transmission and once you are at the Supra Causal Truth Level of Consciousness.

Step 4: The present Natural Emptiness and Openness is that strength and capacity that reveals itself while being in the unwanted.

The present Natural Space and Openness allows you to meet the bondage or limitation and realize that it is just a feeling, just a thing appearing in your seeing, your light of consciousness.

Step 5: When you meet it directly, you illuminate the bondage, the unwanted.

Step 6: The seeing and consciousness are beyond the apparent limitation or bondage, just like the movie screen being beyond the images appearing on it. It does not affect the screen, the seeing.

Step 7: The present Natural Space and Openness reveals itself through humanness, unconsciousness and beyond, like the lotus flower springing from the muddy water.

Step 8: The Self, the Source is the power of a direct meeting and un-avoidance.

Step 9: Take a few moments to feel the larger light, natural space, and openness. Acknowledge that it is okay if there are any smaller energies, any personal energy, any more limiting energy.

Full Consciousness is Not the End

"The best service you can do is to keep your thoughts on God. Keep God in mind every minute." (Neem Karoli Baba)

Despite attaining Full Consciousness, a long period is still needed to integrate this opening into our ordinary life. Inclinations, habits, and tendencies may linger for some time as this integration takes place. It usually takes four to seven years for all aspects of the self to align and integrate into Full Consciousness.

The level of Full Consciousness is not the End, but is actually an ever alive, natural, and open Self. Increasingly more people are nowadays opening to this level of consciousness, even though their soul mission may not have the same far-reaching impact as Buddha, Jesus, and other great Sages and Masters.

After the Self-Realization of Full Consciousness, all spiritual beings continue living and expressing themselves via their own unique way of Self-Actualization. It is an ever-deepening polishing of the present here-and-now experience.

Nothing has changed, yet everything is different. This present moment in pure consciousness becomes more alive, open, spacious, and complete; nonetheless, life goes on within consciousness too.

The levels of advancement of self-realized beings can differ greatly. For example, a newly awakened being to Full Consciousness might have difficulty explaining energy and consciousness, while other spiritual masters may have decades of experience helping seekers and have helped many of them to awaken to higher consciousness.

As we observe many teachers of the past and present time, we may realize that spiritual teachers can also be very different from each other in their multidimensional skills, qualities, and teachings. Enlightenment of Full Consciousness is actually a re-realization of who one really is but then follows what one does with that realization.

When it comes to great beings such as Buddha, Krishna, Jesus, Mahavatar Babaji, and all other well-known spiritual beings, the following question arises: How do they compare to other spiritual teachers who have also realized their God-Self nature?

At New Humanity Divine Marga, we have spent over a decade researching spiritual teachers, and more recently, we have conducted a deeper study on advancement beyond opening to Full Consciousness. This research enabled us to realize that there are actually infinite possibilities, even for spiritual teachers, to grow beyond the initial realization of Full Consciousness.

By researching spiritual teachers at Full Consciousness, we can see different degrees of Soul Advancement[31] of the whole being, including the physical body and nervous system, emotional and mental maturity, personality and psychological development, mastery of energetics, overall spiritual power to affect, transform, and empower others, transcendence of worldly matters, and the advancement of the higher vehicles of consciousness. This multi-dimensional advancement can be truly infinite.

---

[31] Read more at https://www.divinemarga.com/locs-of-past-teachers

Infinite Ascension & Cosmology

At the bottom of the hierarchy of creation, we find the mineral kingdom, followed by the vegetable kingdom, and animal kingdom. Then, we find human beings that are not conscious of their connection with the soul, and thus, they have not yet stepped onto the path of awakening.

Consequently, there are spiritual aspirants who have started on their path of spirituality. Next are disciples who are dedicated to their spiritual development. There are many levels of spiritual discipleship and initiations into higher spiritual domains that should ultimately lead to Enlightenment of Full Consciousness.

Ascended Masters

After many incarnations of spiritual discipleship and even being a spiritual teacher or guru, a person may one day advance to become an Ascended Master. Becoming an Ascended Master does not necessarily mean leaving the physical body and residing in a higher realm. This can be done even while being in the physical body embodied on Earth. In essence, the physical Ascended Master has raised the frequency of the body, having two feet in Heaven and two feet on Earth.

Ascension denotes a mastery of one's own physicality, mental, and emotional bodies, as well as mastery of the lower spiritual realms, and resolution of the lower karma binding one to the cycle of rebirth. It is important to note that not all spiritual teachers have completed this work; thus, becoming an Ascended Master involves much more self-mastery than being a regular spiritual teacher.

There are also Ascended Masters who are non-physical beings, who do reside in higher planes. They are all in Full Consciousness, in their perfected God-Self actualized state. Some of the Ascended Masters are the Lords of the Seven Rays.

Lords of the Seven Rays

1st Blue Ray: El Morya (Will of God, Faith)

2nd Yellow Ray: Lord Lanto (Illumination, Wisdom)

3rd Pink Ray: Paul the Venetian (Divine Love)

4th White Ray/Ascension Flame: Serapis Bey (Purity, Discipline, Hope)

5th Green Ray: Hilarion (Truth, Healing, Science)

6th Purple/Gold/Ruby Ray: Lady Nada (Peace, Ministration, Service)

7th Violet Ray: Saint Germain, Hierarch of the Aquarian Age (Freedom, Mercy, Transmutation)

Maha Chohan is the Lord of the Seven Rays, who represents the Holy Spirit for the evolution of this planet and the elemental kingdom.

World Teachers are currently Kuthumi and Jesus the Christ. Jesus is a spiritual master and the central figure of Christianity, the world's largest religion. His life shaped religion in the western world, influencing humanity in countless ways. His teachings centered on love and forgiveness. He and Kuthumi are currently overseeing the development of humanity as a whole.

The Christ (Planetary Buddha) is currently represented by Lord Maitreya. When Jesus was walking on Earth, Lord Maitreya was overseeing and assisting Jesus in his mission.

Lord Maitreya is regarded as the future Buddha of this world in Buddhist theology. He is said to be the successor of Guatama Buddha, with the mission to reinstate the dharma, the cosmic law underlying right behavior and social order. One of his main functions is to oversee the evolution of humankind.

Lord of the World

Above this level are the Lord of the World, Gautama Buddha, and Regent Lord of the World, Sanat Kumara, who is the planetary entity representing all human souls with complete union with the soul of the Earth. Sanat Kumara is overseer as the director of all the rays and all activities that happen here on Earth. Sanat Kumara's twin flame is Lady Master Venus.

Archangels

Further up are the Archangels that are very well known in the Christian tradition. The seven Archangels and their twin flames are: Archangel Michael and Faith, Archangel Jophiel and Christine, Chamuel and Charity, Gabriel and Hope, Raphael and Mother Mary, Uriel and Aurora, and Zadekiel and Amethyst.

Interestingly, Mother Mary is the only Archangel who was incarnated in a physical body. It was a unique case that Mother Mary incarnated on Earth, giving birth to Jesus, the world teacher.

Planetary Logos is basically the soul of the Earth, known in the New Age as Gaia. Beings at this level must be a Planetary Deva (Sanskrit: deity/divine being) at first, before becoming a Planetary Logos.

Solar Logos is Helios and his twin flame Vesta. Their work is to transmit the seven rays from the heart of the sun through the seven spirits before the solar throne to all the life waves of the solar system.

Galactic Logos

Many levels above the Solar Logos is the Galactic Logos, personified as the cosmic being Averran.

Cosmic Logos

The number of levels of initiation would ultimately depend on the size of the Cosmos because enough souls would have to climb the ladder to ensoul all the stars with stellar logoi and all the galaxies with galactic logos, while providing staffing for their attendant cosmic bureaucracies of angels, archangels, etc.[32]

About this, C.W. Leadbeater explains:

"The ladder of being [i.e., of initiation] extends upward into clouds of light, into which few of us can yet penetrate, and when we ask those who stand higher than we and know infinitely more than we do, all they can say is that it extends beyond their sight also. They know many more steps of it

---

[32] Source:
https://en.wikipedia.org/wiki/Initiation_(Theosophy)#:~:text=The%20number%20of %20levels%20of,cosmic%20bureaucracies%20of%20angels%2C%20archangels%2 C

than we do, but it goes further, onwards and upward to unimaginable heights of glory, and no one knows its end."
(C. W. Leadbeater, The Masters and the Path)

According to Ascended Master teachings, the Cosmic Logos is personified as the beings Alpha and Omega.

Universal Logos, Multiverses & God Source

Considering that God Source/Sat Purush[33] has given rise to ParBrahm, the supreme being, who holds dominion over 700 quadrillion multiverses (ParBrahmanda), and Lord Brahm, is a Being that holds dominion multitudes of lower Brahmanda universes, of which one is ours, then, all other universes would also need to be ensouled and managed by the respective Beings.

---

[33] More information: https://www.divinemarga.com/divine-cosmology-planes-of-existence

CHAPTER FIVE

Spiritual Myths & Clarity

Enlightenment Idealizations

Many people have many idealizations of Enlightenment, like one should be in constant bliss, sitting under a tree or in a cave, become like a saint, or be utterly unbothered by family or work.

Let's face it, this is not what usually happens. Some gurus and teachers may be like that, but it is circumstantial, according to their culture, their current life setup, and their past merits. If you were to give me any example of any guru, upon a deeper investigation of their life, or in their past lives, it would be possible to see that a lot of work had been done before reaching that stage, and that their overall advancement had been earned in their past incarnations.

Additionally, for example, India has a cultural support of gurus, but if a guru were sitting under a tree in the West, being not functional and unable to explain what was happening to them, most likely, they would be taken to a mental institution for help since common westerners have no idea what else to do in such situations. Therefore, teachers who visit or are born in the West are usually more grounded and practical in their expression of awakening.

When I become Enlightened, will all my life challenges disappear?

It is a common fantasy that, after your Enlightenment, you would instantly be a guru, and now, everybody treats you as a celebrity, everyone loves you, and your life would be like roses.

When you become Enlightened and fully realize your essence, you still have to do what you must do. You still need to wash your dishes, clean your house, continue having an income, care for friends and family, be in a relationship, and so on. That is the beautiful challenge that we have in the West. It is very integrative and grounding to be living a practical Enlightenment of everyday life.

After Enlightenment, can you completely relax, or do you still need to work on yourself?

With the opening of consciousness, you see it all more clearly. You see all the patterns, all conditions and all that arise in a clear light. Clarity is another word that can be used for the term Enlightenment.

You start seeing things clearly, and sometimes, it is not easy seeing things clearly because, so far, you have been avoiding, denying, escaping, and resisting; but now, you have this clarity.

Now, coming back to you is recognition that, at whichever level of consciousness you are, you are working through what you have at your hands. You are working through what you call your past, your present, and your future; all in the NOW.

Once you clear things up or decondition, to a certain extent, with inquiry and familiarization with the higher level of consciousness, you move up. Just like getting a degree in college, you have learned the lessons, you have taken your exams, and now, you are ready for the next level up.

Of course, there are some highway approaches that make that quicker, but even if you awaken to a higher level of consciousness very quickly, you will still need to work through your past. When you get to the surface, the light is bright. You are awakened, but those past cycles come back. However, you are no longer going to react the same way, and you are no longer going to be triggered the same way. It is going to be easier.

Some gurus sit and stay in silence, and they do not speak. There are many stories of gurus who became self-realized, and then, they took some time to be alone. Why? To work through the past backlog and to integrate.

A good teacher or guru will keep their focus on the Self, on Consciousness, God, and they continue polishing their energetics.

Like an analogy of the mirror of Awareness, one polishes the appearances in the mirror, polishing the energies in the clear light of the Self.

A guru or teacher continues to strengthen their abidance in the Self every moment. Their energetic capacity has different degrees, and they keep giving a lot of quality time for that 'polish', moment to moment.

After the initial Enlightenment, your work continues to

advance energetically further, to polish up further, to learn more about the universe, how to manage things, how to work with energies, and most importantly, how to help others. Essentially, you learn how to be of service to the world, to others, and to yourself because you are the world, you are the others. You become of benefit to everyone. Your Enlightenment is for the benefit of all.

"Lord, make me an instrument of thy peace. Where there is hatred, let me sow love; Where there is injury, pardon; Where there is doubt, faith; Where there is despair, hope; Where there is darkness, light; And where there is sadness, joy. O Divine Master, Grant that I may not so much seek; To be consoled as to console; To be understood as to understand; To be loved, as to love." (Prayer of Saint Francis of Assisi)

We can also see the principle of Ascension in the Universe. As you ascend, your work takes on a larger scale, a larger capacity to help others, or the whole planet, solar system, galaxy, and so on.

It is essential to know that this work continues. That's indeed the beauty of it. Therefore, we see such a beautiful diversity of teachers and teachings, bringing messages, and trying to clarify how this universe works.

Diversity of Spiritual Teachers

From the ancient Greek philosophers and Eastern Yogis to modern-day spiritual teachers, we can say that these teachers have shared their unique insights on the nature of reality, the path to Enlightenment, and the ultimate purpose of life. We will explore some of the different spiritual teachers and their focus on teachings, highlighting the diversity of spiritual paths available today.

Spiritual teachers may be on different levels of consciousness. Therefore, it is essential to research their teachings and see what fruits they bring. For example, there might be a spiritual teacher at the Awareness Level of Consciousness, the first step of Enlightenment, who might be mature and integrated, and their fruits might be bountiful.

Another teacher might be in, say, Supra Causal Truth, but has just awakened there recently, and has started to teach some students without taking the time to integrate. Therefore, the above two teachers would have different depths in their teachings and ability to help their students; hence, we cannot judge a teacher by the level of consciousness alone.

It would help if the seeker took the time to get to know the spiritual teacher, become familiar with their teachings, understand the depth of their teachings, and, most importantly, see the fruits of their teachings.

For instance, how many other people have they helped to awaken? That is a good measure of fruits. Sometimes, there is a large community around the teacher, but the focus is more on a spiritual lifestyle, rather than awakening. Sometimes, there is a small number of seekers, and everyone awakens fast.

Some spiritual teachers have a more humanitarian focus than others. They might establish global humanitarian organizations; for example, the organization of Sadhguru (Isha Foundation), Sri Sri Ravi Shankar (Art of Living), etc.

Organizational management takes up a lot of time, and the focus of their leaders becomes broader. They can certainly reach more people, but their availability to more advanced spiritual explorers requiring more personal one-on-one time is greatly reduced; thus, more people are helped more broadly, but fewer people awaken to the highest levels of consciousness.

Other teachers are more specialized in their teachings, such as Eckhart Tolle, whose entire focus is on the Presence level of consciousness. He spent many years after his awakening sitting in parks, immersed in the Beingness of Presence. When he started approaching other communities and groups, he began realizing that his experience was different from the common meditation and yoga practices. After several years, he gained a deep and refined seeing of Presence. His success came after appearing on the Oprah Winfrey television show, which made him famous worldwide. Eckhart's teachings on Presence are a big gift to humanity, helping to shift from the common spirituality of Inner Love and Unity into Presence consciousness.

Meanwhile, Jiddu Krishnamurti's story was quite complicated. Theosophical Society leaders were searching for a new world teacher, and they found a young boy in India with a bright aura, Jiddu Krishnamurti. Consequently, the Theosophical Society groomed him to be the new World Teacher, an advanced spiritual position in the theosophical tradition (e.g., Jesus the Christ), but later, Jiddu rejected this mantle, and withdrew from the organization behind it.

Unhappiness unfolded, including in his personal love life. However, Jiddu Krishnamurti was an intelligent and highly realized being. His teachings brought the light of Awareness to many interests, such as psychological revolution, the nature of mind, meditation, holistic inquiry, and human relationships, while bringing about a radical change in society.

A very well-known historical being, Mahatma Gandhi, helped to free India from British rule. He later inspired movements for civil rights and freedom across the world. His message was non-violence, freedom, and unity, thus focusing primarily on Unity consciousness.

We may thus understand through these examples that spiritual teachers have a particular purpose, and that their lives are not always easy. Spiritual teachers bring a particular message, and they deliver specific fruits, according to their life mission or unfoldment of life.

There is also a difference between spiritual healers, teachers, and spiritual masters. Spiritual healers do healing work, with all that it includes. For their part, meditation teachers can begin teaching meditation after some time of integration in Inner Light, Love, and Unity levels of consciousness. A spiritual teacher would generally be at least in the Presence consciousness.

Many spiritual teachers have large followings, creating beautiful gatherings, and giving many talks or amazing experiences to their students. Nonetheless, only a few of their students might be actually awakened to Presence consciousness or above. Therefore, communities, talks, and spiritual experiences do not necessarily mean awakening to a more advanced level of consciousness.

A spiritual master is not only a fully realized being himself/herself but also helps others to awaken and integrate into the highest levels of consciousness, while being able to meet another exactly where they are, knowing all ins and outs of each step of the way.

Giving nothing objective, the master at the highest levels of consciousness helps spiritual explorers to awaken to the open and natural Full Consciousness. If there is something wrong, the spiritual master would immediately tell the seeker that and would also guide the seeker towards their higher qualities, their higher realization, their more natural and true Self.

Spiritual masters can easily express Divinity and can also be fully grounded in Humanity. They would pour the light of consciousness upon seekers via consciousness transmissions and support them at all levels of existence. The masters' support is everywhere, at all levels of our being, in all dimensions and all levels of consciousness; thus, spiritual masters are not easily found.

Note: You may also refer to Chapter 4, the topic entitled 'Infinite Ascension & Cosmology,' for more information about further advancements beyond awakening to Full Consciousness as well as read more here: https://www.divinemarga.com/locs-of-past-teachers

Enlightenment Experiences vs. Full Consciousness

When we meditate, we can quite easily experience Enlightenment, as well as experiences of higher consciousness. However, remaining at these higher levels of consciousness is a different story. This is where the real work happens.

Many seekers might say: "I had an enlightenment experience, I was in bliss, and there was complete emptiness and infinity." Then, they ask: "Am I Enlightened already?" I would reply: "Well, yes, you were enlightened for that moment. When you had your enlightenment experience, for that moment, you were Buddha, but the difficulty is in stabilizing more permanently into that level of consciousness."

The consciousness of Presence is something beyond an idea. Presence means pre-sense before senses. It means being beyond the five senses. We are all familiar with these five senses – smelling, hearing, tasting, touching, and seeing – enabling us to perceive the apparent world, the reality that appears to these five senses.

Many realities can be perceived with the third eye. However, being present is something else. It is being behind, while at the same time being with what appears. In Presence, we are not trying to block anything, and we are not trying to detach or observe, which is a common practice in Inner Light and Higher Self Consciousness when we watch and observe the mind. Being present is being behind the five senses, behind this appearing world, but here and now too.

If you look now, what you perceive is exactly with the five

senses. If you draw your attention back to awareness, you recognize that there is much more than what you can now perceive with these five human senses, or even the inner spiritual senses.

The human body is intelligent and complicated, but it is not the ultimate. We can only imagine in this vastness of the universe how many more sentient beings there can be with many more ways of perceiving reality.

Regardless of how many senses we have, 5, 10, or 20, Presence, and even more so, our own Self is beyond senses and manifestation. Our own Self gives them power, is immanent and permeates all creation.

The degree of Presence is the lessening of resistance to what IS and developing the strength and light of our awareness.

Enlightenment is an illumination of unconsciousness, the very depths, the very deep sleep state, the very bottom of the bottom. Not the conscious mind, not the subconscious mind, but illuminating unconsciousness itself.

The subconscious mind is that part of us that stores memories, beliefs, and emotions that influence our behavior. In contrast, the unconscious mind is that part of us that operates outside of our conscious and subconscious awareness and contains our deepest instincts and impulses.

It takes a lot of patience, strength, and compassion towards our difficulties to be fully present. The mind is usually active. It wants to do everything on the list, but for the real seeker, the following question should arise – 'Is it in doing that we achieve Self Realization?'.

Those who are present, sitting quietly and silently on the top of the mountain, can watch everybody in the valley doing what they are doing. Sitting at the top of the mountain is being fully present. You have already mastered Doing. You have learned the lessons of Doing. You now recognize that the value is in Being.

If you are drawn back into the mind, you can remain present, with the recognition that you are now being drawn into the mind. You tell yourself, let me be there, let me be present with that. It is a great skill of non-resistance. First, you need quite a lot of effort to be non-resistant. People would say: "Oh my gosh, why is it so difficult? Why does it take so much effort?" And my reply is that they are learning to become effortless, to let go completely, dis-identify, and dis-attach from the mind, to become uninvolved and disinterested in the mind.

The mind is like a magician. It can pull all kinds of magic tricks from its sleeves. It is always going to find a way to wow you. The mind would say: "Oh, look at this!" And you are instantly back in your mind. The mind is often called a trickster. It always finds a way of getting you interested in something that appears, that is, the manifested reality in all its dimensions. There is a lot of stuff that can be interesting in the multi-dimensional universe. This is why you need to keep a firm focus on the light of consciousness, because, otherwise, the mind would find ways to make you interested in some appearing phenomenon.

"A mind that is fast is sick. A mind that is slow is sound. A mind that is still is divine." *(Meher Baba)*

All qualities are also fragments of creation; for example, peace, happiness, love, and a sense of freedom are illusionary in the ultimate sense. They are only the tastes that appear in the consciousness, which is the lightless light beyond all appearances.

From Experience to Consciousness

Let's become more familiar with this present moment, with this Now, to become more familiar with experience. Experience includes what you perceive with your five senses, your inner experience, this environment, all these forms, and spaces. This is what makes your experience as a whole.

This experience is witnessed to be happening now. It is witnessed in awareness. It is seen not in the observer, not through the process of observation, but in your awareness.

We may say that there is a present experience, and there is awareness. When these merge, they become boundless consciousness. Your experience has a certain stickiness, which is a pull into the lower forms, such as emotions and surface thoughts. The thoughts are little bubbles on the surface of the ocean. They are the surface of energies, emotions, and feelings. All is just energy and vibrations.

To go deeper and realize the depth of consciousness, you need to swim through this ocean and gain some immunity from the tendencies of the stickiness of experiences. The first thing you can do is realize that thoughts have no real essence

249

in themselves. Emotions and feelings are more substantial as they are more real. They are felt in your body, and when thoughts subside, emotions and feelings become available. You become present with your emotions and feelings, and you become present, here. This presence is positional because it is you being present, and then, it expands. It is a certain field and space.

You may realize that the experience of being present with emotions, feelings, and energies is not excluded from the environment where you are right now because nothing is excluded in consciousness. There is no inside, no physical, no spiritual, or outer world in consciousness. There is no inner or external universe. How can you separate them? Everything is inseparable, but in your individual experience, you have a feeling of separation that seems real. It is a grand illusion.

"True self is non-self, the awareness that the self is made only of non-self elements. There's no separation between self and other, and everything is interconnected. Once you are aware of that you are no longer caught in the idea that you are a separate entity." (Thich Nhat Hahn)

You identify with your story, anger, sadness, and happiness. It is all a story. When you empty yourself of emotions, you do not become a robot, but you are no longer attached to those emotions. For a person identified with anger, their reality becomes as such.

Therefore, consciousness is the clear omniscient Seeing, which comes from recognizing that feelings have colors, and that those deep assumptions have their projections. The biggest assumption is that you are this externally separate form. The original separation is the assumption of a limited position that limits itself and defends that limited position.

The limited self is called the ego. The ego is only defending. The nature of the ego is contraction and attachment to that contraction that becomes a point of reference, known as identification.

You may recognize that there are many emotions, feelings, and assumptions. There is a vast ocean of many layers and interconnected streams. There is indeed a tendency to focus, contract, and identify with these streams. This is how the mind has built up its structures.

Desire comes in the middle of focus and attachment because desire wants it to be this way or not that way. Desire adds another layer of suffering. It pulls you to the left or right of what you want or do not want, and when you come to the neutral position of neither one thing nor the other, you can meet the emotion.

Becoming present is just halfway through the journey. It is the right relationship with what is here. It is midway through the journey because those who are present must then notice that they are aware of, even being present, the being, and how still and peaceful they are. They are aware of how disturbed they are when they are deeply present or balanced when they feel that way.

Therefore, the key to Self-Realization is to go beyond energy, feelings, emotions, thought forms, names, shapes, spaces, and dimensions – beyond Experience.

Awareness that is beyond experience is the key. It is easy to verify this truth because you know experience, no matter what form it takes or how deep it goes. You are aware of yourself being in peace or love, and it is just another experience.

Enlightenment is not about maintaining a blissful state since there is a certain effort to keep it. Your awareness of experience becomes increasingly stronger as you stay as an awareness. As you see and investigate each experience, observe how the experience is attracting you and how sticky it is.

There are an infinite number of experiences that can draw you. Experience has a force of action that makes you do things. Then, there is the balancing force that maintains balance and peace, but that is still experienced.

Three forces of nature make up our experiences. The three Gunas are the three qualities of Nature found in all aspects of life, namely, Sattva (harmony, purity, and goodness), Rajas (activity and passion), and Tamas (dullness, heaviness, and inertia). All three Gunas work together to create each experience in our life.

Therefore, you need to become stronger from the forces of these experiences because you would be sucked into the energies, your emotions, and feelings. Alternatively, you would be spacing out and unsettled with spiritual experiences, such as, feeling your energy centres, having kundalini sensations, or experiencing higher spaces and dimensions.

Energetic sensations and going into blissful states are side effects of your return to the natural state. Altered perceptions are also side effects of returning to the natural state that feels very natural, beyond, and with all as it is.

Expanding and gaining strength in your awareness is the key, and when that merges with what is being experienced, it transforms into Consciousness.

Good practice is to ask yourself what you are aware of. You can further state: "In my awareness, I'm aware of this." This allows you to see the position of your awareness at that moment.

At the moment of noticing, you can release any position. Fighting against external or internal conflict is a position and defending that position or resisting injustice keeps injustice.

When there is fighting, there is a lack of mutual understanding. When you are in an internal conflict, the other person is no longer there, but the fight is still happening inside, within you. Therefore, there is a certain resistance in that position. Softening both sides of the resistance allows you to transcend both: the position of what is right and resisting what you feel is wrong.

You may see that holding a certain position is always limiting. The ego is defending a position, denying the truth, and protecting that position.

Neutral awareness, on the other hand, is unconditional allowing. It is not concerned with experience. When this final resistance with experience is transcended, that becomes Natural Consciousness.

Readiness for Non-Duality & Self-Enquiry

Advaita Vedanta is a spiritual tradition, looking at reality not as distinct, separate objects or identities but as an indivisible ONE.

Contrastively, Self-Enquiry is about discovering the unreality of the 'I-thought' that is the root cause of the Ego.

Integrated Non-Duality is the recognition of openness and present aliveness. The Self is here. It is open. The present experience can take any shape or form and go deeper and deeper, infinitely more.

A direct Non-Dual approach is suitable for those who are more mature, who already have good experience with meditation and have experienced various states of consciousness, even blissful (Samadhi) states, and who have settled into the Presence of their Being. At that point, a person is truly ready for Non-Dual inquiry.

Suppose a person approaches Non-Dual inquiry with a philosophical attitude, trying to understand it from the mental place, not even being awakened to the Inner Light. In that case, it is not a good time for Non-Duality.

Non-Duality is not about mental contemplations. It is, in essence, an inquiry deeper within one's Being beyond energies and phenomena.

A ripened way to use inquiry is to see what is truly here, to recognize the true nature of existence, the true nature of the

Self.

In the early stages of Non-Duality, a person is taught the practice of negation. It is helpful practice, but at the same time, it is meant to be done using a 'middle way' approach as the means of dis-identifying from various fixations.

An example of negation practice is to say: "I have the body, but I'm not the body. I have thoughts, but I'm not these thoughts. I have feelings, but I'm not these feelings. I feel energies or I have energies, but I'm not these energies only either."

This is healthy dis-identification or negation, enabling the seeker to detach and dis-identify from phenomena to experience fewer fixations, thus more openness.

If a person, or even a teacher, is not so mature in Non-Duality, they would adopt extreme negation, and would say such things as: "there is no world, there is no me, there is no you, there is nothing." This kind of negation has a particular flavor of being too dismissive or lacking aliveness and openness.

I have seen so much trouble being caused to students with this approach because it can cause a mental breakdown, total confusion, even more isolation, lostness, and even existential crisis.

This is not a healthy way as it can create a traumatic experience and psychological or mental breakdown. However, there is a better way to help someone. There is a way to go beyond the mind without breaking a person's psychology and creating another traumatic experience.

Therefore, Non-Duality is best approached with a certain

maturity in Presence consciousness once you know how to meditate and manage your emotions, different states of mind, and meditative states. That is a ripe time for a Non-Dual approach.

There are also higher degrees of Non-Duality. Some mature teachers, for example, Sri Ramana Maharshi and Sri Nisargadatta Maharaj, came forward with higher terms, such as, Absolute Self, no other than the Self, etc. They were entirely correct in the context of their talk, in the context of those who were capable of receiving this directness. Ramana used to say that Self-Enquiry is for mature Souls.

At the highest level, Non-Duality is a very direct and piercing approach, and it is addressed to those seekers who are capable of receiving this directness and who have prepared for it.

There is a saying that the teacher appears when the student is ready. The danger nowadays is that direct Non-Duality is accessible to anybody today on the internet, whether one is ready for it or not.

Therefore, throughout the ages, spiritual teachers held spiritual lineages to pass on their teachings. They would offer teachings to those seekers who were ready. However, with technology, many things have nowadays shifted and changed, and everything is available instantly.

It is essential to evaluate yourself, feel, and see whether it is the right time, especially regarding Non-Duality. There is indeed a very easy way to check: If you feel that it helps you and makes things clearer, then that is good, but if you feel more confused, then maybe you should not do it.

If you stumble upon the truth,you are ready for, it will be

experienced like a lovely peeling-off effect of an old layer.

Non-Duality is best approached when the seeker is ready for it because the truth at this level of consciousness is very sharp. This is the beauty of Jnana Yoga, the Non-Dual approach. It is a very sharp truth, but it is meant to have more of a peeling-off effect to avoid causing drastic psychological disturbances.

Subtle Planes – Do They Exist?

Spiritual experiences can be a spiritual playground as people can get those experiences with various meditations, yogic practices, breathwork practices, etc. Many people can easily experience and see subtle planes, altered states of consciousness, and planes of existence.

Yes, subtle planes are here. Scientists have found that many layers make up the universe and there is intelligence within it. At the same time, every major world religion recognizes higher dimensions and higher beings. For instance, Christianity recognizes the existence of heavens, Angels, and Archangels, and Islam mentions many heavens too. Meanwhile, in Hinduism, the most elaborate tradition, some say it acknowledges 330 million Deities. Buddhism also has a cosmological perspective with many beings occupying different planes of existence.

We can see the wonder of subtle planes even within our physical bodies. The human body that we carry is composed of different components, such as, eyes, ears, arms, fingers, etc. Those major components of our physical form are made of smaller components. We thus have trillions of cells dancing together in perfect synchronicity and harmony to create this appearance of a physical form.

When we are asked, "How are you doing? How are you feeling?", and we answer, "Oh, I feel fine", that means that all of our trillions of cells are giving us a sense of well-being. It's just beautiful how things are.

Scientists have further found many different layers of the structure of matter. In fact, matter is made of atoms, while atoms are made of subatomic particles (protons, neutrons, and electrons), and even those are made of yet smaller particles, with the latest discovery of the 'God molecule' that gives matter its matter.

This is how nuclear reactors work. They smash atoms together, producing so much energy that they can power up the whole city for a while. There is increasingly more energy as we go into smaller and smaller components of creation. Paradoxically, as they get smaller, the energy becomes bigger.

We can confirm that major world religions have seen subtle planes, scientists have discovered molecules that make up everything, and, of course, spiritual teachers saw it all a long time ago.

In a very generic model, we know that there are twelve main dimensions. However, that model is quite abstract since every dimension has many sub-dimensions and sub-frequencies within them.

Indeed, we can witness that even here, on Earth, because we are all walking on this third-density Earth. Nonetheless, the experience can be so different for people at different levels of consciousness.

Path of Devotion

The path of devotion is the path of love, devotion, and surrender to Divine, God, Self in all its forms by all different spiritual traditions. The path of devotion turns our heart to the Divine, letting go of the personal self, personal needs, and desires, while surrendering ourselves completely to the Divine. It is where Divine will is above all, and every moment becomes a reflection of surrender and devotion to the Divine.

"Love the Lord your God with all your heart and with all your soul and with all your mind." (Jesus, Matthew 22:37-40)

In the Christian tradition, Jesus was the ultimate devotee of God. Meanwhile, in yogic traditions, this is known as the Bhakti. Kabir path is focused on Nirguna Bhakti, together with Sikh religion on Sat Purush, and Islam is focused on Allah. All other major religions and spiritual traditions have their ways of devotion and practice of love.

It is important to study scriptures, read books, and contemplate the nature of not only the Divine, but the obstacles of the Ego as well in order to purify the conditioning and impurities of the mind, heart, and soul, and to see how the mind clings to the world.

Divine Love is a way of self-offering and self-expansion. It is not one of earthly renunciation or asceticism, but a middle path, where the seeker has the opportunity to renounce or transform the negative qualities which stand in the way of union with the Divine. Meditation on the heart brings the light of the soul closer to reaching the highest Love.

"Wear a crown of flowers on your head, let its roots reach your heart." (Kabir)

The practice of devotion helps to shift the flow of energy towards the Divine. Different kinds of organizations and movements offer various practices, mantras, songs, and dances, elevating the seeker to an ecstatic state.

Some years ago, after a retreat in India, we organized a group trip to Vrindavan, the birthplace of Lord Krishna and the world's capital of Bhakti (devotion). While there, we visited the main temple of the International Society for Krishna Consciousness for the evening Kirtan (a call-and-response song or chant set to music, where multiple singers express loving devotion to a deity). Everyone had so much fun singing and dancing for hours on end, feeling uplifted to devotional ecstasy.

We also noticed other seekers who were engaged in more integrative Bhakti practices. They had their mala beads for silent, inward mantra meditations, and were also studying Bhakti scriptures.

Many people see only the beautiful and fun side of Bhakti, but a lot of hard work is also required for the purification of the heart, mind, and soul to become one with the Divine.

Unity of All Paths & Openness

The Non-Dual Advaita Vedanta tradition of Self-Enquiry, traditions related to the subtle planes, and the path of devotion all merge together at some point. They are actually intertwined and related to each other in many ways.

We should not become spiritual extremists, just like those people who say that there is only the Christian God, or only Allah, or only this path or the other. Beyond all forms and all paths, there is Consciousness, our own essential nature of Self to be realized.

"The whole universe is our home and all residing in it belong to our family... instead of trying to see God in a particular appearance, it is better to see him in everything." (Neem Karoli Baba)

Consciousness is actually all unifying and endless. Beyond ecstasy, there is more bliss, and beyond bliss, there is more peace, and beyond that peace, there is more love, and there is even higher light, and so on. A true spiritual master knows that, and never says that this is the end, there is nothing more.

In our universe, time moves forward. However, there might be another universe where time moves backwards. There might also be a universe that is not expanding, but contracting, and another universe where the energy is combined differently. Maybe there is a universe which is totally 2D flat, like those old computer games, and another universe which has 100 dimensions.

Consciousness and its creations are really endless, the number of vibrations and frequencies are immeasurable, and the possible experiences are infinite too.

It is best to be open, to see what is here, and be open to know that, perhaps, you do not see everything. Be open to see that, perhaps, there is more than you can ever imagine, sense, or perceive.

Consciousness is the source of all and is all manifestations. It is the Self that is truly infinite and endless, where all the diversity of all manifestations is experienced in one Consciousness, God, Self. All paths are within the same ONE.

Challenging Energies, Emotions & Triggers

If I am at the level of Presence or Awareness or Non-Duality, why am I still experiencing challenges? Should I no longer have any problems? Should I no longer feel emotions?

These are common questions that people ask, and I will tell you this: you still have the body, don't you? But you know that you are not only the body. Similarly, emotions can still come, but now you know that you are not those emotions.

You still get various energetic sensations and various clouds arising. You know that you are not those clouds, and this is a big illusion breaker because the most common thing after helping many seekers and seeing how they take everything in is that they assume and believe that, at the Awareness level of consciousness, or higher, they would no longer have any emotions or experience challenges.

The questions to ask are: Who are You? What is your essence? What is your identity? Nothing has changed. The garden is the same. The woods are the same. The water is the same.

If you have past traumas, and you have not fully healed them, many of them would still be there to be healed. Maybe you would need to work through some of them to get to the openness of consciousness. Still, it does not mean that you would heal and solve all of them because that takes a lot more time, and they are not relevant to your True Identity. This is akin to a back pain that is not relevant to your True identity since it is simply a bodily pain.

People say that, if you are Self-Realized, you cannot be sad anymore, and you should always be happy.

Wait a moment, are we trying to pretend to be somebody else and live someone else's life? Or are we trying to be ourselves, our real selves?

Guess what it means to be your real Self. Being your real self means being authentic, being real, being true to yourself, and being honest with yourself in your own life, right now.

There is no denial, no argument, no protection, and no defensiveness. These were the luxuries of the Ego, and you cannot afford them anymore. However, these mechanisms would only arise to indicate that some more healing needs to be done.

In Full Consciousness, there is a certain sense of self-honesty and self-truthfulness. Nothing is taken personally. There is a lightness of being behind any circumstances. Even if some troublesome stuff comes up, there is lightness behind it because there is no more identity. Things are easier overall. It becomes easier to continue healing and living your life too as there is no more stick in the wheel.

Does being at Full Consciousness mean that I will no longer get triggered?

To open up to Full Consciousness, we have to unblock the key blockages. Nonetheless, the secondary ones are not that important since they do not block consciousness permanently. They might merely come as a temporary cloud. Being triggered is not a problem. It is just indicating that something is unresolved, that it needs more work and integration of consciousness into our lower vehicles.

Suppose you had a very traumatic childhood or adolescence. In that case, some things have even been hard-wired, becoming a blind spot in your nervous system. It is thus going to take some time to continue the healing process, but it does not mean that you cannot open to Full Consciousness. Just like losing a limb in a car accident, it does not mean that you cannot realize who you really are.

Therefore, do you see how many assumptions about Enlightenment can contribute to creating or keeping more distances? I am trying to close those gaps, to bring you closer to your real Self, beyond all conditions and assumptions.

Non-Dual Emotional, Psychological & Trauma Healing

"Your task is not to seek for love, but merely to seek and find all the barriers within yourself that you have built against it." (Rumi)

From the perspective of Non-Duality, emotional, psychological, and mental healing are all necessary because some locks need to be opened for consciousness to be freed to reach Full Consciousness. These specific locks need to be found, healed, and unlocked. I mention 'specific ones' because not all mental, psychological, or traumatic issues block access to Full Consciousness.

On the highway to Full Consciousness, you do not necessarily need to pay attention to everything on the road, and you do not need to stop at every corner. Therefore, opening to Full Consciousness does not mean that everything will be resolved. When you open to Full Consciousness, you are open, and in that openness, past cycles return for healing too. However, it becomes easier with supportive openness, while the mind and identity are no longer holding you hostage. When the 'I' is no longer holding you hostage, it is much easier to continue healing.

In healing, major issues are called traumas. Traumas create certain blind spots that shift one's psychology into alternative options. This is how coping mechanisms are born, such as escapism, avoidance, denial, aggression, protection, and so on. The subconscious mind tends to avoid those blockage points, thus creating various limitations in the psychological state.

Trauma healing takes a lot of time. I have seen many people who needed to clear layers of associated emotions and beliefs to gain deeper access. We remove one layer on the surface, then another layer in the middle, and then, we gain access to the actual trauma, which is the deepest layer.

It is possible to heal traumas. However, the level of consciousness Presence is usually where we encounter some key challenges. By the time someone has moved into Non-Duality or above, many of the key major life challenges have been worked through. In Non-Duality, one feels a certain liberation which increases one's sense of freedom, strength of presence, and openness because the key obstacles have been worked through.

When you heal key blockages and issues on the way to Full Consciousness, you already gain a certain experience and knowledge of self-healing.

My role is not to be a doctor or healer, but to help you to come to Full Consciousness, and to teach you how to heal yourself. By experiencing the healing of the key issues that you were unable to deal with yourself, you get the experience you need for healing. Therefore, issues become smaller, and I trust that you manage more on your own and continue healing yourself.

My role here is to help you to increase your capacity for openness, space, and strength, and to provide all the tools for healing. It is then up to you to do your own polishing throughout those cycles.

For those who choose to advance and ascend further after their opening to Full Consciousness, we continue working on that together.

At New Humanity Divine Marga, we teach many healing techniques and meditations. You can do many practices yourself, but at times, you may need some help because some things are too deep or too big, and you might need additional support to work on them.

One more important thing to mention is that I encourage people to develop understanding when it comes to psychological and traumatic experiences. I encourage everyone to learn about traumas, and how they function. There are a lot of resources available online about trauma healing. Any spiritually mature being should learn that.

I know this is not the most exciting topic because everyone wants only bliss, happiness, and freedom. People may even wonder why they should learn about traumas and all those things since their wish is to escape them and to be spiritual. They do not want to have anything to do with all of that.

However, if you want to be truly free, I suggest learning about traumas and their mechanisms because this makes you much stronger. Awareness of these mechanisms would indeed liberate you.

The brighter the Consciousness is, the brighter it shines into every corner of your Being.

You must investigate every corner of your being and turn every pebble upside down. The bigger light gives you a bigger capacity to handle deeper and more complex mechanisms and see the functions of the deepest and darkest places of the human psyche.

If you want to be strong in consciousness, you need to see deeper. However, do not try to do too much at once either as the healer should not get sick. You should not drown in more problems because that is not the point. The real intention is to see more clearly how all things work.

Essentially, for psychological and traumatic blockages, it is very important to learn, understand, inquire, and heal yourself and help others. It brings more compassion to you, as well as more humility and strength to help someone who is experiencing something difficult.

When people re-experience something traumatic, they get triggered, and through those blind spots, they may say bad things or even act out in the worst cases. They can become quite angry, rageful, and even abusive. Your ability to realize that this person is acting through the blockage would thus help you to not take it personally.

You can develop an ability to see what is really going on, to have compassion for what is going on, and of course, you might be on the receiving end of the trigger because you are helping someone. Sometimes, you may take a lot of fire, but once again, do not take it personally because you know what they are experiencing. You know that you are doing your best. Ideally, the more you learn, the more you know how these mechanisms function, and the better you would be at helping someone.

Dealing with Challenges at Higher Levels of Consciousness

Even if you are Enlightened, you might face many conditional situations that are typically brought about by life, such as family life, going to work to earn an income, and being in a relationship.

You need to learn how to deal with challenges because it is not all roses. Indeed, it has never been only roses. Unfortunately, if you expect only roses, your illusion will certainly face reality very quickly. What makes life easier is learning how to deal with challenges and how they work.

With time and continuous purifications, you polish yourself, sharpen, and have a certain transcendence. There is a release and liberation when energy gets polished on both ends (the highs and lows), to a certain degree. This energy becomes a transcended energy. In other words, you are no longer triggered by it and can be non-reactive to that type of provocation or trigger. That is how we polish those cycles. We call this Non-Dual transcendence.

Unfortunately, people often watch videos, idealize, and fantasize that all spiritual teachers and enlightened beings are like saints. However, they are not aware of all life challenges that these individuals face because these are not talked about on YouTube. Seekers must thus realize that every person has to learn how to deal with life challenges.

Some spiritual teachers may deny any life challenges or try to show only perfectionism. They may completely ignore these topics and try to avoid them. This may be done in order to uphold a certain image, but it does not mean that they do not have any life challenges to deal with and to overcome.

The best thing is to acknowledge the complexity of human interactions and psychology, particularly the complications of psychological blockages and traumas.

My advice to those of you who face challenges is to seek and receive help, learn, and educate yourselves. It is good to learn and educate yourselves when things are good because, when you are burdened with a challenge, you will be ready for it. If it suddenly hits you out of nowhere, and if you have not learned anything about trauma healing, you will still go through it, but in a hard way.

Sometimes, we need to re-ground ourselves and understand that trauma is trauma, and a psychological issue is a psychological issue. Even if we consider ourselves spiritual, trauma is still trauma.

Some people try to sugar coat and spiritualize their issues, but they are still a problem that needs to be worked through and healed.

Insight into what is blocking consciousness is needed, as well as the ability to identify and see those deepest hooks and heal them so that higher consciousness can open up.

CHAPTER SIX

Consciousness Integration

"When both body and mind are at peace, all things appear as they are: perfect, complete, lacking nothing." (Dogen Zenji)

Nervous System Capacity

The importance of the Nervous System for Consciousness Integration

There are three stages in opening consciousness. The first is the opening of consciousness, which is how we return to our true nature. Various energetic sensations may arise as we start to become aware of our subtler being. The second process is when our energy system adjusts to the new level of consciousness, while the third process is stabilization and integration of a higher level of consciousness which takes years to be fully integrated.

The nervous system plays a key role in stabilizing and integrating the new higher vibrations, frequencies, and energies with our body. Our nervous system is composed of the brain, spine, and the nerves that stretch throughout the body. The brain and spine comprise the central nervous system that performs the major functions, while the nerves stretch throughout all the organs and muscles, all the way to

271

our fingers and toes.

The nerves through which electrical signals travel are composed of neurons (nerve cells). This is a vast network of neuron pathways, with a single neuron, making up to 15,000 connections. The nervous system is the micro version of the universe.

If our nervous system were unblocked entirely, everything would flow in harmony. We would already be fully realized and enlightened. If the electricity and light flow were unobstructed, we would be filled with light. This is called En-Lightenment.

Our nervous system is like the motherboard of a computer. For example, our solar plexus is one of the major channels where many nerves meet. These channels are like a microchip, where the nerve force is traveling, electricity is transmitted, and signals pass through our nervous system to give instructions for certain actions. The nervous system connects with all meridians and distributes all the life force energy throughout the body, connecting with chakras, kundalini, and all the nadis (Sanskrit: (energy) channels).

Eleven million bits of information per second are sent to the nervous system from the five senses of sight, hearing, touch, smell, and taste. The whole experience that is happening now is being processed via our nervous system.

What may negatively affect the nervous system?

The nervous system is very sensitive. Therefore, negative or traumatic experiences significantly impact the nervous system. Physical injuries and traumas may damage the nervous system because they block the neuron pathways. Traumas can create literal blockages in the nervous system, where the light can no longer flow through.

It is common for the average human being to have a huge nervous strain, depletion, and nervous system exhaustion. As one ages, the nervous system keeps depleting, blocking, and getting denser. Nervous strain can be experienced through various stresses and tensions due to the inability to process and deal with situations and circumstances.

It is further known that various psychedelic drugs (especially chemical ones) can harm the nervous system because a person can overdose and be overwhelmed by experiences. When people experience something beyond their capacity to handle it, their nervous system blocks or gets damaged in one way or another.

When there is a block in the neuron pathways, the neurons start to rewire to different pathways to avoid that blocked area in the nervous system. As neurons rewire themselves to avoid these blocked areas, blind spots and defense mechanisms start to form, such as fears and denials.

Another problem is social and psychological programming that wires our brain and nervous system to create suppressions and limitations, known as conditioning. Over time, if these psychological conditions are reinforced, the physical wiring of the nervous system establishes itself.

Our nervous system creates our experience on autopilot. Nervous system wiring becomes physically manifested. That is how this current experience is perceived automatically.

Can the nervous system be healed?

The good news is that the nervous system is quite malleable and can be rewired. This rewiring process is not easy though, and requires effort, including repeated practice or effort, called deconditioning.

Once you release the conditioned wiring, you are free from that blockage. Therefore, the next time the same situation arises, you will not act the same way because you have physically rewired your nervous system.

You can access increasingly deeper levels of your nervous system. When you unblock your nervous system pathways, you release the suppressed material, you turn the dark pebble upside down, and electricity and light can now flow through easily. This is how you can increase your nervous system capacity thereby uplifting your experience in the present moment and future to a higher vibration.

Your nervous system is a significant asset and an excellent investment because it affects your future. It determines your actions and reactions. If you establish self-observation, self-awareness, healing protocols, and practices, you ride the right wave, and surf through life experiences without reacting negatively, or even self-sabotaging your life experiences. You can then surf the waves of life experiences with enjoyment.

Although working with the nervous system is not easy, it is worth it. When people rewire their nervous system, their life experience constantly changes for the better as life experiences align with a higher light of expression.

"The wound is the place where the light enters you." (Rumi)

Healing the nervous system is essential to sustain higher consciousness because this higher light shines through the body and the nervous system. Consciousness opening is number one, and nervous system development is number two. It bridges the gap between the top and the bottom.

How can I know how good my nervous system is?

The nervous system has a capacity that can be measured using Kinesiology on a scale from 0 to 1,000. 1,000 represents a perfect nervous system.

However, no human being is perfect because life itself takes a toll on us daily. It is thus impossible not to be affected by external conditions. The exception would be somebody who manifests themselves from a higher dimension, taking on a human form, never being touched by the conditions of normal life. That being would be at 1,000 on the scale, with a perfect nervous system.

According to our research at the New Humanity Divine Marga, the average person's nervous system (who hasn't done any spiritual work) is measured somewhere between 50 and 80.

At higher consciousness, nervous system sensitivity increases in a relaxed way. You become more sensitive, but relaxed, and can process a lot more energy.

For instance, a decade ago, when I used to give public meditations and Satsang, I would be quite tired afterwards. However, nowadays, giving a Satsang and facilitating Full

Consciousness Transmissions are effortless since my nervous system has adjusted to that capacity, and it has become normal and easy.

You can also increase the bandwidth and range of the spectrum of sensitivity that manifests in a higher perception and ability to sense more deeply and subtly what is happening now. It is a very relaxed, yet highly aware state.

When new energy that you have not experienced before comes into the nervous system, you might need some time to process and get used to it. A new environment can also take some time to adjust to, but this is easier with a relaxed nervous system. Over time, you can handle much more complex situations with ease and stability.

How can I increase my nervous system capacity?

The first thing that we suggest at New Humanity Divine Marga is the Five Tibetan Rites. This is a daily practice that everyone can learn from day one, irrespective of their level of consciousness. This immediately starts to increase your Life Force energy. We suggest you take up to six months to reach 21 repetitions of each exercise because you need a gradual increase in vibration. It is not about physical stamina, but about gradual and sustainable vibrational growth.

Kriya practices and Pranayama breathing exercises significantly increase the nervous system capacity and Life Force energy flow through your nervous system. Life Force energy flows through the chakras into the nervous system.

Another way to increase your bodily vibration is with super nutritional supplements. At New Humanity Divine Marga, we have done extensive research on what helps most, and all the information is presented on the webpage called 'High

Vibrational Heath'.

A lot of everyday foods are highly processed and lack life force energy. Meanwhile, they have heavy metals, pesticides, and toxins. It is thus best to look for organic foods to avoid this. Detoxification helps to remove heavy metals and toxins from the system.

There are also healing devices for the nervous system. You can even carry a small portable device to help you keep a higher vibration and protect your energy field. These devices are listed on the 'New Technologies' webpage.

Furthermore, using certain crystals, orgonites, etc. helps to create a high vibrational space in your house and at work.

Lastly, transmissions of higher voltage energy and higher consciousness from a teacher at a higher level of consciousness also help greatly to increase nervous system capacity. It is a certain attunement and adjustment of voltage for the receiver's nervous system to start energizing, unblocking, and reopening. More open consciousness means that there is more space for the nervous system to harmonize, balance, and heal.

Reality and Illusion: Overcoming Optional Suffering

Everything is real, and from the perspective of the absolute now, everything is free. The illusion is real, dreams are real, and this present experience is real. Even something unreal is also real.

Something which you feel is not real is also part of the now. Therefore, this is direct recognition that even the feeling of unreality, the feeling of illusion, is also real. It is also part of the bigger Now.

From the absolute perspective, even wrong assumptions are real. Everything is thus included in the present moment. Everything is included in consciousness. And that is the beauty of consciousness – it has manifested all these forms and shapes.

Consciousness has even manifested the ultimate idea that you might be separate from consciousness. This is the most curious and ultimate feeling, this idea that you might be separate. It is the ultimate idea and experience because it is completely at the furthest spectrum of truth.

The truth is that you cannot ever be separate, it's just impossible. But the feeling and idea that you are separate is also real and can be experienced as real.

It depends on from which perspective of absolute this idea of separation and experience is real, but it is experienced within consciousness. Therefore, it is fully allowed, fully accepted, and fully supported. It is just here. However, if we look at the perspective of a person who is assuming the reality of separation, then, of course, it does not feel so good. It creates suffering, challenges, and problems.

A seeker might say that, yes, in their experience, it is like this, and that's completely real for them. That is, however, where complications arise. From the average human perspective, there are a lot of challenges and problems. The sense of separation seems real. The mind assumes many problems to be here that are troublesome and challenging.

From the perspective of the position of the one who assumes, it is a challenging experience. But when we open our minds, hearts, and consciousness, we start to investigate if it is true. Is it really so? Because having a fixed idea is a certain closure that reinforces it further.

Therefore, with ignorance or not knowing whether it is really true, we assume the reality of a problem, limitation, and separation. And to make it worse, we reinforce it with additional feelings. And that is very common.

We start to reinforce an already challenging situation with additional mental stories. Indeed, there is a saying that pain is unavoidable, that if we hurt our arm or leg, we feel physical pain. But psychological suffering is optional.

All those stories and judgments, all of that is quite optional. That is what is called suffering. If we look at the average human life, 95-99% of all suffering is psychological, emotional, and mental.

These things have been pre-programmed and pre-installed in our minds. We did not know how to manage our thoughts. What are your thoughts, and how do we manage them?

Where did they come from? Why are they here? How do we make them subside, and how do we resolve them?

What are those additional feelings of anger, judgment, sadness, depression, cravings, longings, desires, and dissatisfactions? All of these things are also optional only because of mismanagement, not knowing what to do with them, and not knowing how to manage them. Indeed, 95-99% of all suffering in the whole of human existence is quite optional.

Unfortunately, our society is not helpful, the government does not help us, and the educational system is not concerned about that. They want to prepare us for a good job, but not for a happy life.

Essentially, it is a recognition that the entire society is still ignorant of the very reason why people suffer.

Overcoming Resistance

Many of you are open to investigating this resistance. If you notice that there is immediate resistance, it means that something inside you is reinforcing suffering. This is important to bring to your awareness.

Start gently by bringing it into your awareness. If you feel resistance or objection, or if some thoughts arise (e.g., 'no, it can't be so'), it means that there is a subconscious or unconscious pattern of reinforcement that is based on assumption.

And, of course, you may make a valid point that you have had much suffering in your life, that you have gone through so much trouble and so much suffering in your life, and it was all real. It was all absolutely real. It was as real as experiencing pain when you are in a dream. It is also as real as in this life. You have your past experiences, and they all happened.

If you assume that you are limited, your assumptions are real. If you feel that you are limited, then these feelings are real. From the absolute point of view, this whole play is real. Here on Earth, human life is considered a tragic comedy. It is tragic because it is all assumed to be real. It is, however, a comedy because it is actually not.

Therefore, it is not easy to awaken to this because it forces you to realize that many things are optional and unnecessary. Some people start laughing at themselves. Some people start crying.

From the absolute perspective, everything that happens energetically, emotionally, mentally, and psychologically is real. Even the Maya, the illusion, the veiling, the conditioning, it is all real, it is all happening, it is all manifested.

But the big question is, who are you? Are you this entity who assumes that all these things are real, who suffers because of assumption and ignorance, who suffers because you unconsciously reinforce suffering?

You consciously understand that you do not want to do this. But subconsciously, you feel resistance, you feel objection. This means that, somewhere, there is enforcement of illusion, of ignorance. Some programs and conditioning are running.

Self-Kindness is Empowering

The best approach is to recognize the truth with loving kindness. Approach this truth with self-compassion and softness.

If you become very sad, you support suffering. If you judge yourself or others, you hurt yourself. Therefore, you need to notice in this instant what reactions and feelings or energies arise. Notice what objections arise and stay in this aware instant. You can have self-compassion and self-kindness.

You can empower yourself with the necessary tools to support yourself in this process of disillusionment, thus allowing self-compassion to be born. It is your right-hand support.

Loving kindness is your left hand, and instant present-moment awareness is in the center. If you lose your power and start stepping into objections and feeling that you cannot do anything about it, you lose your power.

The most important thing is to return to your power. If you start losing your power, stop investigating, and start returning to your power. If you are no longer in the present, instant awareness, and instead go in the energy and feelings, you get wet since you have fallen in the river of life.

Therefore, look closely at what is going on right now, what you are assuming, and what you are taking as real. How has your power of Awareness leaked into the river of life?

To be free, you have to see through what is truly real in your present self-awareness. Although you are generally aware, you still have all kinds of habits, patterns, and assumptions, and you are swinging left and right.

I invite you to return to your present instant Awareness, notice what is going on, and bring the unconscious into the light of Awareness. Then, everything which is subconscious and unconscious will come to light.

This is not easy because there is a lot of momentum and strong waves, and you are pulled and dragged. Even sitting peacefully, it sometimes grabs you and drags you into some pattern.

You need self-compassion, loving-kindness, and recentering to reset over and over again. Meanwhile, various other spiritual practices, transmissions, and private sessions are necessary to facilitate and quicken the process, enabling you to gain more clarity, in essence, and assisting you in coming back to the power of your own Full Consciousness.

The Middle Way

You always need to be in your power to do your work. You can get support, but then, you need to do your work to strengthen yourself. Sometimes, you need more help at the beginning of your journey.

Subsequently, you reach spiritual adolescence, and you start rebelling, wanting to do it your way, see the world your way, speak your truth, etc. But the mother allows her children and teenagers to do their things and learn for themselves what works and what does not.

The journey is about the middle way. You constantly need to monitor if you are victimizing yourself or if you are boosting the ego. Or maybe you are temporarily exploring things and options, which is fine.

There are many cycles in life, and they are all fine. These cycles in life need to happen. That is how you test yourself. It is how you test your strength, your centeredness, and your weaknesses. You pinch yourself, and then you evaluate yourself, asking whether you are still in your centered self-awareness.

The most important thing is your clarity every single moment. Then, you allow this experience to play out in this or that way, you allow things to happen as they happen, and you allow the train to go where it needs to go. You recognize that you are the passenger of life while, in a sense, being the one who is experiencing this life unfolding.

When you remove all subtler separations, you are actually life itself. You are this experience, you are all of it, every sensation, every energy, every thought, every feeling, every space, every cloud, every tree, every bird – all of it is in your experience, without separation.

Try to avoid pushing yourself somewhere quicker, higher, and further if it means that you may be in pain and feel distressed, which can affect your life and disbalance things. My message on your path is to grow in the Middle Way. Sometimes, you need more support or a little push.

If you feel you need more healing, more love and compassion, then that is what you need right now. That is the middle way, which is supportive, and the quickest way. It is not about the destination but about the journey. It is about having a lovely journey, the most optimal and empowering journey.

Grounding & Stabilizing into the Present Moment

Grounding means stabilizing in the present moment.

The deepest meaning of grounding

Grounding is essential because it allows you to center, feel balanced, and integrate into higher consciousness. When you work with energies, they can get out of control quickly, and it may be hard to focus on everyday life and physicality, which is an integral part of consciousness.

You cannot remove physicality from reality and from spirituality. You certainly cannot remove it from consciousness. It is right here. It is very stable, and this is a big benefit of physicality. Even while you experience significant energy flows, your body is still stable. Even if your mind wanders five miles away with entertaining ideas or troublesome thoughts, your body acts as the anchor of the present moment.

The deepest meaning of grounding is being present here, fully, even if big energies are flowing through, your mind is feeling lost, or there is deep anxiety or worry. You can stay with any experiences. The capacity of consciousness can sustain any experience. Even if you are resisting this experience, it is still within your ability to resist it. Therefore, whatever is happening in the now, the IS-ness of it is your unrecognized capacity to sustain this experience. That is the deepest soil that allows any emotional weather or experience, no matter how high or low.

Everyone has the capacity to sustain this experience exactly as it is. It is unrecognized because our focus is usually on what we want to change in this experience. And guess what? Our capacity allows our desire to change, avoid, or escape this experience. Looking deeper into this capacity also allows us to inquire into our experience. The deepest Self is usually entirely unrecognized for most of its capacity.

There is also the balancing aspect of grounding. When we speak of grounding, it is commonly considered as a balanced energy system. Although it is usually understood as being balanced, its true meaning is the capacity to sustain whatever experience is happening in the now.

What are the techniques of grounding?

Grounding is related to our root energy center (root chakra). There are many techniques of grounding.

A very root-activating technique is to visualize yourself sitting on the top of a volcano, with the volcano beneath your root energy center. This is a very activating technique for the root chakra, and you may immediately start to feel your root chakra settling in. If you want something milder, you can visualize simply sitting on Earth, instead of a volcano.

Another technique is to imagine yourself sitting at the base of a beautiful tree with the roots coming out below you and the tree. You are the Tree of Presence. You are here, and remain rooted as thoughts and emotions change, cultivating your grounded Beingness.

You are always in the present moment. Maybe you have other feelings right now, perhaps you may have many thoughts, but you are in the present moment because you cannot be separated from the present moment.

You are not separate from the present now. This is the fundamental truth. It is immediately verifiable and obvious. That is the fundamental grounded aspect of you.

You are still here. Wherever you go, whichever galaxy, planet, altered meditative state you abide in, you are still in the present moment.

However, you may not feel so as there may be feelings obscuring your focus on being in the present moment. It is indeed a paradox because, although you are in the present moment, you might feel that you are not.

There might also be other disbalanced energies. Therefore, you may feel that you are only partially here and now since your focus is entangled with those disbalances, and that is fine. It means there is a disbalance, but the good news is that you are always in the present moment. You cannot escape it. You are engulfed in consciousness, reality, and the present moment. That is the deepest ground, the deepest soil, the truth of Being.

* * *

Grounding in the Present Moment Meditation

Step 1: Take a few moments to gently feel your breath, taking some time to slow down.

Step 2: Slow down any processes, any thoughts, any feelings, any sensations.

Step 3: You can make an intention to bring your energies back into the energy centers, into the chakras.

Step 4: You can start by visualizing approaching a beautiful tree and sitting down

at the roots of the tree. It further helps if you can imagine a volcano beneath you, and you are sitting on top of it.

Step 5: Feel into that stillness as you bring all the energies back to the base, the root.

All the energies are coming back to the root from below.

Step 6: Return to the lower spine, the hips, your lower belly area, your sacral.

Step 7: Now, return to your belly and lower spine, from 360 degrees, all the

energies that are coming back to your body.

Step 8: Now, return to your upper belly area, mid spine, your solar plexus. The energies are returning and staying here, returning to the being, to the here and now.

Step 9: Now, return the energies to your lower chest, your arms.

Step 10: The energies are returning now to your whole chest, your heart, and upper

chest area.

Step 11: The energies are also returning to your shoulders, upper spine, neck, behind the neck, and your throat.

Step 12: Return the energies to the back of the head, the face, forehead, and third eye.

Step 13: All the energies are returning to the head, you are not looking out, and everything is returning, and you are simply here, present here.

Step 14: The energies are also coming back to the crown, from the top, back to the head.

Step 15: Now, you are back in the body, being present, here, now, grounded in the present.

Liberated Authentic Personality

Integrated approach of awakening

Consciousness awakening can be a fast and challenging process because the aim of self-realization is to disidentify from the ego, mind, and that which is not the essential Self. This often leads to the disregard of personality, and, many times, its suppression while the seeker is exploring deeper spiritual aspects within. That is why some personal problems with family members and friends may arise in the process of awakening.

A need arises for a more integrated approach to awakening, where changes of personality can be fully understood and acknowledged. Personality starts to develop immediately from birth, feeling a disconnection from the essence that is referred to as the original sense of separation. This separation has a sense of lack within it, and thus, personality develops with compensating mechanisms.

It is helpful to realize that the Levels of Consciousness

represent a more general layout of the spiritual journey. They are the big picture of the road ahead, and the key milestones to the destination towards awakening to Natural Full Consciousness.

When the seeker approaches higher levels of consciousness, such as Presence and above, it becomes very important to develop a comprehensive understanding of their own personality and its ways since there is a greater capacity to access deeper parts of the subconscious mind and certain parts of unconsciousness.

The healthiest approach is to be eager to see yourself more clearly, especially as ordinary life situations unfold. In other words, to know what is natural to your own personality, that not everything personal is a problem, and to understand that certain qualities, reactions, and responses are normal.

Other people have different qualities. That is, they could be more social, self-preserved, or intimate. These are distinct instinctual drives; thus, behavioral patterns can be very opposing, and there is nothing wrong about that. Just like cats have their own behavioral patterns, even dogs, birds, fish, and all other animals have their own unique ways.

It is possible to transcend the limiting personality traits by deconditioning, healing work, and keen self-awareness. With openness of Full Consciousness, giving some time for integration, the soil becomes ready for a liberated and authentic personality to shine forth.

Therefore, the healthiest way is to learn about yourself, what is natural to you, and that it is okay to be yourself. Knowing your natural personality, you would be able to see more clearly the natural ways of others too, thus removing any judgment, unnecessary arguments, and misunderstandings. This provides a tremendous sense of unconditional love for others in order to be accepted as they are.

* * *

Heart's Longings Practice

Understanding your heart's longing may help you to break the psychological mechanisms of separation, lack, and fear, and to bring you closer to your essential Self.

Try to slowly feel into these messages of the heart's longings:

1. 'You are good. You are good as you are.' Understanding this message may help to remove struggle and self-judgment from your life.

2. 'You are wanted for just being you. You are wanted for just being yourself, for just being you.' It is incredibly satisfying to hear that you are wanted just for being yourself.

3. 'You are loved and valued for being yourself; you don't need to achieve my love.' Since many people have childhood issues related to their parents transferring their own expectations onto their children and always demanding more, this creates a subconscious belief that love needs to be deserved or earned; thus, this message for the heart might help to alleviate this subconscious conditioning.

4. 'You are seen for who you are, special and unique.' This heart's longing may help to alleviate the feeling of inadequateness, while trying to look for a

relationship to compensate for that.

5. 'Your needs are not a problem.' This heart's longing may help to soften a sense of lack and seeking for more in different ways.

6. 'You are safe.' This heart's longing may help to perceive the world as benevolent, rather than threatening.

7. 'You are taken care of. You can slow down. You can relax. Everything is fine. You don't need to continue looking and searching for things.' This heart's longing may help to know that it is the Self, or God, who is taking care of you, your mind, and your life.

8. 'You will not be betrayed.' This heart's longing may help to know that the Self, the Divine, and God will not betray you. It always has your best interest.

9. 'You don't have to resolve all the conflicts. You don't have to try to solve everybody's issues. Your presence alone is enough.' This heart's longing may help to bring all efforts to rest and peace.

Spiritual Maturity & Integration

Full Consciousness is a Natural State, all embracing and all encompassing.

How can one integrate Spiritual Freedom into daily life?

A mature being does not distinguish between spiritual and non-spiritual life. An integrated life is life without separation, with a sense of equanimity that spiritual things are not exaggerated and any more significant than everyday life.

In reality, any life activity is special because it is a life activity. It is a source manifestation. Suppose we can see the simplicity of any action, and that it is the mind that distinguishes one thing as special and another as mundane.

It is a common issue in spirituality because spiritual people try to behave very spiritually, showing off to others, and then, facing issues because of their feelings of specialness.

Paradoxically, many people experience a loss of their spirituality when they awaken to higher levels of consciousness. It becomes a loss because the spiritual role has been cultivated for many years and has become a way of living for some people.

Therefore, some people are reluctant to open all the way because it can be a loss of what they are holding onto.

Some people in their 20s or early 30s become rebellious, not wanting to be part of society and following the rules. First, they prove to themselves how free they are; then, there comes a time when they discover what real freedom is.

Real freedom is not about rebelling, but about becoming open and without resistance, about letting go of ideas of how things should be.

Integrated living means that you are no longer escaping anything. You are no longer escaping doing the dishes, cooking, or helping somebody in a simple way.

Full Consciousness integrated living feels normal, but this is where words start to fail because of the openness and aliveness of every moment. It is much more real than any dualistic feeling of specialness. It is the only thing that is real. Think about how you feel at the end of the day – relaxed, without trying to do tomorrow's things, while forgetting about the day. It feels indescribably content.

Can you see my chakras?

People are also very fascinated with kundalini energy and chakras, and many spiritual teachings focus on kundalini awakening as the ultimate goal, rather than Full Consciousness. At one of my Satsang in India, I was discussing Self-Enquiry and the nature of Awareness. One Indian man who was present was very impatient and wanted to ask me a question so badly. Finally, when his turn came, he asked: "Can you see my chakras?" I had just spoken for an hour about the importance of Self-Realization and Awareness, and all this person could think of was if I could see his chakras.

People get so interested in these insignificant things. Chakras are energy centers like guitar strings – they need to be balanced and taken care of, but they are not who we are. It is like thinking that bodily organs such as our heart and liver are who we are.

Do spiritual experiences affect consciousness?

Experiences wear off. The only reality is in the present background of all experiences. Even after I returned from months of travel with many activities and experiences, it was like nothing had ever happened. I am here and now, always, settled into unmoving consciousness itself. Experiences are the only thing that moves. This can be pretty shocking and disappointing for many people when they realize that, in consciousness itself, experiences ultimately do not matter.

Most people carry the past in their present; thus, they are not truly present. This also applies to spiritual people because they are often fixated on their past spiritual experiences. It shocks people to learn that, in natural consciousness, we are here, now. Holding all the memories and experiences is like carrying around our luggage, whereas the present moment is open, alive, and light. People say the present is boring, but that is because they have not discovered what the present really is. They are living in the past or future, and thus, they do not know the real present. The real present is open consciousness. It is where experiences happen, and not so much about what experiences take place.

How do I live my daily life while my sense of identity is dissolving?

Life manifests that which needs to happen. If you are meant to meet a specific person or get a particular job, it will happen. It may help you to know that, when you focus on the

Source, you do not need to bother so much about goals and other achievements. Everything that needs to happen will happen, and other things that are not of the highest importance will change or will not happen.

Full Consciousness is the best thing to focus on. Even if somebody were to promise me gold, riches, and fulfillment of all desires, if I am not in Full Consciousness, I would refuse it all. I know many wealthy people who are slaves to their wealth. They are stressed, often in poor health, and are usually never truly satisfied. They are limited in their experience because they dream about that ultimate happiness that never comes via material means.

Similarly, many goals and objectives that people have are not meant to be. So much time is spent chasing fulfillment. People get what they set their focus on and often lose it later.

A story that illustrates a way of Natural Law is that of a Zen Master, a Boy, and a Horse:

A little boy who lives in a small village is given a horse as a gift. All the villagers say: "Isn't that fabulous? Isn't that wonderful? What a wonderful gift."

The Zen master says: "We'll see."

A couple of years later the boy falls off the horse and breaks his leg. All the villagers say: "Isn't that terrible? The horse is cursed! That's horrible!"

The Zen master says: "We'll see."

A few years later, the country goes to war, and the government conscripts all males into the army. However, the boy's leg has healed very badly, and thus, he does not have

296

to go. All the villagers say: "Isn't that fabulous? Isn't that wonderful?"

The Zen master says: "We'll see."

Psychological Maturity

Your ultimate journey is to become a fully conscious, integrated being, and heal in a mature way. That is how you can be happy along your entire path, and your ego will be under control. You would further employ wisdom, rather than impulses, while your relationships would be preserved, and your journey beautiful.

A person can be at the highest levels of consciousness, even at Full Consciousness, and still be psychologically immature. Arriving at the destination does not necessarily mean that all emotional problems and psychological issues are resolved and all traumas healed. Therefore, a person's level of consciousness does not imply that they have worked through all their issues.

I have witnessed people at lower levels of consciousness with mature psychology and way of dealing with emotions. I have also seen people at higher levels of consciousness, who, despite being in Non-Duality, Awareness, or Full Consciousness, are immature in their own personality, and do some seemingly unwise things.

If someone opens to Full Consciousness as a teenager, which is possible, they would still be teenagers. They would not be as mature as a person who is 40 or 50 years old with some life experience. They would still explore, have fun, and make mistakes because they are still teenagers, and that's what it is. Psychological maturity has its own path and growth, which develops into an integrated personality.

Maturing happens in two ways. The most common way is that a person matures by learning life lessons. The second is that some maturity comes from the previous lifetimes of a person. Some people are older souls with more mature beingness.

Psychological maturity is usually very dependent on a person's upbringing, especially their childhood. It is also very dependent on past traumatic experiences. If someone has major traumatic experiences, they will come up to be healed as they open to higher levels of consciousness.

Healing traumas is not a quick and easy thing to do, and it can take years. It might seem that the person has healed from a specific trauma, but then, a couple of weeks or months down the line, something would trigger it, and they realize that it is still there.

What does integrated Enlightenment mean?

Full Consciousness is Enlightenment, but it is not integrated Enlightenment. Generally, it is good to spend four to seven years for Full Consciousness to become integrated.

People tend to expect that, when a person is at a higher level of consciousness, they are saintly, angelic, and wise. Some teachers may develop a certain way of expressing themselves, which may be very mystical or confusing. One moment, they are talking about peace, balance, and stability, and the other, they are saying something very different, thus possibly causing many instabilities for their students, hence shaking up the mind, which can be helpful in some instances.

However, somebody in Full Consciousness, after some time and reasonable integration, would be generally more consistent and able to help someone in a more integrated way.

Additionally, the level of consciousness where one is integrated brings a flavor to how one presents information. I know some lesser-known teachers who are integrated into Non-Dual consciousness, and they developed a very strong flavor of negation. It is the common 'Neti-Neti' (neither this nor that) approach, but too much negation can cause challenges and confusion to peoples' psychology and mentality.

Can you give an example of this negating attitude?

Someone in Non-Dual consciousness may negate the world, life, and the body in an unhealthy way. They may negate things in a way that suggests that nothing is important. This is not an integrated negation.

Meanwhile, compassionate negation is a healthy way of opening the mind, while harsh negation may be very disbalancing.

Some people who get attracted to harsh negations may have had childhood traumas, and thus, they resonate with abusive behavior.

What is psychological maturity all about?

Essentially, psychological maturity has to do with overcoming abusiveness and/or victimization. The shadow side are subconscious and unconscious patterns, unseen, avoided, or not yet met. Every person has them, and they contribute to psychological blind spots.

Maturity is how we meet those patterns and deal with issues. The number one rule is to not cause harm to others. Meanwhile, the second is to own our issues, and have a sense of responsibility for all of our reactions. If we know that we sometimes get angry, we should own it as our own issue.

What is Shadow Work?

Shadow work is a New-Age term for working on subconscious and unconscious patterns, especially avoided ones. It involves recognizing impulses, conditioning, and stuck energies, and bringing them into conscious awareness for healing.

What are some (Ego) pitfalls on the way to maturity?

Many people like to find flaws and faults, especially at a certain stage of spiritual development. They see their truth and think that everything else is wrong. This commonly happens in the mid-levels of consciousness, after spending some time in Inner Love, Unity, and Oneness consciousness. People tend to start owning their truth, fighting for the truth, and proving to others their one-sided spiritual truths. These are the spiritual ego pitfalls.

I usually ask them what is important to them now. Do they want to continue proving their truths? Or do they want to continue growing on their journey and becoming mature beings? Truth can be relative, arrogant, and one-sided.

Instead, individuals should ask whether it makes any of their friendships better, and whether it makes their family life better. The person proving their truths no longer has harmony as their priority. That is why rule number one is to not harm others. It is thus important to express yourself in a way that does not cause trouble to others. Do not be disillusioned by spiritual truths. Instead, have the common sense of what is really happening now. Spiritual argument is still an argument.

In the context of psychological personality development, the goal is harmonious growth, healing, respecting others, and acknowledging that everybody has challenges and issues, no matter their level of consciousness.

Living Beyond Time in the Instant Now

"Now is the time to have a direct introduction to this moment. This moment is free of time, of mind, of any notions. Introduce yourself to this moment." (Papaji)

Time exists in your experience only because you place your attention on the continuity of time. Time is a stream of energy. Sometimes, it passes very quickly when you are enjoying yourself, and sometimes, it seems like you are in a slow-motion movie.

Time is like a stream, and just like any other energy, you can come out of it. I usually give the example of a river: If you are in the river, you are wet and are going wherever the river goes. When you step out of the river, you are no longer wet; therefore, you can change your direction. Therefore, in essence, time is a river. That is why it is called a timeline.

There is continuity from point A, this moment, to point B, the destination.

This present moment, Now, gives you an opportunity to step out of time by changing your focus. It is very easy to shift your focus somewhere else, but sustaining your Presence beyond time is more difficult because people have been supporting the experience of time and getting used to it for decades.

The mind, emotional experiences, thoughts, and even thinking about the future are all past. They are all already old. Even this ordinary life experience is already old. From the perspective of the Self, of instant Awareness, everyday life flow is slow and already outdated.

It is the Self, instant Awareness, the Source, God, or Consciousness that is instant reality-existence. From that instant existence comes high vibrational energy that slows down and takes on shapes and denser forms, eventually resulting in physicality.

Physical forms are already the end product of an old thought of source. It is already a baked cake, a done deal. Imagine you are a chef. You envisioned a beautiful cake and went through the process of baking it. Now, the cake is on display in a coffee shop. But, for the chef, that cake on display is already old, a done deal.

The average human being is living only 4% of their whole life in what we could say is real-time reality, while the other 96% is already old. People have normalized themselves in the old version of reality, like trying to catch the wind which is already gone.

Beings who are one with the Self are truly alive. They are

living in real-time, instant Now, not in the past.

When you slow down and stop, look around and see that everything is alive and fresh. It is essential to taste this aliveness of existence because it allows you to see the contrast between that which is alive and real and that which is not.

I am pointing to a recognition of the present instant existence, which is always alive, always fresh. It is available to all.

Daily Life in Full Consciousness (Sahaja Self)

Moment to moment, there is Seeing, the primordial Seeing, the essence Seeing, where Consciousness, your own Self, is Seeing, here and now.

Primordial Seeing is the Natural Self

Consciousness is already aware of what is here and now, of the body, of what is within and what is around. This Seeing is sometimes referred to as direct knowing, not knowledge per se, but direct self-luminous knowing.

This Seeing is deeper than the eyes because, even if we close our eyes, we still see. This Seeing is recognized as the Self. It is recognized as the Natural Self (Sahaja Self) because it is the most natural and closest way of being.

Seeing is more natural than thinking, feeling, sensing, or perceiving. Thinking feels slightly more distant than seeing or being. Seeing is so much closer than any process, such as doubting, worrying, contemplating, or even inquiring and discerning, which are helpful processes.

Whatever functions you use of the mind, you must recognize that they are just a tool. But the Seeing being is your Self. You cannot say that it is the closest because there is no distance. It is that close. The gap collapses, and you are truly yourself, the Self.

It becomes evident that, when a less familiar or challenging emotion arises, it does not feel natural being inside that emotion and assuming that this emotion is somehow your identity. You see clearly that this is what is arising, and it is apparent that you are not this emotion. It is just a passing cloud, a passing energy. There is no denying or avoiding the 'I'. You can see that it is just an emotion passing by. Even if some very nice energies arise, such as love or peacefulness, you do not attach to them.

This is what is meant by pure love, joy, or peace. Pure means not being mixed up with attachments and conditioning. There is no story attached to it, no confusion about it, and no identification with it. You do not identify with even the nicest things because, if you identify with peace, this identity becomes a certain fixation. Maybe peace is more natural to you, but you are more than peace. You are the Seeing of peace.

You are no longer confused, and you do not identify with that which is passing by and is subject to change. There is this spaciousness and openness in which you experience what passes by. You see openness, spaciousness, experience, and whatever is happening.

Even if your attention diverts slightly into the past, you can see clearly that one part of yourself is looking into the past. You can also see that other parts of yourself are looking into the future. Sometimes, you need to plan some things. It's okay. But you see how this system is planning. The planning is what is happening now. You can be functional, and do whatever you need to do, whether shopping, gardening, driving, etc.

Usually, people are more dysfunctional when they have altered perceptions, also referred to as altered states of consciousness. They might experience these while they are still in the process of opening to Full Consciousness. For example, some may temporarily have trouble thinking or planning due to a great sense of peace.

But you generally become increasingly more functional, attain a higher capacity, and can do whatever comes up in the Natural Self (Sahaja Consciousness). Whatever comes up is what comes up. You are no longer avoiding, denying, resisting, or wanting to change what comes up.

The beautiful part is that, once you settle into this spacious, open, natural Full Consciousness, older cycles of experiences return for the clearing up. For example, if you had a problematic relationship that ended badly, memories and emotions about it may arise. You no longer resist, avoid, or deny them when they appear. Subsequently, they can be processed and released for you to re-harmonize.

"For the person who has learned to let go and let be, nothing can ever get in the way again." (Meister Eckhart)

As you open up more, you heal the past and free your future because the past conditions future events. Any future you can think of is mainly about the past and in relation to the present. Your history is still functioning because your thoughts of the future are based on what you know – the past. You only need to take care of the Now though, and that is how you can heal the past. Trust in life arises.

Older cycles naturally come up even in Full Consciousness for further integration. People who take a slower approach deal with most cycles on the way to Full Consciousness. Full Consciousness is the Self-Realization of who you truly are, but not an immediate resolution of all your problems.

As soon as you heal something, there is space for newness, freshness, aliveness, love, being, living, and direct wisdom. There is more of whatever is aligned with you.

Looking closer to this present openness, in the beginning feels like a spacious transparency. That is the initial phase of Full Consciousness.

As you settle in and integrate more, you start seeing that it is not only transparent, but there is a transparent light or lightless light. As you look more into this lightless light, there is bliss.

You go further to a deeper Seeing, which is natural and always present. This is called the Sahaja Samadhi, which means natural blissfulness. This transparent light is the Seeing itself.

Practical Life in Full Consciousness

In Full Consciousness, day-to-day life continues. You can go to work and do whatever is aligned with you. What has changed is that you no longer identify with what you are not.

When everyday life is lived from this place, everything transforms because you are no longer misidentifying, fantasizing, or living in worry.

The ordinary or more mundane moments in life no longer feel boring because there is this aliveness, openness, and clarity. For example, it is quite enjoyable to do the dishes. It feels lovely feeling the water flowing through the hands.

For the more repetitive daily tasks, sometimes, they feel aligned, and you can do many of these functional tasks. At other times, it does not feel that this is what you want to do. You could do some other tasks in the meantime. For example, if you are an accountant and must work through a large stack of paperwork, it might feel somewhat unnatural because it is slightly draining, and then, you might need to rest a bit.

When you take some time to rest, balance, and re-harmonize, you can continue in the best possible way. It does not mean that you become superhuman, doing 10 hours of Excel sheets, and feeling okay about it. It is unnatural because the body is not designed for that. But sometimes, you do what you must do and become more functional over time since there is no resistance or avoidance anymore.

That is the truth about daily life in Full Consciousness, just like in the Bhagavad Gita, where Krishna showed himself to be down-to-earth and practical, advising about the War, while also revealing the true nature of reality.

These are examples of this down-to-earth practicality, clarity, and decision making in Full Consciousness. You might claim that this is not for you since you are merely an 'accountant'. But you do whatever you need to do in a more grounded, present, diligent, and clear manner. Whatever your thing, you can do it with a larger capacity. That is the very practical side of Full Consciousness.

Beauty & Value of Natural Emptiness as the Nature of Reality

"When mind soars in pursuit of the things conceived in space, it pursues emptiness; but when man dives deep within himself, he experiences the fullness of existence." (Meher Baba)

There is only one conscious and open emptiness, but different degrees of familiarity with it.

At the beginning of a spiritual journey, a person starts by familiarizing himself with the inner space located around the chest and heart. They can also realize that there are some gaps between their thoughts. There are additional moments of pauses between one set of thoughts and another, where the person can see the gap between each thought.

There are also gaps between breaths. When we breathe in, there is a little pause. When we breathe out, there is another little pause.

That is how we start to get to know the inner space and natural emptiness.

In Buddhism, there is a saying that the mind is like a bowl. It has a certain capacity, a certain amount of stuff that you can fill up in the present size of the bowl of the mind.

When you meditate, you can make this bowl bigger, you expand the bowl of the mind, expand the space where the mind is functioning. The more space there is, the easier the mind can function. It has more room for everything.

As the seeker progresses along their journey, they familiarize more with the importance of emptiness and space. Because it is actually a place of restfulness, the seeker can discover peace in the emptiness.

Indeed, you can realize that every night you are joyfully going into emptiness to rest, sleep, and turn off. It is very healing, that is where your mind rests. Restful emptiness turns off tensions and stresses of the mind.

As you go deeper into meditation, you can observe dreams as well. They are in between the waking and sleeping state. They are like a flowing river.

In a deeper state of meditation, a beautiful emptiness reappears once again, where you can rest even from dreams.

Because dreams are sometimes also quite busy and stressful, they are not always joyful and restful. They are a reflection of your inner state, sometimes, simply processing the activities of the day, because you did not give enough time to deal with everything consciously.

When you catch up with the day and dream state, you are ready to go into a deep sleep state, into emptiness, to rest, recover, and re-energize, where the body is in a state of rejuvenation.

Recognizing the value of healing, recovery, restfulness, we tend to go into meditation more often. That is where meditation starts to get deeper, and once we reach a certain stage, we recognize that, perhaps, since we are always resting in the emptiness, in a meditative state there might also be energies, and, perhaps, we should rest even deeper from energies in the restful emptiness.

Feeling, healing, and balancing our energies is also quite a busy thing to do. It is a certain management, a work to be done. We may then recognize that our home is actually emptiness, it is not in the energies. Energies may be nice, sometimes even beautiful and harmonious, while, at others, they are somewhat messy.

When you harmonize all your energies, all your chakras, your kundalini, and everything is totally harmonious, you may enter into temporary homeostasis. But if you fail to recognize the value of emptiness, you only enjoy homeostasis for a while, and go back into energy because something changes, and then, you need to balance that again as well.

Homeostasis is where people really long to come back to,

into this perfect balance and harmony. There is a certain longing because it feels like everything is absolutely fine. But it is hard to maintain homeostasis because it happens in the background of emptiness.

To stay longer and more in homeostasis, in perfect balance and harmony, we need to go one step back into the emptiness. That emptiness becomes a supporting background where our energies are supported. That is where the value of Beingness arises. The value of beingness, rather than doingness.

Managing our energies is an activity that we do thereby recognizing the value of Beingness in terms of supporting emptiness. That is where we start touching the ground of something much more real and essential. This lays a foundation for continuing our work all the way to Full Consciousness, familiarizing increasingly more with natural emptiness.

We recognize more where our true home is, and as I mentioned right at the beginning, there is only one emptiness, but different degrees of familiarity.

There is a saying that, when it comes to all sorts of energies, like love, and joy, it is like a dance, but how long can we dance for? It is nice to dance, but then, we need to rest, don't we? Where do we rest? In the same place where we go every single night, very joyfully, very peacefully, hence going to sleep, rest. We may look at our day as a dance of all activities, while the night is a coming back home to rest.

However, to make this place of restfulness more permanent, we need to dive deeper into the void. What is the void? It is where we really empty ourselves of content. We look closely at what other content we might be holding. We become aware of the unconscious energies we carry within our consciousness, unaware of their impact on us.

Stepping into the Great Void[34] is like surrendering everything back into emptiness in order to be freer from content. It is the deepest surrender, letting go, giving it all up. It is not scary, not destructive. It would only bring up fear if we are not familiar with the value and beauty of emptiness as the foundation for all content and dance of life.

This is the only reason why fear of unknowingness arises, or the fear of disappearance, of getting lost, or non-existence. These fears arise because of a lack of familiarity with emptiness.

As we recognize the value and beauty of emptiness as our true nature, we surrender easily and recognize its wholeness.

Our home is not another star system, not another planet, not another dimension or place. These are temporary places where the soul has incarnated in the past and has spent some time there.

Buddha introduced the term emptiness because he recognized that it is the fundamental background, the fundamental home and reality.

The same applies to other terms, such as, Awareness. We first recognize the light of Awareness, and we recognize that we are always aware. We then recognize the transparency of Consciousness. That is what I call natural Full

---

[34] See Chapter 4 on Level of Consciousness Great Void (The Unconsciousness)

Consciousness.

Even when we are dreaming, we are aware. When we are in a deep sleep state, that is where we are aware of absence, it is where we are absolutely surrendered to the emptiness, and we are that emptiness.

As you develop a certain strength of the light of Awareness, you may start letting go of Awareness. You do not need to hold onto it and focus on it. This is a process of deeper and subtler familiarization with your deeper Natural Self (Sahaja Consciousness).

That is very relaxing. It is a relief from tensions. The only thing you may lose is your control and tensions. There is no need to try to keep Awareness, to try to control it. In this emptiness, you recognize the final state of Consciousness, which is natural and effortless Consciousness, fully awakened emptiness.

The Great Void is a transitory step. The Great Void is where you let go of all content, of the stuff within unconsciousness that you did not even know you were holding onto.

There are things that we take for granted. For example, we hold onto certain identities that are completely normal, like knowing that we are human. It is entirely normal, but we take it for granted because we are very familiar with being human beings. However, we should not be conditioned or limited by this.

These are the deepest hard-wired functions and software. If you know a bit about older versions of computers, this is like the BIOS, the fundamental code. Being a human is one of the fundamental codes that are taken for granted.

Therefore, these are some things that we can meet in unconsciousness. However, we would most likely meet something that is a bit more conditional, limiting, suppressive, and interfering with the Natural Self (Sahaja Consciousness).

That is what we normally release into the void because we are already familiar with emptiness to such a degree that we feel really okay going there and revealing those deepest identities and attachments within unconsciousness.

Generally, it is not so challenging or difficult, of course, with some help. That is where we uncover the deepest conditionings within unconsciousness that we may have forgotten or did not even know we had or were holding onto them.

We illuminate unconsciousness, we En-lighten the deepest parts of our being and clear the way for the Natural Self.

No matter what comes up, no matter what appears or disappears, there is stability. There is an unshakeable ground of this natural emptiness, naturally aware and awake emptiness.

This is the only ground, reality, or absolute reality, which is unmovable and unshakable, no matter what appears, no matter what happens.

Everything we see is an appearance. Dreams are an appearance, the World is an appearance, all experiences, all energies, and all the Gods and Goddesses are appearances in the ultimate reality of natural awake emptiness.

314

This ultimate reality is very familiar. You are already familiar with it somewhere deeper within you because, if you did not know it, it would not be natural. It would not be real. It would not be stable.

Something in you, somewhere deeper knows it as your real home. That is why there is longing and desire to return. It is your inner GPS. In other words, you must know what the wholeness is. If you know what a limitation is, then you must automatically know what it means to be restful and free.

What is bothering you is something which is no longer needed. If a person is happy with their mental or emotional roller coaster, they have no idea that there is something deeper, and they just live habitually automatically. But when people start awakening, they know that there is something more, something deeper. Similarly, you automatically know that you no longer need what is limiting you.

This is the clarity and immediacy of the intelligence that you have. Intrinsic intelligence, beyond thoughts, beyond understanding, beyond mind. Something in you already knows the awakened natural emptiness.

The Self recognizes that which is not awakened emptiness, that which is an obstacle, that which is a stick in your wheel.

Change is on its way; therefore, approach it very gently. I wish to emphasize taking a very gentle approach to that which is bothering you. You could even do a meditation to bring to the fore what bothers you, bring it in front of you as another person.

Let's say it is a judgment, or fear, or at a deeper level, the 'I', or something else. Just bring it in front of you as an entity. Gently allow this entity to tell you it's story, why it is there.

When you bring it as a separate entity, you may find that resolution and healing that is needed. That is how you can resolve it and return to the natural emptiness that you are.

That is what we usually practice between the Great Void and Full Consciousness. We look at what is being held. What is our point of reference? Many people can recognize what is different when they are experiencing from emptiness and when they are experiencing from something more limited that feels uncomfortable. Then, they would want to get rid of it, and the best way is, as I described above, to meet it gently, softly, as a separate entity. Talk to it, just be with it, heal it, reconcile with it, and be liberated, be free.

As you approach Full Consciousness, and even, as you awaken into Full Consciousness, you realize that you are this background, aware, naturally awake emptiness.

That is why it is called pure consciousness. Pure means that which is untouchable, it cannot be limited, it cannot be stained.

How can emptiness be touched? How can emptiness be stained? How can emptiness itself be limited in any way? It simply cannot. The only thing that can be limited is the point of reference that you may narrow down into, feeling a discomforting experience from that point of limited being. But even as you do so, natural emptiness stays in the background. It is still here, but more in the background.

Stabilization into Full Consciousness is the realization that it is okay if your point of reference sometimes arises because it is just another appearance. When you become okay with the points of reference, or the points of limitation, it means that emptiness is becoming stronger than those points of reference.

Get familiar with emptiness, with being okay not to know, to be here, to be open. Open for pain, open for love, open for heartbreak, open for anything. This is the way of cultivating openness, naturalness, and being your true Self.

Being authentic means being fully open to being yourself in natural emptiness. You are not only emptiness, but you are all that is within it too. You are fully yourself with all your qualities, your body, and personality, as well as all that makes up this form. As you integrate more into your own naturalness, you polish your conditioning along the way.

Various qualities become more natural and purer, like heartful qualities, intelligence, or peaceful qualities. What is natural to you arises, becoming purer. That is the beauty of naturalness, authenticity, and newness.

Be patient with yourself, without any expectation of something sudden, because your mind may want to jump somewhere. Having less expectations and assumptions enables you to reach natural emptiness sooner.

You can slow down and relax into emptiness because that is how you get there sooner. If you chase, for example, super intelligence, super consciousness, highest bliss, and most Godly love, you would quickly be stuck, in one way or another.

When you work on natural emptiness, this super intelligence becomes obvious to you. It comes to you. It just appears, and you would know more and more automatically. Therefore, it becomes available without chasing.

Why? Because you created space for it. When you chase something, it means that you are limited, and you are projecting a limitation and need. There is not enough space for that which you want. To get what you want, you need to create space for it.

Of course, that which you want, ideally, would be that which you need and that which is natural to you. The first step is to create space for it, and then, trust that, that which you need and that which is natural to you will come to you.

That is the art of manifestation. If you chase what you do not really need, or what is not natural to you, even if you get it, it will not satisfy you, and it will not last long.

In this art of manifestation, you need patience, wisdom, and unwavering determination. What I mean by that is meditation, to know what you are doing. If you do not know what you are doing, you are merely fishing around. You are just jumping like a monkey on a tree. You are simply grabbing whatever appears in your awareness. You thus need to know what you are doing. Consequently, with space and a clear intention to know what you are doing, things will come if they are natural to you.

Things will come when they need to come. Things will happen when they need to happen. You will receive what you need to receive, what is real to you. It is just a question of time.

Many other things are generated from the mind, from desires, from expectations, from all sorts of incompletions. These things are but transitory, and they do give you lasting happiness and fulfillment. When you receive something that you truly need, then, you are truly grateful for it, and you value it.

Start by creating more space inside you, familiarizing yourself with emptiness. Align yourself with the deepest way of your being, with your Presence, Awareness, and eventually, with your Natural True Self.

Like the sun shines through the clouds, emptiness comes forth through the form, through objects and energies, revealing its beauty, value, essence, unwavering stability, and the ultimate reality of your own Natural True Self.

About Sat Mindo Dev

"Here is a man of truth, great compassion, and honor. The sparkle in his eyes reminds me of the infinite. Nothing can contain him. The heaven and stars sing to him. This man walks on earth so that others can return home."
(Lyonne Premananda)

Sat Mindo Dev is a spiritual teacher, author, and founder of Divine Marga, an international organization for God-Realization, Soul Liberation, and Divine Living.

For over a decade, Sat Mindo has been dedicated to helping seekers worldwide with opening up to Non-Duality, Enlightenment, Divine and Natural Sahaja Self via Full Consciousness Transmissions, and assisting with Soul Liberation via the Divine Light and Sound Current (Shabd).

Sat Mindo Dev is available to anyone who truly seeks for the Freedom, Joy, and Bliss of their Natural Full Consciousness and God-Realization.

Sat Mindo offers crystal-clear insights on the steps of Enlightenment, Soul Liberation, and Divine Cosmology, supporting and guiding you through every aspect of your Soul returning to the True Divine Home of God Supreme Source.

Sat Mindo holds weekly online Live Meditation Meetings, Satsang, Meditation Teacher Training Courses, and International Retreats.

Weekly LIVE Group Meetings:
https://www.DivineMarga.com/events

More about Sat Mindo Dev: https://www.SatMindo.org

Journey of Self-Realization

Birth Memory

Sat Mindo has a clear memory from the 1970s about planning his incarnation on Earth. This was more than ten years before his physical birth. On the day of his birth, he remembers entering his mother's womb as a Bright Light. Several events took place during birth, symbolizing the end of karmic cycles for the family tree that he chose to be born into.

Re-Awakening Period

In 2009, at the age of 24, Mindo went to live in New Zealand. There, he resided in a sacred home on a mountain in

Wellington, where a rare and spontaneous Re-Awakening and Ascension event took place.

His Consciousness was lifted out of the body, and he witnessed his body being infused and transformed with Light particles. This process lasted about 1.5 hours, and subsequently, all his energy system was fully activated. Furthermore, his psychic powers and gifts from his past lives were restored in this single event.

After this awakening, he went to live in Auckland, where he began very intense and rigorous training in the subtle planes with guides who showed all possibilities of his new abilities.

At this time, Mindo's deeper inner Self told him that he was Awareness Itself, and thus, a conscious process of returning to Enlightenment began.

While residing in New Zealand, he met some of the best-known spiritual teachers and psychics in the country, who confirmed that he was a being of Great Light.

Mindo was Initiated into the teachings of the Masters of the Ancient Wisdom, Ascension Path, and the Order of Melchizedek. He further received a blessing from Sri Chinmoy in spirit.

Mindo learned and mastered many spiritual practices, meditation, healing methods, and energy work practice with great ease and joy, quickly and effortlessly. He spent over 10,000 hours immersed in a deep meditative state.

Public Appearance

In 2012, Mindo was guided intuitively to move to the Maltese Islands in the Mediterranean, where he settled and started to teach openly to the public.

While living in Malta, he took a few years to mature into Presence and Non-Dual Realization. During this time, he delved deep into all aspects of the higher Levels of Consciousness, mastering meditation techniques, practices, and energy work.

Enlightenment Re-Realization

In 2014, at the physical age of 29, Mindo returned to the first state of Enlightenment, called Awareness Level of Consciousness. He has received Grace and Blessings from countless Enlightened guides, Avatars, and Ascended Masters in the subtle planes to allow this re-realization of Enlightenment.

2015 was the year of the beginning of the New Humanity Divine Marga when Sat Mindo met with his beloved, Lyonne Premananda. Together, they have been working on uplifting the collective consciousness of humanity ever since.

Sat Mindo opened to Full Consciousness shortly after and had a strong connection with Mahavatar Babaji and Sri Ramana Maharshi, whose Presences were coming through spontaneously and were over-lighting Sat Mindo, while giving Consciousness Transmissions to individuals and groups around the world.

Sat Mindo received blessings and further support from numerous spiritual guides for further deepening and integration of Full Consciousness and while hosting Satsang retreats across India, Sat Mindo had the privilege to visit numerous Samadhi Ashrams, such as:

Neem Karoli Baba Ashram in Vrindavan
Anandamayi Ma Ashram in Haridwar
Sri Aurobindo Ashram in Pondicherry
Sri Ramana Maharshi Ashram in Tiruvannamalai
Sai Baba of Shirdi Ashram in Shirdi
Upasani Maharaj Ashram in Sakori
Hazrat Babajan Ashram in Pune
Avatar Meher Baba Ashram in Meherabad

He also visited many other sacred places and Ashrams from the East to West of India, from South through the Himalayas.

Divine True Home

It was in 2024, exactly 10 years after his realization of the first state of Enlightenment, that Sat Mindo Dev attained mastery of the 6 Divine Regions in multiple lineages and was bestowed with the title 'Adi Sat Guru.' This sacred title is given only to those anointed Souls who bring forth a unique Divine Lineage as a blessing to Humanity.

Lineages

Sat Mindo Dev works with various spiritual lineages, beings, and aspects of subtle planes. Different guides offer their help at the right time to assist spiritual seekers on their journey of God-Realization and Soul Liberation (Moksha). Perhaps, you are familiar with some of the lineages or beings below:

Kabir lineage: Sant Kabir Das

Jnana/Advaita lineage: Ramana Maharshi, Papaji, Nisargadatta Maharaj, and Adi Shankara

Sufism Reoriented lineage: Avatar Meher Baba, Hazrat Babajan, and Upasani Maharaj

Bhakti lineage: Krishna, Rama, Neem Karoli Baba, and Sai Baba of Shirdi

Sikh/Sant Mat lineage: Guru Nanak, Hazur Baba Sawan Singh, and Kirpal Singh

Mudrashram lineage: Swami Prabhu Maharaj and Swami George A. Boyd

Buddha lineage: Palden Gyatso

ParamShiva lineage: Mahavatar Babaji and Haidakan Babaji

Masters of the Ancient Wisdom lineage: Saint Germain, Serapis Bey, Hilarion, El Morya, Lord Lanto, Paul the Venetian, Lady Nada, Melchizedek, Jesus the Christ, Maitreya, Gautama Buddha, Sanat Kumara, and Mother Mary

Brahmanda Region: Kuan Yin, Kali, Durga, Saraswati, Lakshmi, Parvati, Tripura Sundari, Ganesha, Shiva, Brahma, Vishnu, and Lord Brahm

ParBrahmanda and Divine Regions: ParBrahm, ParamShiva, MahaVishnu, Svarupa Shakti, Sat Purush,

Alakh Purush, Alaya Purush, Agam Purush, Anami Purush, and Adi Sat Purush

Yoga Lineages: Sat Mindo has various degrees of mastery in Jnana Yoga, Bhakti Yoga, Kriya Yoga, Raja Yoga, Karma Yoga, Kundalini Yoga, Nada Yoga, Mantra Yoga, and Agni Yoga.

Note: Different traditions may have other names for these beings. Many more lineages and higher beings are known to humankind, but the above are the ones that Sat Mindo works with.

Teaching Meditation and Satsang Teachers

In 2019, Sat Mindo started to give a formal Meditation and Consciousness Transmissions Teacher Training Course[35].

Some more advanced students of Sat Mindo started to give public Satsang[36].

Current Positions

Currently, Sat Mindo Dev is a Founder of Divine Marga International, New Humanity Foundation in Malta, New Humanity International Ltd. in the UK, and New Humanity Life Non-Profit organization in Nepal and in the USA registered 501(c)(3) status.

---

[35] More information: https://www.divinemarga.com/ttc-new

[36] More information: https://www.divinemarga.com/testimonials

About Full Consciousness Transmissions

This is a unique opportunity to receive a direct Full Consciousness Transmission from an enlightened teacher, Sat Mindo Dev, that unblocks your mind and raises your Level of Consciousness. Sat Mindo transmits the highest Light from Adi Sat Purush, the highest Divine Region of Supreme Source Consciousness, which is the purest and highest energy in the world. It is a Highway to the Higher Consciousness opening!

A common feeling during the energy transmission is passing through of the Light, expansion of the crown at the top of the head, and a feeling of Oneness. Your whole nervous system is attuned to the level of Full Consciousness, as well as your Aura, Electromagnetic field, Shakti/Kundalini, and all 7 energy centers.

It is one of the most effective consciousness transmissions currently available in the world. It allows the Divine Source light (like the Sun) to flow through you harmoniously, connecting you to the purest Consciousness, unblocking the mind, which is the cause of all problems, and assisting your Soul in ascending closer to the True Divine Home (Moksha).

Sat Mindo has helped over 1,000 people to raise their levels of consciousness on their journey to Enlightenment and to live a life in deep harmony, love, joy, and oneness with life and the Universe.

Full Consciousness Transmission allows the source light (like the Sun) to flow through you harmoniously, connecting you to the purest Consciousness, unblocking the mind, which is the cause of all problems, and opening into a higher level of Being.

After Awakening to Full Consciousness – Integration Transmission Session

Since there are more and more students at Full Consciousness at Divine Marga, the next step is to work on Full Consciousness Integration via Body Nervous System and Energy System Integration, and, most importantly, to clear all remaining Karma for your complete Soul Liberation, as per Divine Cosmology.

In this session, you will receive a supportive Full Consciousness Integration Transmission, your Personal Chart, and advice on any questions and any further integrative support needed.

Book a Session

To book an appointment in person or via Zoom, you can e-mail: satmindo@yahoo.com

Sessions are done via Zoom by people from all over the world and are as effective as meeting in person.

Sat Mindo has a special gift of seeing your aura over the distance, as well as your chakras, your energy field, the density of the mind and consciousness, and the Advancement of your Soul; so, the sessions via Zoom are very effective and powerful.

Included Support & Recording of Practice

At each meeting with Sat Mindo, you will receive personal advice on any question you may have, as well as a recording of meditation/transmission/practice that you can download for your personal keeping after the meeting. It is advisable to repeat the practice for deeper integration until the next meeting.

Sat Mindo will also advise you on further supportive readings, videos, and practices to continue with your Integration after the session in your own time.

Experiences & Openings of Students

Esther T.

"Sat Mindo's meditations and transmissions are absolutely profound. From a place of wholeness, purity and wisdom, he encourages us to join him in the present moment, which is full of aliveness, joy and love.

Sat Mindo's transmissions cut through the depths of our being so that everything that is unhealthy and conditioned can be seen and dissolved in the openness and space of awareness itself. Mindo points out and encourages us to unfamiliarize with the disempowering way how we look at ourselves. Rewiring in love, wisdom and power is possible! Inner wisdom can be seen more easily. Mindo's knowledge and nearness gives everyone an opportunity to get familiar with and develop their levels of consciousness. Mindo shares all the wisdom unconditionally with a big, big heart. A teacher who is so 'near' and so willing to help us is rarely found."

Ryan D.

"I have prayed and hoped for Full Consciousness this lifetime, beginning at a young age. I feel immensely blessed to work toward and complete the journey into Full Consciousness, and the beginning of true living with Sat Mindo. The transmissions are, of course, very powerful and Sat Mindo's presence is palpable. I highly recommend you step into the Full Consciousness Transmission and be sure to go the full route."

Mechele T.

"Sat Mindo has assisted me in raising my consciousness and initiated profound healing in my being that has benefitted me beyond description. He is a huge gift to humanity!"

Manvir D.

"Sat Mindo is a very grounded, down to Earth, practical, and amazing teacher. My evolution since working with Mindo and delving into his easy and precise teachings has been quantum, to say the least. He has developed such an effective way to enlightenment and evolution and has created such effective practices actually to go with it.

Enlightenment finally has an easy and efficient roadmap, as well as an amazing guide to show you the way back home. Thank you! With Lots of Love and Gratitude."

Anna L. E.

"Sat Mindo's openness and integration in full consciousness and beyond and his presence and powerful guidance is unique. He is one of the very few spiritual teachers in this world being and teaching at this level of consciousness, so it's very precious to come across someone like him. If you are ready to open up more and more to higher levels of consciousness, this is the place to go. He will safely guide you there. Deeply thankful."

V.

"Sat Mindo is a very down-to-earth, honest, compassionate and practical teacher. Meditating with him was very powerful and his pointers were always helpful. I achieved LOC 1,000 by working with him for 6 months. I highly recommend him for the evolution of one's individual consciousness and he will work with sincerity for the spiritual growth of the individual. He made himself available all the time in spite of his busy schedule and helped me grow spiritually! Wonderful human being and felt like a good friend whenever I worked with him as he is very unassuming for his spiritual stature."

Rustan P.

"I connected with Sat Mindo in June 2018 and It was a big breakthrough in my spiritual journey. At that time, I did not know how to move on and was really pessimistic about my life. I've had about two sessions with Mindo every month with guidance and deep meditations. These sessions are always very transforming and also fun.

Sat Mindo knows every step in detail on the road up through the different levels of consciousness. This is a tremendous shortcut to a state of peace, love and happiness. I strongly recommend the videos of Mindo as they explain all aspects of the spiritual journey and the different levels of consciousness."

Angie M.

"Since I met Sat Mindo it's been one big adventure that never stops amazing me. I've been having sessions with Sat Mindo where each time I feel happier, lighter, freer and filled with love. I have a deeper connection with the world and the people in it, and people comment that I have a very good aura. I wouldn't be genuine if I told you that challenges don't come up, but I've learned that these are only things that are ready to be healed. Sat Mindo is very gentle and caring and has the ability to meet you wherever you are in your journey, bringing you towards where you are meant to be."

Ron G.

"Sat Mindo is a wise and gifted teacher of consciousness and enlightenment. He uses the Levels of Consciousness to offer effective practices to raise the consciousness of students at every level. My one-on-one Zoom sessions with Sat Mindo have helped me immensely."

Anne K. A.

"Sat Mindo offers a very clear mirror where you have the opportunity to see yourself - As you are. The heaviness and pain of your survival patterns and the sweetness and freedom of your true being."

Santi C.

"Sat Mindo is an excellent teacher. He guided me to recognize the obstacles blocking my growth and suggested practices for overcoming them. I would recommend his counseling to anyone who finds themselves resonating with his teachings.

I also attended his online retreat and it was very powerful and inspiring. It is a great gift to have a teacher who has mastered enlightenment and can show you step by step along your path!"

Elisabeth B.

"Sat Mindo's Satsang meetings have become a regular weekly highlight for me between New Humanity Divine Marga courses and retreats. They are life-changing moments of joy, stillness and peace in an absolutely safe and loving space where Sat Mindo guides and meets us wherever we are in our journey, as a group or individually. His insights, guided meditations, transmissions and his kind, clear words regularly turn out to become the most important „missing puzzle stone" for that given moment, bringing me further in my personal and professional journey and integration. With love and gratefulness."

Deb M.

"Sat Mindo helps you to understand yourself and why people are the way they are. Mindo's Full Consciousness Transmissions are life-changing to experience and his clarity and teachings have provided such valuable guidance and wisdom.

Within six months of private sessions with Sat Mindo, my awareness and presence have increased noticeably. He is kind and supportive during the sessions and afterward, all previous feelings of stress and heaviness are removed and replaced with high positivity, happiness and peace. Each session is a unique experience and always my level of consciousness is raised.

I feel very grateful to Sat Mindo for all the positive changes and progress I have made."

Alexandria D.

"Sat Mindo is among the few modern-day Sages that inhabit the planet at this time and bless the collective consciousness with Divine guidance and loving inspiration. Sat Mindo's energy is constantly evolving and creating a new expansion in the collective as well as the individual. My capacity to receive Divine love has increased under Mindo's tutelage and resulted in the release of negative energetic patterns and has reshaped my daily reality."

Yvette C.

"After my second transmission, I feel Eternal Gratitude to you for helping me heal my Heart. To know inner Love is always available to me. Not to push so much, instead allow me to melt into that soft, Gentle Love and to be immersed with Inner Love. Wow!!! It is Amazing. Honestly, l have benefitted immensely. From the effectiveness of your practices, Meditations and Transmissions, You are showing me The Art of Living, Truly living. This journey of Ascension has given me True Purpose. I feel so blessed to have connected with you. Brightest Blessings to you, Dear Soul. Love Yvette."

George J.

"Please do not miss out on Sat Mindo's sessions. You will experience a permanent elevation in consciousness each time you do it. It is a blessing to have him in our lives."

Betty M.

"A trusted friend recommended that I have a session with Sat Mindo, so I booked one. I went into it not knowing what to expect, what the experience would be like and also thinking that I'd just try it once and that would be it. Several sessions later and I haven't thought to stop. I've noticed a shift in my mind, my body and my life that at first felt subtle, but when I reflect on the changes, I see them as being significant. My level of awareness and peace and the relationship with myself and others have improved. For this, I Am grateful, Sat Mindo!"

Paul G.

"Sat Mindo is an amazingly bright and pure-hearted enlightened spiritual Teacher. The depth and clarity of his sessions, including advanced meditations and transmissions, are outstanding. It allowed me to make great progress in my level of consciousness in a short amount of time. This has improved my life in unimaginable ways already, for which I am very grateful. The retreats are a great and effective way to dive into his teachings' vastness in wonderful surroundings. I'm looking forward to continuing my journey under Sat Mindo's guidance."

About Divine Marga

New Humanity Divine Marga, founded by Sat Mindo Dev and Lyonne Premananda, is an international organization of God-Realization, Soul Liberation, and Divine Living. Over the past decade, over a thousand students worldwide have come closer to Home on their journey to Non-Duality, Enlightenment, Divine, and Natural Sahaja Self via Full Consciousness Transmissions and Soul Liberation (Moksha) via the Divine Light and Sound Current (Shabd).

Many spiritual paths exist, but not all lead to the Highest regions of the Divine. Divine Marga (Path) is beyond Non-Duality. This Supreme Path ascends beyond the Cosmic Deities and beyond the Awareness stage of enlightened consciousness, soaring past the pinnacle of the most advanced Hindu spiritual traditions.

This holistic approach ensures an integral and balanced awakening, resolution of karma at all levels, and the mastery of Soul Advancement[37] – a privilege only a few Souls on Earth have ever received.

Experience Pure and Divine Consciousness, which is the Source of all creation. Full Consciousness is a Natural State called Sahaja. It is a natural openness that is as blissful and bright as a thousand suns. It is alive, eternal Love, and unshakable Truth.

Divine Marga offers crystal-clear insights into the steps of Enlightenment, Soul Liberation (Moksha), and Divine Cosmology, supporting and guiding you through every

---

[37] More information at: https://www.divinemarga.com/locs-of-past-teachers

aspect of your awakening to the Natural Sahaja Self (Full Consciousness) in the most harmonious and integrated way.

Our signature Teacher Training Course:

* Meditation, Spiritual Life Coaching and Consciousness Transmission Facilitators Course

Divine Marga Offerings

Weekly online events include meditation and Satsang on such topics as Spiritual Growth, Non-Duality, Self-Enquiry, Path of Love, Soul Liberation, Divine Cosmology, special events with Consciousness Transmissions, and more.

Retreats are organized regularly, both online and in person, to meet the needs of students from around the world. Some past retreats have focused on Awakening Consciousness, Practicing Presence, Soulful Journey, Divine Living, and Non-Dual Life. These deeply immersive retreats include Satsang, Meditations, Full Consciousness Transmissions, and time for individual sharing. In-person retreats are offered in Europe, India, Nepal, and the United States.

Full Consciousness Transmissions from Sat Mindo Dev and Lyonne Premananda are the spiritual highway to spiritual evolution and a key offering of New Humanity Divine Marga. These transmissions dissolve blockages on your path, while giving direction and practices that are helpful to you at your stage of evolution.

One-to-One sessions are offered by Sat Mindo Dev and Lyonne Premananda and New Humanity Divine Marga certified teachers for spiritual guidance tailored to your stage of the spiritual journey. Our New Humanity Divine Marga teachers are trained by Sat Mindo Dev and Lyonne Premananda, and are empowered to transmit energy for opening, balance, and healing.

Levels of Consciousness teachings assist students in gaining insight into their consciousness and the path of advancement available. Detailed descriptions of each level of consciousness, obstacles to growth, and resources to assist in healing are included for each stage of the spiritual journey of awakening.

Advanced Research on consciousness, spiritual teachers, ascension, Divine Cosmology, and advancement beyond Full Consciousness are key teachings offered by New Humanity Divine Marga.

Daily Practices for beginners are crucial for smooth spiritual evolution. Therefore, New Humanity Divine Marga teaches practices, such as, Pranayama, Five Tibetan Rites, nervous system purification, and energetic support for raising consciousness.

New Technologies to accelerate human consciousness development is researched and tested by New Humanity Divine Marga team. Bio-resonance, neurostimulation, Chi generators, and PEMF therapies are some of the suggested technologies to enhance spiritual growth and nervous system healing.

High Vibrational Diet is our suggested way to help support the physical form for higher consciousness.

Enneagram teachings are offered to assist students in understanding their strengths and weaknesses on their spiritual journey.

Online Store gives access to many offerings for students to learn, heal, meditate, and receive transmissions in their own time. Each video has a transmission that speeds evolution and can be repeated as many times as needed.

YouTube videos from Sat Mindo Dev and Lyonne Premananda cover a wide variety of topics suited to both beginner and advanced spiritual seekers alike.

Question and Answer videos are available on the New Humanity Divine Marga website to answer the most common queries from students around the world.

Volunteer opportunities (Seva) are available for many roles at New Humanity Foundation. We are always looking for help with transcriptions, video editing, writing, proofreading, or donations to our foundation that allow us to make teachings accessible to more people.

New Humanity Foundation is dedicated to promoting conscious living, self-realization, and the advancement of human consciousness in the US, Canada, UK, Europe, India, Nepal, Thailand, and other countries through educational programs, community-based projects, and humanitarian assistance.

New Humanity Foundation supports the teachings of Sat Mindo Dev and Lyonne Premananda by making them available to all who sincerely yearn for peace and freedom.

New Humanity Foundation is a non-profit, tax-exempt, charitable organization. We welcome sincere students of any race, ethnicity, ancestry, gender expression, national origin, disability, religion, sexual orientation, or socioeconomic background. We welcome all to our community of friends practicing the teachings together, bringing depth and clarity to our lives.

Founded in 2018 on the Maltese Islands, the New Humanity Foundation today reaches people around the world who are naturally drawn to the sincerity and depth of Sat Mindo Dev's and Lyonne Premananda's message. Our team and many dedicated volunteers work together to bring these teachings forward through In-Person and Online Programs, Publications, Live Online Meetings, and Media. We bring support to our Community through various Support and Financial Aid Programs. Our organization is run by the principles of integrity, sincerity, and a loving awareness of ourselves, each other, and the world around us.

We are registered as a non-profit organization in Malta as New Humanity Foundation VO/1644, and in the United States as New Humanity Life Inc. Non-Profit organization registered 501(c)(3) status.

More about New Humanity Foundation:
https://www.newhumanityfoundation.org/

Next Steps to Support Your Awakening

- Browse our website www.DivineMarga.com for more info, videos, and Q&A.

- Try our recommended Daily Practices for beginners.

- Attend a Live weekly online Satsang meeting and Meditation.

- See the schedule of upcoming Physical and Online Retreats.

- Join a Meditation, Spiritual Life Coaching & Consciousness Transmissions Teacher Training Course.

- Explore our Online Store for practices for each Level of Consciousness.

- Watch the latest videos on YouTube @SatMindo

- Receive Free Access to the upcoming event with a **Full Consciousness Transmission** by:
  - Leaving your review on Amazon book page
  - Send a screenshot to DivineMargaInternational@gmail.com

Made in United States
Troutdale, OR
05/18/2025